# MUSIC MAKES
# THE NATION

# MUSIC MAKES THE NATION

## Nationalist Composers and Nation Building in Nineteenth-Century Europe

*Benjamin Curtis*

CAMBRIA
PRESS

AMHERST, NEW YORK

Requests for permission should be directed to permissions@cambriapress.com, or mailed to: Cambria Press, 20 Northpointe Parkway, Suite 188, Amherst, NY 14228.

Library of Congress Cataloging-in-Publication Data

Curtis, Benjamin W., 1972-
    Music makes the nation : nationalist composers and nation building in nineteenth-century Europe / Benjamin Curtis.
        p. cm.
    Includes bibliographical references and index.
    ISBN 978-1-60497-522-2 (alk. paper)
    1. Music and state—Europe—19th century. 2. Nationalism in music. 3. Ethnicity in music. I. Title.
    ML3917.E85C87 2008
    780.9'034—dc22

2008010667

# TABLE OF CONTENTS

# PREFACE

This book is an intellectual and cultural history of a pivotal movement that broadly stamped nineteenth-century culture—namely, nationalist music. The nineteenth century is in many ways the century of "building nations," and all across the European continent, nation building is incomprehensible without an understanding of the role that art played in it. This book examines the social and political functions of nationalist music to reveal how artists and their works transformed society, politics, and culture. As society was transformed in this process, so too was art, becoming a political tool for effecting social change. While in previous eras, art had indeed served various political functions, never before had art forms such as music been used to influence a mass audience to achieve extensive sociopolitical goals. There is another, final transformation I examine as well: composers became political activists, with distinct social and cultural agendas that they advanced in society through their works. The social, political, and intellectual story behind some of the great musical works of the time and the composers who created them is the focus of this book.

What links all of these themes together is the fundamental goal of nationalist composers to create a national art. This art, in turn, would serve as a constitutive element of a broader national culture that was itself supposed to be an essential building block of the national identity. This effort by cultural and political activists to create a national art and culture is deeply intertwined with many of the most important questions in the history of European nationalism. It demonstrates nationalist intellectuals' ideas on how art and culture could become the unifying elements that would bind the members of the national populace together. It also forces us to consider the tension between nationalist intellectuals' simultaneous primordialist and constructivist attitudes toward the national identity. As one final example of the many important issues involved, the effort to create a national music also exposes how politics and culture were supposed to work together in nation building.

The complex of themes and strategies for creating a national art and culture will be familiar to any student of nationalism. What is new in this book for scholars of nationalism, European history, and musicology, however, is the comparative study of nationalist music specifically as a sociopolitical phenomenon. Though few previous works have examined these issues from a perspective of both politics and culture, nationalist music and art unmistakably deal with *both* politics *and* culture. Therefore, this book seeks to make a lasting contribution to the understanding of what role art—and specifically music—played in nationalist movements, which will benefit historians, political scientists, and musicologists.

The research for this book was supported by a number of generous grants from the departments of Political Science and Germanics at the University of Chicago. Archival research in Norway was additionally funded by the Sons of Norway Foundation and a Fulbright Fellowship. For their help during the research phase in Norway I want to thank Karen Falch Johannessen, of the Grieg Archive at the Bergen Offentlige Bibliotek, as well as Dr. Hans Weisethaunet and the faculty and staff of the Department of Music at the University of Bergen. In Prague, Dr. Olga Mojžíšová and the staff of the Bedřich Smetana Museum and Archive provided invaluable assistance, and my research in Munich was facilitated by the staff of the Bayrische Staatsbibliothek.

# MUSIC MAKES
## THE NATION

# INTRODUCTION

In 1848, as the flame of revolution spread across Europe, Richard Wagner was hard at work on the prose poem of what was to become his opera tetralogy *Der Ring des Nibelungen*. This work was conceived explicitly as an indictment of the contemporary social order, and soon after he completed the text, he turned his creative energies to a new project: fomenting an uprising in Dresden. He edited a revolutionary newspaper, he rallied the combatants on the barricades, and he literally dodged the bullets of the Prussian troops sent in to quell the unrest. When it finally became clear that the revolutionaries had lost, he took flight under an assumed name, evading the secret police and a likely death sentence, and one fair May day, he crossed on foot the borders of Saxony, into exile.

Also in 1848, a few hundred kilometers south of Dresden, Bedřich Smetana took up arms in Prague's own revolution. He was a member of the revolutionary national guard, assigned to defend the city's Malá strana district against the oncoming Austrian troops under General Windischgrätz. His more important contribution to the Czech cause, though, took the form of several pieces of music: a "March for the Student Legions and the National Guard," and his "Song of Freedom," designed to spark the battle against the forces of reaction with its opening words of "War, war, the flag is fluttering, arise Czechs!" Likewise, his *Jubilation Overture* expressed his own hope for the success of the Czech cause. As in Dresden, however, the revolutionary forces were defeated, and much like Wagner, Smetana was forced to flee his city, taking refuge at his parents' house in the Bohemian countryside.

Edvard Grieg was only seven years old during the events of 1848–1849, living snugly with his family in faraway Bergen, Norway. Instead of manning the revolutionary barricades, his own involvement in a political upheaval came much later, in 1905, when he was already an old man. However, during that year's crisis over the breakup of the Norwegian-Swedish union, Grieg, as one of the most internationally famous Norwegians of his day, did what he could to prevent an escalation into violent conflict, dispatching letters to his admirers such as Kaiser Wilhelm of Germany and King Edward of England, urging their intervention in the dispute. When the crisis was peacefully resolved and Norway had gained its independence, it was Grieg's music that led the rejoicing. At the first concert attended by the new Norwegian king and queen, Grieg sat with them in the royal box while his *Sigurd Jorsalfar* was performed, a piece that glorified an ancient Norse monarch and simultaneously celebrated the modern victory of Norwegian national aspirations.

What do these three men, and these three historical turning points in which they participated, have in common? In each case, we have an example of an artist taking an active role in politics—and not just any politics, but specifically in *nationalist* politics. Furthermore, while Wagner's and Smetana's escapades at the barricades figure among the most heroic examples of artists' politics, engagement in politics was by no means unusual for many artists in the nineteenth century. Indeed, one of the most compelling stories in the cultural history of that long century (1789–1918) was the role that so many artists took in political matters. Art in this period became more actively political than it had been in centuries. And very often, the politics that such art and artists were concerned with were a politics of *change*. As intellectuals from Jean-Paul Marat, to Karl Marx, to Vladimir Lenin were concerned with effecting social change through their writings, so a great many artists expected to support or bring about social change through their art.

No better example of this campaign exists than with nationalism. Nationalism, together with socialism and liberalism, stands as one of the earth-shaking social movements of the decades between the French Revolution and the First World War. The effort to forge a single people united culturally and politically in a single state—which fanned out from Jacobin Paris right across the entire European continent—swept up not just politicians, soldiers, writers, and peasants, but artists as well. These are artists of all genres and lands, including the painter Jacques-Louis David in France, the poet Pushkin in Russia, the architect Gottfried Semper in Germany, and musicians such as Wagner, Smetana, and Grieg, in their respective countries. Nationalism—perhaps even more than the other two great-isms of liberalism and socialism—inspired some of the most gifted creative minds of the century, deeply impacting both their artistic works and their engagement in society.

For Wagner, Smetana, and Grieg, their moments of dodging enemy bullets or brokering the creation of a new kingdom were unquestionably the most actively political in their lives. However, their involvement with their countries' nationalist movements stretched over their entire adult careers, as artists fervently engaged with political and social change. A nationalist music was the principal vehicle for both their artistic and political ideas. These ideas, and the goals they sought to realize, are consistent among these three composers—and indeed, this is what unites them with other nationalist artists across Europe. What nationalist artists are fundamentally engaged in is an epochal project to build a *national culture*. This culture was intended to be an expression of a nation's past, future, landscape, language, and artistic aspirations. Even beyond that, though, in nationalist artists' minds, the national culture would actually help *to create the nation*, in particular by creating national citizens, the bearers and representatives of that culture. One of the paramount purposes for national art was to forge a national populace. Art, these artists believed, had the power to build the nation culturally, and could thereby make an absolutely vital contribution to the larger nationalist project.

The nationalist artists who undertook this project are a fascinating combination of artist and political activist. Fascinating, because in many cases these are creative geniuses—among them some of the greatest that humanity has ever produced—who dedicated their careers, their hopes, and the very fruits of their incredible artistic inspiration to their country's nationalist movement. In so doing, these artists were simultaneously creating something besides art, and besides a national culture. Through their engagement with politics, society, and culture, nationalist composers were also helping to fashion the role of a social actor who had never existed previously in history. They were becoming *nationalist intellectuals*, the activists who deserve most of the credit for launching the movements that would reshape Europe's, and eventually the world's, political order.

Nationalist intellectuals operated on many levels and in many areas to promote their country's nationalist movement. They wrote historical tracts uncovering the supposed history of the lands aspiring to autonomy. They wrote speeches and articles declaring their movement's demands and protesting oppression by other peoples. They led rebellions, argued in parliaments, and waged wars. They also authored poetry, painted pictures, and composed operas. Nationalist artists were, in fact, often closely involved with other political actors in the nationalist movement, and count as a fundamental subset of nationalist intellectuals more generally. Most nationalist movements depended on this division of labor among the activists, where some dedicated themselves to writing, others to combat, and others to art.

The examples of Wagner, Smetana, and Grieg reveal precisely what the goals were for nationalist artists such as composers—and they also reveal the *process* by which they sought to realize their goals. This process, the actual practices these men engaged in to bring about their political and artistic goals, is best understood as a process of creation. More concretely, there are actually three creative processes involved here that, once we grasp them, make fully clear the role of artists in nationalist movements. The first creative process is the constitution of nationalist music itself. To understand how nationalist music was created—the why, the how, and the what for—we have to examine the ideas of those who created it. What, in the composers' vision, was the purpose behind nationalist music? What would it do, what would it accomplish? How, exactly, did music become "national"? And how, above all, would this art form be made to serve sociopolitical ends?

The second creative process is that of the national culture. The national culture was the symbolic, aesthetic fabric that nationalist artists intended would weave national citizens into a unified and whole populace. The ultimate purpose of nationalist music was to contribute to the establishment of this national culture. But, what precisely were the mechanics of this somewhat mystical power of culture to unify people? How were these national cultures constructed? Here again the composers' own dreams and plans can provide the answer. Their ideas and achievements help to explain the function of culture, and particularly art, within a nationalist movement.

The creation of the role of nationalist artists themselves is the third process. This is the elaboration and evolution of a particular role within the movement and within the larger society. How did nationalist artists such as composers carve out a place for themselves in nationalist movements? How did they, in short, elaborate their own role? There can be no doubt that nationalist artists were indeed active participants in elaborating their own role, since they consciously set about developing the tools and techniques they then used in their political project. We will see that both ideas and practices figure in this process of creation. On the one hand, a preexisting complex of beliefs about the nation and ideas on nation building formed a kind of intellectual structure that shaped these artists' practices. Like all such structures, the ways of thinking about the nation and nation building both constrained and enabled the activists' practice. The intellectual structure provided a universe of ideas and possibilities for *how* nationalists could create nations and national cultures. As these ideas and possibilities were applied—that is, translated into actual practice—so these practices came to define the role of the nationalist artist, since the practices are what defines the role: what nationalist artists *are* is what they *do*.

Stated succinctly, the effort to create a national music illuminates the emergence of nationalist intellectuals as social actors and lays bare the cultural strategies for "building" nations. That is why the story of nationalist music is such a significant one, because it is inextricably bound up with some of the most far-reaching political, social, and cultural developments of nineteenth-century European history. All European nationalist movements are unthinkable without some cultural content. The culture was, again, what would give meaning to the national identity. And it was the job, above all, of nationalist artists to create that culture. Without them, where would the content of the culture come from? What works, whether of poetry, prose, visual arts, or music, could there be to constitute the nation's cultural uniqueness? The creation of the national culture, then—along with the other two creative processes, that of the actors who would create the culture (nationalist artists) and of a specific form of that culture (nationalist music)—are all central to the development of nationalism. As they are fundamental to the world phenomenon of nationalism, so too must they be understood as fundamental to world history.

It was the individual nationalist artists, naturally, who fueled this phenomenon, and in order to reach any kind of understanding of these three processes of creation, we have to study individuals who put these ideas into practice. Thus the nationalist composers Richard Wagner, Bedřich Smetana, and Edvard Grieg are my lens for exploring the phenomenon of nationalist art, and of music specifically. Though (in a strange coincidence) they were all just slightly over five feet tall, each man nonetheless assumed a towering position within the nationalist movements in his own country—Germany, the Czech lands, and Norway, respectively. In the course of this book we will follow these composers along the path of the three creative processes they were engaged in.

First, in terms of their art, Wagner, Smetana, and Grieg sought to establish through both their artistic creativity and social activism a uniquely national music, a music that would meet the highest standards of art and hence both enlighten and nationalize the audiences who heard that music. They all viewed the creation of a national art as an essential means of rescuing their nations from a historical and cultural decline. All three employed similar means in the production of their national artworks: they set to music texts in their national language, they evoked their country's landscape, and they incorporated elements from the history and legends associated with their homeland. They also all relied extensively on sources stemming from the peasant classes—which were perceived as the purest repository of the nation's cultural values—in order to elevate those folk songs, dances, and tales into a high art.

Second, we will see how these three composers contributed to the creation of a national culture. As part of their projects, they sought to draw boundaries between their nation's art and that of other nations. They were concerned to create something distinct, different, and unmistakably German, Czech, or Norwegian. At the same time, though, they also wanted to transcend boundaries with their art. They wanted to create music that, through its nationality, would go out into the world to testify to their nation's cultural achievements, and that would, like all great art, be universal. However, the ultimate function of such art, as a critical element of the national culture, would be to produce national citizens.

Finally, the ideas and tools that Wagner, Smetana, and Grieg employed to achieve their ends simultaneously helped constitute the role of nationalist artists such as composers. Their ideas and tools are essentially identical to those of all European nationalist composers: they are consistently applied, across countries and generations, to meet the previously mentioned two goals of creating national music and national cultures. Within this broadly similar picture, however, the variations in how the composers used these strategies will in fact help reveal the intellectual, artistic, and functional content of the strategies that define the role of the nationalist composer. Through the story of these three composers' ideas and works, then, we will read the larger story of nationalist music, and indeed, of nation building itself.

The remainder of this chapter offers a biographical overview of Wagner, Smetana, and Grieg for readers who may be unfamiliar with these composers' lives and works. The second chapter outlines the key concepts of nationalism that the book is grounded upon. I propose a reconsideration of two theoretical traditions: first, of the relationship between nationalism and culture, and second, of the relationship between nationalism and music. I argue that art and politics are fused in nationalism as in few other social phenomena, such that culture becomes an essential political tool for building nations. Second, I show how previous understandings of nationalist music *as music* need to be refined to take into account the fact that nations and nationalism are social constructions consciously manipulated by activist artists. Nationality in music is therefore similarly a construction and a political tool, the result of concrete social and artistic aims on the part of those activist artists. Readers who are well versed in theories of nationalism may wish to skim the first half of this chapter to focus instead on my discussion of nationalist music.

The third chapter answers the question of exactly *how* Wagner, Smetana, and Grieg sought to make their music national. Their approaches were a combination of inherited ideas representative of broader intellectual trends of the time, and innovations that nationalist composers themselves pioneered. All three composers reacted against what they perceived as a decline in artistic standards and taste that prevented the public from recognizing its own true national art. So, building upon the contemporary conception of art's power to edify and educate, these men determined to apply that power toward educating the populace into the values of the new national culture. These composers also each engaged in institution building—establishing orchestras or opera houses in order to realize their educational goals and simultaneously to inculcate audiences with the national culture. Finally, I analyze how Wagner, Smetana, and Grieg all brought their own artistic genius to bear on these goals by actually creating artworks that would establish the new national style and serve as pillars of the national culture.

The fourth chapter deals with one of the most prominent, and thorny, issues in nationalist music—the inspiration of folk sources—to provide a new understanding of the relationship between "the folk" and nationalist art and nation building. It begins with a historical overview of how the products of peasant culture (such as songs, dances, or tales) became conceived as "national" through the efforts of nationalist collectors and researchers. I demonstrate how later artists such as Wagner, Smetana, and Grieg regarded these folk inspirations primarily as raw material for a nationalist art. These composers insisted that folk material had to be elevated or "idealized" before it itself could actually count as art. This process of elevating folk sources into a national art, I argue, reveals one of the fundamental goals of the effort to build a national culture: the fusion of the "low" folk inspirations with the "high" artistic forms represents and effects the way the nation was supposed to become one people, unified across the rural-urban divide.

The effort to build a national culture was not without conflict, and in the fifth chapter I explore two bitterly fought conflicts, namely, the conflicts *between* national cultures, and also *within* national cultures. These conflicts arose as a result of nationalists' desires to create boundaries between their cultures and those of other peoples. I explore Wagner's campaign to free German music from what he saw as the encroachment and corruption of French and Jewish music. Smetana, for his part, was a committed Wagnerian, and he accepted some German influence on Czech music. To other figures within Czech cultural life, however, Smetana's Wagnerian leanings were traitorous, and they accused him of trying to "Germanize" Czech musical culture. Grieg represents a third variation on this theme, in that he, too, accepted some German influence, but was subsequently attacked mainly by German music critics for departing from the supposedly universal standards of German music to trifle in the particularity of Norwegian folk inspirations. At the heart of the battles in all three of these cases was an obsession with the "purity" of the national culture, and to what extent foreign influence was admissible in national art.

Nationalist artists' obsession with creating rigid boundaries, difference, and particularity in their art coexisted with simultaneous aspirations to universality. The sixth chapter stands as the opposite side of the coin from the preceding one, and it shows that for all their inward-looking drive to create a unique national art, Wagner, Smetana, and Grieg were also looking outward, at the function of the national art on the world stage. Ultimately, besides constructing a national culture at home, these composers' works were created to represent the nation's values and artistic achievement abroad as well. Three themes in particular run throughout the nineteenth century's discourse on nationalist music: prestige, dissemination, and universality. Composers were concerned that their music be disseminated internationally, to secure prestige for their nation's art. In this way, their music would benefit not just their own nation, but would rise to the universal standards of all great art. Through this example of national art, I establish that despite the particularity and difference inherent in nationalism, nationalism can also contain within itself appeals to universal and cosmopolitan values.

Moving from the detail of the preceding six chapters, in the Conclusion, I widen my lens for a sweeping view of many more nationalist composers. Incorporating figures from Carl Maria von Weber to contemporary Latvian composer Zigmars Liepiņš, I demonstrate that the constitutive features of nationalist music that I identify in Wagner, Smetana, and Grieg are indeed present throughout the nineteenth century and into the twentieth. With this broad historical overview, I once again tie together the three guiding themes of the book—the creative processes of nationalist music, national cultures, and nationalist composers. The incredibly consistent goals, techniques, artistic output, and achievements of nationalist composers all the way from Spain to Russia demonstrate the seminal importance of these processes as aspects of art, politics, and society in Europe in the nineteenth century, and point to the continuing relevance of these cultural and political phenomena today.

## BIOGRAPHICAL OVERVIEW

There were dozens of nationalist composers I could have chosen for my investigation, but I settled on these three for three main reasons. First, it was important to study composers who were generally credited with being the founders of their country's "national style." Such a criterion narrowed the focus to composers for whom the national in music was truly a crusade, and in turn such composers would be the best for studying how nationalism and the arts intersected. Smetana and Grieg both count as "founders," though Wagner does not, since there is no generally acknowledged founder of a German national style. Nonetheless, his rabid support for the foundation of such a style, and his expression of that support in his voluminous prose works, identified him as a good candidate for study. Second, it made sense to consider only major composers, and so lesser nationalistic lights such as, for example, Moniuszko in Poland or Erkel in Hungary, were ruled out. Third, I elected to focus on nationalist movements that were both state building and nation building: this criterion excluded countries such as Russia or England that were already unified and fully independent in the nineteenth century. The motivation behind this stipulation was that it allowed me to observe the interaction between nationalists involved in both sides of the movement—the more narrowly political and the more broadly cultural. It also enabled closer investigation of how nations are built via art in the absence of a national state.

Even these criteria, admittedly, did not reduce the choice only to Wagner, Smetana, and Grieg. So, perhaps a final, purely subjective criterion was simply that I like their music and was interested in their countries. Indeed, over the course of writing this book I came to feel as if I got to know each of these three men personally. Each proved to be an intriguing companion over the years of research. While I became intimately familiar with their life stories in the course of this project, I recognize that not all readers may be as prepared as I am to answer abstruse trivia questions about Smetana's favorite foods. Therefore, a biographical crash course will be appropriate at present; as the book proceeds, it will be easier to tell the story of Wagner's, Smetana's, and Grieg's ideas if I have already briefly sketched the stories of their lives.

Reducing the life of as controversial and gigantic a figure as Richard Wagner to two paragraphs may seem impossible, but then again bringing

Wagner down to size would not be such a bad thing. Born in Leipzig in 1813, Wagner grew up in a prominent theatrical family and from an early age was inclined to make a career in the arts. His musical training was rather piecemeal and almost haphazard, learning from books and a variety of teachers, and though he eventually did acquire a phenomenal technique through which to express his genius, his earliest operas *Die Feen* (1834) and *Das Liebesverbot* (1836) are today largely ignored. He in fact experienced some difficulty in getting his musical career off the ground, taking positions in Würzburg, Königsberg, and Riga before trying his luck in Paris in the early 1840s. There he met with very little success, much to his annoyance, though it was in Paris that he wrote *Der fliegende Holländer* in 1841, now considered his first mature opera. A longtime fascination with German mythology began to bear fruit in *Tannhäuser* (1845, revised 1860).

Wagner had also long been preoccupied with politics, and took such an active role in the 1848–1849 revolution in Dresden that, once the revolution failed, he was forced to flee Saxony or face a possible death sentence. His years of exile from Germany were spent mostly in Switzerland, where he busied himself with writing some of his weightiest philosophical tracts such as *Oper und Drama*, and then produced *Lohengrin* in 1848. With this opera, he finally began to win wider recognition. In the mid-1850s he started working on what would become *Der Ring des Nibelungen*—whose music was composed over almost twenty years. Also in the 1850s, he began his romance with Cosima von Bülow, a daughter of Franz Liszt. She was already married to the prominent pianist and conductor Hans von Bülow, though that did not stop Wagner from stealing her away and eventually making her his own wife. Thanks in part to his characteristic impecuniousness, Wagner was in a state of despair about his career when in 1864 a miracle occurred: King Ludwig II of Bavaria invited him to come to Munich to rely on royal financial support so he could compose his music in relative security. Also characteristically, Wagner eventually managed to sabotage this incredibly lucrative relationship. However, it was nonetheless thanks to Ludwig's support that he managed to complete *Die Meistersinger von Nürnberg* (premiered 1868) and the *Ring*; the latter was finally performed as a complete tetralogy in 1876 in Wagner's own theater in Bayreuth, also largely bankrolled by Ludwig. Though at the peak of his worldwide fame, Wagner nonetheless was upset that the newly unified Germany failed to appreciate his music in the way he had hoped for. He composed *Parsifal* (1882) before dying in Venice in 1883.

In comparison with Wagner, Bedřich Smetana's life was in many ways as difficult and ultimately rather tragic. Born in 1824, he grew up in a rural environment around the brewery that his father owned. From a relatively early age, he had contacts with Czech nationalists such as his teachers Josef Jungmann and František Josef Smetana (the latter was Bedřich's cousin), so by the time he arrived in Prague in the early 1840s he was already a committed nationalist. His earliest musical works are dances for piano, but his ambitions expanded after his musical training in Prague and his meeting with Franz Liszt in 1848. Smetana was actively involved in the 1848 revolution in Prague, and though he avoided any sort of prosecution, he found the cultural and political climate of the postrevolution reaction so severe that in 1856 he took a job as the music director in Göteborg, Sweden. His most notable compositions from the 1850s include several symphonic poems—a form he explored under Liszt's influence—such as *Richard III* (1858), *Wallensteins Lager* ("Wallenstein's Camp"—1861), and *Hakon Jarl* (1861), none of which are especially nationalistic. Also during this time his first wife died, wounding him deeply; his second marriage was often unhappy.

In the early 1860s, repression of Czech nationalism subsided, and when Smetana learned that there was an opening for the post of the director of the Czech opera, he enthusiastically applied and was accepted. In 1864 a competition was held to select the best new Czech national opera, which Smetana entered with his first opera, *Braniboři v Čechách* ("The Brandenburgers in Bohemia"), and won. His status as one of the leading figures in Czech culture rapidly consolidated. Some critics of *Braniboři* complained that it was too "Wagnerian," and Smetana responded by turning in his next opera to a decidedly lighter mood, creating what has become perhaps the paragon of a folk opera; *Prodaná nevěsta* ("The Bartered Bride") went through several revisions before taking its final form in 1871, but enjoyed enormous popularity almost immediately. Nonetheless, with his third opera, *Dalibor* (1868), his critics resumed their attacks and Smetana found his position at the opera and within Prague's cultural life increasingly embattled. He completed his next opera, *Libuše*, in 1871, though it did not receive its premiere until almost ten years later, because Smetana reserved it for the opening of a new Czech opera house. Disaster struck in these years as he began to go deaf (a result of syphilis) and was forced to retire from his theater post. He continued to compose, however, producing what may be his most famous work, the cycle of patriotic symphonic poems entitled *Má vlast* (1874–79), as well as two impressive string quartets, a cycle of *Czech Dances* for piano, and several more operas, including *Dvě vdovy* ("The Two Widows"—1874) and *Hubička* ("The Kiss"—1876). Money worries dogged Smetana for the rest of his life, and by the time his contribution to Czech culture came to be widely revered, he had only a few years left to live. By then he was already suffering from the incipient dementia that would see him committed to an insane asylum, where he died in 1884.

Never as stormy as those of his two predecessors, Grieg's life was on the whole a happy one, despite his often frail health. Born in Bergen in 1843 to a prosperous merchant family, Grieg's early musical talent was such that his parents sent him, on the urging of the renowned Norwegian violinist Ole Bull, to the Leipzig Conservatory, regarded as the foremost of its day. Upon his graduation, Grieg began associating with young Scandinavian musicians in both Christiania (the former name for Oslo) and Copenhagen, and together they encouraged one another's interest in folk music. In Christiania, Grieg founded a music school and conducted orchestral concerts, though he was often frustrated by what he saw as the Norwegians' lack of interest in art music. The work that first brought him to wide international attention was his piano concerto (1868); chamber works such as his violin sonatas and miniatures for piano also grew popular. The incidental music (1875) he composed to a production of Ibsen's play *Peer Gynt* enjoyed enormous fame thanks to his arrangements of the music into two suites.

Grieg also collaborated with a number of other prominent Norwegian artists of his time, including the writer Bjørnstjerne Bjørnson, with whom Grieg had a close though sometimes quarrelsome friendship. Bjørnson and Grieg planned on writing a national opera, though their project was never completed. Indeed, as he grew older, Grieg realized fewer and fewer large-scale works and instead focused his productivity on songs such as his cycle *Haugtussa* ("The Mountain Maid"—published 1898) and shorter works like his various Norwegian dances for orchestra or piano, including the *Symphonic Dances* of 1898. Still, his fame continued to grow and Grieg began touring extensively throughout Western and Central Europe, usually returning home to Western Norway in the summers to compose. His stature as the leading Norwegian musician granted him the opportunity to undertake projects like the music festival he organized in Bergen in 1898. His international fame was such that, besides counting many of the greatest composers of his time as friends, he was also a favorite of figures such as Kaiser Wilhelm II. Among Grieg's last works were an edition of Norwegian dances, known as *slåtter* for violin and piano of 1902, and the *Four Psalms* for male voice choir of 1906. He died in Bergen in 1907.

As important as nationalism was to these artists' careers, it is admittedly not the exclusive concern of their art. None of them were so one sided as that. Nationalism is simply the lens through which I view their careers in the present work; there are obviously many other valid ways of studying Wagner, Smetana, and Grieg. That said, there should be absolutely no doubt about their intent to make their works national, and so to create a national art music for their respective countries. Some, however, might dispute the extent to which these three composers' activities could be described as a self-conscious program. And it is in fact reasonable to ask whether Wagner, Smetana, and Grieg can really be considered social activists with a cultural/political project of their own. However, Wagner, Smetana, and Grieg do all count as committed and conscious nationalists, as "nationalist intellectuals" as per the definition in the next chapter.

It is true, though, that their activism did not necessarily take the form of a program strategically planned out in advance.

These three men, after all, were composers and not philosophers or theoreticians. They were not concerned with elaborating a philosophical system. Their ideas are not flawlessly logical nor, in many cases, all that deep. Of the three, Wagner is the most theoretical, the one who thought hardest about what he was doing. However, even his thought lacks the internal consistency we find in, for example, a Kant. Nonetheless, it is not only philosophers whose ideas have import. Indeed, it is as innovators and implementers of the ideas behind nation building and national art that Wagner's, Smetana's, and Grieg's thought is worth examining. They practiced what they preached. Further, what they were involved in was a *project* and not a *program*: the imagining of the nation proceeds not according to an inviolable five-year plan, but instead contingently in response to a variety of factors. Together with fellow nationalists in their respective movements, Wagner, Smetana, and Grieg were impacted by the intellectual, artistic, and social developments of their time. They elaborated their ideas and techniques as they went along.

That said, their projects for creating a national music and culture were predicated on a certain logic. We can read the intellectual, artistic, and practical principles that informed these men's activism from both their own accounts of their motivation and inspiration, and from their concrete achievements. These principles, their motivation, and their achievements all lead to the overriding question of precisely how, according to Wagner, Smetana, and Grieg, the project of creating a national music should proceed, and what, ultimately, it should accomplish.

# CHAPTER 1

# NATIONALISM AND MUSIC

The objective of this book is to study what people (and particularly nationalist artists) of the nineteenth century thought about music and nationalism: how they viewed the interaction of those two phenomena, and what they expected to come out of that interaction. This study is a historical analysis of ideas expressed by important historical personages who were intimately involved with the interaction of nationalism and music—namely Wagner, Smetana, and Grieg. Their ideas, needless to say, are no longer current, and the way we understand nationalism and music today has for the most part changed. In my analysis, however, I take these composers' ideas largely at face value—the objective, again, is to know first *what* they thought, and only then to evaluate according to contemporary theories of nationalism the role that nationalist music actually did play in the nineteenth century.

This chapter provides the necessary first step on this historical and analytical project by outlining contemporary theories of nationalism. I begin with an overview of modern scholarly understandings of several critical elements in nationalism theory—elements that will underpin my discussion in the rest of the book. I elaborate in particular upon nationalist intellectuals and national culture, since they form part of my key theoretical arguments. Then, using the lens of modern nationalism theory, I examine the typical and traditional understandings of nationalism and music in order to correct possible *mis*understandings. My intent is that the framework I establish in this chapter will structure the entire account of nationalism, music, and the three composers' own ideas in the chapters that follow.

## Nationalism: Key Concepts and Definitions

While many of the key theoretical concepts in this book, particularly those having to do with nation building, may seem well trodden to scholars of nationalism, we will also be following these ideas down roads less traveled. As important as nationalist intellectuals are both historically and historiographically, our knowledge of how these activists developed their political tools remains quite limited—and in the case of nationalist artists, our knowledge is thin indeed. Likewise, the actual theoretical import of national cultures and particularly nationalist music has been barely explored hitherto. However, in order to understand how Wagner, Smetana, and Grieg effected their simultaneous goals of artistic and social creation, we have to approach this question from a clear understanding of precisely what nationalist intellectuals, national culture, and nationalist music are.

One can approach the nineteenth century's legacy of nationalism not just theoretically, but physically, too. In Prague, walking along the bank of the Vltava river toward the spires of Charles Bridge, one comes across the great neo-Renaissance pile that is the Czech National Theater. Much of Czech history of the latter half of the 1800s is bound up in this building; indeed, at least by the measure of its role in Czech culture, there is perhaps no more important monument in all of Prague. Its exterior is crowned with statues of Czech artists made immortal, as well as two enormous, rather martial chariots in bronze. The interior is no less overpowering, as lavish as any nineteenth-century opera house ought to be, a gleam of gold and crimson everywhere the eye happens to glance. One thing in particular draws my eye in this theater, though: it is the bold letters above the proscenium arch that proclaim, "Národ sobě!" or "the nation to itself!" This is a slogan, almost even a shibboleth, that expresses the entire import of this theater to Czech nationalists. The idea is that the Czech nation has given itself this theater, a sacred shrine of the national culture, in which that culture is both created and worshiped.

In one sense, the Czech nation did "give itself" the theater. The campaign to build a theater in Prague for the Czechs—one that was separate but equal to the German theater in the city—was the fondest wish of many of the most prominent Czech patriots over the course of several decades. It took that long just to raise the money to begin construction on the building, which commenced in 1868. It was more than another decade still, in 1881, before it was finished. And then something so unfortunate, so unlucky happened as to be scarcely credible: a few nights after the first performance in the theater, it burned down. While not completely destroyed, the damage was extensive enough that reconstruction took another two years. That is in fact an astoundingly short amount of time, given all the years it took just to reach the point of laying the foundation stone. What made that rapid rebuilding possible were the countless donations that poured in from all over Bohemia, from Czechs of all walks of life who had been appalled at the tragedy of the first theater's destruction. Thanks to that outpouring—both of finances and sentiment—this shrine of Czech art and culture at last opened its doors to the mass public in 1883, with a performance of Smetana's opera *Libuše*.

So, the Czech public certainly did make it possible finally to establish such a cultural institution in the capital. Yet the phrase "Národ sobě!" actually supposes a quite remarkable bit of magic: the nation, which would be created at least in part via this theater, was nonetheless already in existence enough to *give itself* a theater. Somehow, then, the nation in fact creates itself. That, at any rate, is the nineteenth-century view; according to contemporary understandings of nationalism, however, nations do not create themselves.

A "nation" is in fact only an idea of a communal grouping, one in which people conceive of themselves as united across social divides on the basis of a shared, distinct culture, with common rights and duties for all members of the community. Part of this conception is that the community is entitled to rule itself politically through such means as territorial autonomy or its own state. The quotidian understanding of "nation" is that a nation such as the United States, France, or Brazil has had a distinct identity throughout its entire history, and that nations are real things that exist independently of what people think about them. This understanding is demonstrably deficient, however: historiography shows a process of "nation building" by which a group of people are inculcated with the idea that they belong together as members of the same nation. Nation building also involves the establishment and inculcation of ideas about what the cultural characteristics are that constitute the nation. This book's subject, as per its subtitle, is nation building through music in the nineteenth century.

There is, however, some dispute among scholars of nationalism about precisely how long nations have existed. One school of thought, known as the perennialists, holds that there are certain nationlike features, extending all the way back into ancient history, that help define a people.[1] So, the ancient Greeks, perhaps, might have been close to a nation. Perennialists believe that there are certain raw materials of identity, history, and culture that have persisted into the modern period; these raw materials serve as building blocks of national groupings today. The other major, and dominant, scholarly school of thought is known as the modernists. Modernists hold that the very idea of the nation (as per my aforementioned definition) is something that did not exist until roughly the eighteenth century.[2] Most modernists identify the French Revolution as the birthplace of the national idea, though some scholars look back earlier, for example, to sixteenth-century England.

Regardless of the historical timeline of nations, both modernists and most perennialists agree that nations do not just exist naturally and objectively. They thus dismiss the now historically obsolete claims of primordialists, according to whom nations are eternal, omnipresent, and objectively real (if sometimes latent) in a people's consciousness. This empirically unjustifiable view stems primarily from eighteenth-century writers like Johann Gottfried von Herder, and is now only held by nationalists themselves. Instead, scholars now affirm that nations are "invented" or constructed. As Ernest Gellner, one of the godfathers of nationalism scholarship, observed: "Nationalism is not the awakening of nations to self-consciousness: it invents nations where they do not exist."[3]

Nationalism is best defined as the ideology of the nation. It is the belief that the nation is the central, most legitimate form of large-scale sociopolitical organization. Nationalism advances the claims and conceptions of (the concept of) the nation in virtually all realms of society, including culture, politics, economics, and even theater building. Nationalism is the ideology that inculcates a person's and a people's belief in their shared nationhood, that constructs from a disparate and often divided populace a more unified community that believes in its shared duties, right to political autonomy, and common culture.

Nations, in sum, are not *things*, and they do not build themselves theaters. People build theaters, and people motivated by nationalism build national theaters. And, in actual fact, it is not nationalism but nationalist intellectuals who advance the claims of the nation such as mobilizing mass support to erect artistic institutions or going to war. Nationalist intellectuals are the political entrepreneurs who "imagine the community," in Benedict Anderson's famous phrase, and who then attempt to disseminate and inculcate their imaginings in among the ostensible national populace.[4]

Intellectuals in general are "those who create, distribute, and apply culture," according to Seymour Martin Lipset.[5] Nationalist intellectuals, it follows, are the individuals concerned specifically with promoting *the nation's* culture. They are the creators "not only of nationalisms, but of the more universal discourse of the nation, of the very language and universe of meaning in which nations become possible," as Ronald Suny and Michael Kennedy explain.[6] Nationalist intellectuals historically have worked both against states and within states to promote nationalism. The Czechs, for example, while part of the Habsburg Empire, were politically largely powerless, and Czech nationalist intellectuals worked against the Austrian state's Germanizing policies in order to develop a sense of Czech nationality. In contrast, intellectuals within the French state worked with state mechanisms such as the education system to build a French nation. Whether at the state level or the substate level, through their discourse and activities nationalist intellectuals constitute the social, cultural, and political meaning of their putative nation.

The applicability of such definitions to nationalist composers should be obvious. Nationalist composers create, distribute, and apply culture in the form of music. After writing the music, they then distribute it via performance or publication. They apply culture, as we shall see, with their claims that their art represents their nation's inherent values, character, and cultural aspirations. They are applying this culture onto the society, and that is why the products of their creativity are never "just art," but rather are essential social products created with both artistic and political goals. These goals were that the national culture that intellectuals claimed to be creating would be not just representative of the nation, but also constitutive. Wagner, Smetana, and Grieg believed, as we shall see, that their art actually had the power to create national unity.

## Nationalist Intellectuals and the National Culture

This book studies not only nationalist intellectuals' creation of the nation through music—it also studies nationalist intellectuals' (and specifically composers') creation of their own role within society and politics. How do nationalist intellectuals create themselves? Let me approach this question by considering these actors from a categorical perspective. As the previous definitions suggest, nationalist intellectuals are a category of analysis, in that scholars have identified these activists as the ones primarily responsible for imagining nations. This is not purely a post-hoc characterization, however: men like Wagner, Smetana, and Grieg—not to mention their counterparts in the nationalist movements of their own and many other countries—were quite well aware of what they were doing. They were conscious of their position vis-à-vis the mass public, namely that they formed part of a vanguard that in a certain sense was going to "enlighten" that public about its own, neglected nationality. Wagner, Smetana, Grieg, and their colleagues generally believed that they had a mission, and that their mission was to contribute to the formation of a nation. Given that this was their mission, nationalist intellectuals developed certain tools to realize their sociopolitical goals.

And it is in this way that we can refer to nationalist intellectuals as another kind of category, as a category of practice: an essential means of defining what nationalist intellectuals are is by what they do. Their typical practices help determine what nationalist intellectuals' role is in politics and society. By developing their relevant practices, quite simply, nationalist intellectuals are simultaneously fashioning their own sociopolitical role. Particularly for nationalists in the historically earlier movements—in regards to the rest of Europe, especially the Germans—there were relatively few models from which to draw inspiration for their activism. The very idea of nations, and the dream of *making* them, were really quite new in the early nineteenth century. The main model for the early German patriots was the example of the French Revolution, and they set about borrowing certain tools like rhetorical formulas, or the manipulation of symbols, or gatherings such as festivals, and applying them to their own particular ends. In so doing, these activists were not only establishing a universe of meaning for nationalism; they were also creating a universe of possibility for other nationalist intellectuals.

Both these universes, of meaning and possibility, comprise what can be thought of as the intellectual structure of nationalist activism. Simply, it is the structure that establishes the boundaries of conceiving what the nation is and how it can be created. In turn, the intellectual structure is essential for constituting the nationalist intellectuals' typical practices. Again, it is the universe of possibility. It first involves that which is possible on a conceptual level—what nationalist intellectuals think they can do. There is no precedent for them thinking something ahistorically absurd, like using television to communicate a message (though they did use other, earlier forms of mass media). Similarly, they are conceptually constrained by what they believe about the nation, such as that it is something spiritual, and in most cases, "in the blood."

Second, the intellectual structure establishes boundaries of the possible tools that can be used in the nation-building project. This structure proceeds mainly from the example of other nationalist movements and nationalist intellectuals, since the latter learn from each other. Seeing what worked in one case, nationalist intellectuals assume such a technique to be effective, and thereby a certain possible toolkit or blueprint of strategies comes to be established. This blueprint then impinges on what an individual nationalist intellectual will do to achieve his own goals.

The particular practices of the nationalist composer are geared toward his specific sociopolitical goal of creating a national high culture. As an artist, his goals are most often concerned less with the overtly political tools of international diplomacy or winning votes. Instead, he conducts his politics primarily in the realm of aesthetics. Aesthetic products hold an enormous power in creating national identity—and this is not just in the view of nationalist artists. Even other nationalists ungraced by artistic talent share this belief; among obvious examples witness Hitler's investment in Nazi iconography. As the talented ones, though, the task of bringing forth such powerful, nationalistic aesthetic works falls to the nationalist artists. So, the products of the nationalist composer's activities—his art—are designed to form a fundamental building block of the culture. And art is one of the paramount areas where the elaboration of the "meaning of the nation" takes place. That is so because the existence of an identifiably *national* culture was, to an enormous extent, predicated on each nation being able to boast of having a high art.

The term "culture" admittedly connotes a bewildering array of things. As regards specifically a national culture, though, the last two of Raymond Williams' (four total) possible meanings for culture are most apposite: culture is both "the works and practices of intellectual and especially artistic creativity" and "the signifying system through which necessarily (though among other means) a social order is communicated, reproduced, experienced, and explored."[7] Thus artistic works such as Wagner's *Ring* or Smetana's *Czech Dances* count as "culture," as does the larger end they were working toward, of creating a national culture—that is, the social order that would help constitute the nation.

How is the national culture a social order that helps constitute the nation? The national culture is essential to nationalism because it is what binds the people together. It is the common, shared element that unites individuals into national cocitizens. The prenational social group is transformed into the unified nation, in part, via educating the masses in "national values, myths, and memories."[8] Ernest Gellner's conceptualization of the role of culture in nationalism is also especially relevant here: in his formula, culture replaces structure as the source of a person's identity in the modern world. That is to say, with the decline of the rigidly hierarchized social structures characteristic of feudalism, it is instead a culture, as the means of communication between people, that orients individuals in society and tells them who they are.[9] In the modern world, according to Gellner, people are loyal "not to a monarch or a land or a faith...but to a culture."[10] This is the unifying national culture. By communicating the meaning, values, and structure of a society, the national culture also orients people toward a polity. This goal is of course based on the assumption that every nation is entitled to rule itself. The national culture, then, both fuses the populace into a whole and delimits who belongs; in many senses it is the actual basis of the imagined community.

To be genuinely *national*, though, that culture must be monopolistic, as the exclusive, unified high culture associated with a particular society and polity. It is assumed to belong equally to all members of that society. Interestingly, though, nationalist intellectuals do not take the national culture for granted, as a given. Rather, they are concerned with creating that culture, with weaving the web of meaning that unites the (sometimes splintered) populace. While certain elements of that culture come, in a sense, premade (with folk tunes and tales as the best examples), nonetheless the culture as a whole must be constructed. Nationalist artists are typically most concerned with making it a "high culture."[11] Though they do not reject the need for the "lower" elements of a national culture, they attach the most value to the higher realm for reasons of prestige and for its supposed power to educate the populace.

This educational power of the national culture again ties into its function of creating national citizens. As this culture is transmitted to people, they learn the history, symbols, values, and meaning that supposedly belong to them by virtue of being members of the nation. In other words, people are taught that, in fact, they do *belong* to the nation. Most commonly, the national culture is transmitted through schools, where it is quite literally taught to people. However, there are in fact other means of transmission, often neglected in previous scholarship. Music is one of the most significant of these alternate means: public and private performances of nationalist music are additionally responsible for propagating and inculcating the national culture. Particularly given that music (whether in the opera house, the concert hall, or the drawing room) was one of the main forms of public entertainment in the nineteenth century, it comes as close as anything the era had to a mass medium. "Mass" does not connote lowest common denominator, however. When nationalist artists like Wagner, Smetana, and Grieg emphasize the more socially elevated forms of music (generally disregarding that which is played in dance halls or taverns, for example), that is again because of their design for the national culture to be educational. The higher forms like symphonies, sonatas, or operas were presumed to be better at enlightenment and uplifting than the ostensibly lower forms such as folk songs or dances.

## NATIONALISM IN MUSIC

Music, in the minds of nationalist composers, was thus supposed to fulfill not just artistic but also *social* goals. In Wagner's, Smetana's, and Grieg's hands, music was actually a political tool. In studying some of the ways in which politics interacted with music in the nineteenth century, a necessary first step to that end is to come to a solid conceptual understanding of music as a social product, and in particular, of *nationalist* music as a product of society and politics. Given the many common misconceptions of nationalist music, though, I first want to answer a (seemingly) simple question: what is nationalism in music *not*?

To some extent, answering this question requires cutting through many centuries of inherited belief in nations and nationality as fixed essences, as inherent or given. Often, such beliefs stem from the composers who propagated them. Whatever the source, archaic understandings of nationalism can lead to the assumption that the nationalist content in music actually resides in the music itself and not in the *ideas* about the music. To reaffirm, nationality is not a thing—not in music nor anywhere else. It is not even, as Richard Taruskin in his otherwise admirable entry on nationalism and music for the *New Grove Dictionary of Music and Musicians* claims, a "condition."[12] Nationality is, once again, simply an idea, an idea of a condition, perhaps (that condition presumably being a person's relationship to her communal group's culture and history), but nothing more tangible than that.

Nationality, since it is not a thing, an essence, or a condition, cannot be found in music—it cannot be found on the printed page of a score or in the music as pure sound produced by a piano, a choir, or an orchestra. Rather, since nationality is an idea, it can truly only be found in the ideas about music. How do people think about nationality, and how do they think about nationality in music? Where do they think nationality in music comes from—from a "national spirit," from the influence of the landscape on a people, from the rhythms of a people's language? (Again, for our purposes we have to remember that according to contemporary theories of nationalism, nationality in music comes *only* from ideas such as the national spirit, and not from any such national spirit itself.) How do they think music can be made national? What is the purpose of nationalist music? These are some of the key questions surrounding nationalist music, and thus the best way to comprehend its sociopolitical content is by answering those questions via discourse analysis. The statements, thoughts, and practice of the people who actually believed in and employed the ideas behind nationalist music are where we must look.

Building upon this ideational base and applying contemporary understandings of nationalism, we will come to realize what nationalism in music is not. I will examine five particular themes or pitfalls: these are primordialism, a fixation on folk tunes, an obsession with stylistics, the role of the nationalist composer, and the reception of music. The first, primordialism, refers to the idea that there is some kind of eternal, innate national spirit of a people. Primordialism views nationality as something eternal and natural, as if it were "in the blood." In a musical sense, this primordialism is exemplified most influentially by Herder and his idea of the *Volksgeist*. The Volksgeist is the immutable national identity of a people that finds expression through music. In particular, Herder claimed that every people (Slavs, Germans, the Latin "races," etc.) has its own unique musical style. So, every people has its folk music, which stems innately from that people's national character. The primordial view takes for granted a preexistent "Norwegianness" or "Germanness" or "Frenchness." Nationality in music supposedly proceeds from this inherent character of the people, and a French person could thus not write music that is "truly" Norwegian, and vice versa.

We must be careful, however, not to buy into the idea of these primordial identities, of the inherent and unchangeable characteristics of different races of people. When we understand national identities as social products rather than as metaphysical spirits, we see that the Volksgeist is an insufficient explanation for musical nationality. Today the idea of national spirits is entirely discredited; current theories of nationalism argue that there is no preexistent Volksgeist that motivates Norwegian, or German, or French composers. There is simply no evidence for innate, eternal national characters that reside somehow in ethnic bloodlines. Rather, the Volksgeist is nothing but an imagining of nationalist intellectuals, an invention just like the nation itself. Also, a belief in a primordial, preexistent nationality can lead to a misconception of the role of the composer. If one accepts the idea of the Volksgeist as the root of national music, then the composer becomes little more than an expressive tool for this vague and mystical spirit of the people. The spirit speaks through the composer, because he or she is innately Norwegian, and hence the music that the composer writes is this national spirit made audible, so to speak. This idea is patently untenable, though, as I will discuss later.

Impelled in large part by Herder, ideas about the Volksgeist led many nineteenth-century nationalist composers to seek that Volksgeist in folk tunes, and hence reference to folk material is one of the most common features of nationalist music. However, contrary to what some writers have claimed, the incorporation of folk material into art music by no means summarizes the phenomenon of nationalist music. Some composers, like Wagner and Sibelius, admittedly were relatively less concerned with folk tunes than were others, like Grieg or Bartók. However, that does not mean that Wagner and Sibelius are any "less nationalist" than the latter two (indeed, it is hard to imagine anyone who could be *more* of a nationalist than Wagner—throughout his prose writings, he is positively obsessed with the idea of nationality). In fact, Wagner and Sibelius are excellent exemplars of the ways music can be nationalist, even minus the prominent role for folk tunes. They demonstrate that there are so many more themes beyond just folk tunes that define the interaction of nationalism with this art form: the need to educate the populace, the goal of establishing cultural boundaries, the aspiration to international prestige, to name but three from the chapters that follow. Fixating solely on folk tunes can be a case of not seeing the forest for the trees if it leads one to neglect these other themes. Indeed, this fixation is reductionist and short-sighted: just because a composer did not write a "Fantasia on Folk Tunes" does not exclude the possibility of his being a nationalist composer.

The next potential misunderstanding of nationalist music involves an obsession with stylistics. What I mean by this is the endeavor to pinpoint certain musical features that are "uniquely" Norwegian, or Czech, or representative of some other nationality. Engaging in this endeavor can often lead to the primordial fallacy, and hence to a claim to identify the "unique and characteristic" features of Norwegianness in music. The idea would be that a particular rhythm or harmonic sequence is exclusively a Norwegian feature, and the claim is often made by nationalists that it somehow represents the national character. One example would be the insistence that the prominence of minor keys in Czech music results from an inherent melancholy in the Czech national character. However, even without subscribing to the primordial belief, it is still possible to be sidetracked by stylistics, as in debates about what genuinely constitutes "Czech music." The error is one that Carl Dahlhaus has pointed out. As he says, the bagpipe drone or the sharpened fourths that have been claimed as "quintessentially Polish" also appear with some frequency in Scandinavian folk music.[13] So, how can these individual musical features be either "natural expressions" of the Polish spirit (according to the primordial idea), or more simply the quintessence of Polish music?

The answer, of course, is that they cannot. The fixation on stylistics as somehow providing the clue to the national in music is misplaced precisely because individual musical features are incapable of embodying or independently communicating some kind of national content. First, obviously, there is no such thing as Polishness or Norwegianness to begin with: these are socially elaborated concepts and not fixed "essences." Also, there are no musical features that can be called absolutely and *exclusively* Norwegian. Again, since the national is merely an idea and not a thing, features such as certain tunes or rhythmic patterns do not automatically qualify as national. Musical style cannot be somehow "naturally" nationalistic. We must not look for the defining features of "Czech music" in the music, but rather in the ideas about the music.

These sorts of misconceptions threaten to lead, as an end product, to a misunderstanding of the role of the nationalist composer. In historical, nationalistic accounts, this misunderstanding has most often taken the form of describing the composer's task as "the awakening of the national spirit." The idea is that a composer, by writing music with a national character, automatically taps into a reserve of patriotism that is ready and waiting in the populace. Ralph Vaughn Williams, in his essay "National Music," which amounts to a kind of compendium of the primordial understanding of national music, asks in regard to national composers,

> Is it not reasonable to suppose that those who share our life, our history, our customs, our climate, even our food, should have some secret to impart to us which the foreign composer, though he be perhaps more imaginative, more powerful, more technically equipped, is not able to give us? This is the secret of the national composer, the secret to which only he has the key, which no foreigner can share with him and which he alone is able to tell to his fellow countrymen.[14]

In a similar vein, even the musicologist Otto Brusatti has claimed that national operas "awake...the national consciousness of the listening public" through "the latent roots of a musical understanding for the color of that opera music."[15]

Instead of this unconscious, innate expression of nationality, we should instead conceive of nationality in music as the product of *intent*. A piece of music is nationalist, above all, because its composer *wants it to be* nationalist. A piece of music is nationalist by design. As Leo Treitler has persuasively argued, in order to understand a work of art and its place in history, we need to understand what the artist's intentions were for the work. This sort of knowledge allows us to place the artist and his or her work in context, to analyze art and the production of art not in an intellectual vacuum but as inextricably linked to developments in society.[16]

Logically, then, we can identify a work as nationalist by investigating the composer's intent. Whether he assigns a title to it (like the *Má vlast* or "My Homeland" of Smetana) or a descriptive program, or what he says about it in his diaries or his letters—that's where we have to look. An anecdote from Grieg's life illustrates what I mean precisely. In Copenhagen in the 1860s, toward the beginning of his career, Grieg took a copy of one of his recent compositions and showed it to the Danish composer Niels Gade. Gade looked it over, grumbled a bit, then asked, "So, Grieg, this is supposed to be Norwegian?" Grieg replied: "Yes, it is, Maestro." My interpretation of this incident is that there was nothing on the musical page that would tell Gade that this was somehow national music. He had to be told by Grieg himself that, yes, Grieg intended it to be Norwegian. Plainly, nationality resides not *in* music but in the *discourse* about music. There are admittedly some identifiable differences in musical expression; music written by a nineteenth-century Norwegian sounds different from music written by a nineteenth-century Chinese. However, simply listening to the music itself, devoid of any external knowledge about that music's creation, does not permit one to identify the music as "national."

In turn, establishing a national musical style proceeds from the discourse to how the ideas in the discourse are realized in the artwork, and then finally into the reception of the work as national. My demotion of reception in favor of intent may seem surprising. Reception is certainly another way we can identify a work as nationalist. Carl Dahlhaus actually assigns pride of place to reception: in his formulation, music becomes nationalist when the public regards it as such. Reception of a piece can even make nationalist a piece that was not intended by its composer to be nationalist. The best example of this latter phenomenon is with folk music. As part of the process of "nationalizing" culture in the nineteenth century, local and regional peasant traditions came to be regarded as belonging to the putative nation as a whole. In the realm of music, the various peasant songs and dances were accepted by the public as belonging to their national culture, despite the fact that the origin of such songs is rooted in local practices and in no way in some mystical, overarching "Norwegianness" or "Czechness."

What reception of music as national really means is that a piece is *configured* as national in the public perception. The popular acceptance of a piece as national rarely happened spontaneously, to some kind of automatic mass acclaim. In actuality, there is almost always some behind-the-scenes process by which writers or composers argue for a piece's nationality. It is their discourse that configures the work as national before the public. Mr. and Mrs. Ole Nordmann did not just suddenly, independently start regarding the peasant dances known as *slåtter* as the cultural inheritance of the whole Norwegian nation. Why I focus on composer intent over public reception, then, has to do with my goal of relating nationalist music to the larger nation-building project. The aim of that project is to build a national public. Composers, playwrights, journalists, painters, historians, and other politically minded activists are all engaged in the effort. All these nationalist intellectuals sought to create a fund of cultural values that would be identifiable as belonging to (and thus constitutive of) the nation. In the musical realm, the goal was to establish and elaborate the national musical characteristics and then to celebrate and propagate them in works of art.

In order for music to be eventually "received" as national, though, there first must be a public that is nationalized. The public has to, on some level, be aware of and accept the theses on the constitutive characteristics of their national communality. And before there can be a national public that receives works as national, there must first be a project to construct that national public. A not uncommon feature of the careers of nationalist composers—this certainly holds true for Wagner, Smetana, and Grieg— is that early on, their national music found very little enthusiasm with their publics. For example, both Smetana and Grieg complained bitterly about the indifference that the people of Prague and Christiania at first showed to the kind of music they were writing. I suspect that the reason for this indifference can be attributed at least partly to the fact that in the 1860s in both the Czech lands and Norway, the idea of what would constitute the musical characteristics of the nation had barely begun to make inroads among the general populace. That is to say, the national public was still very much "under construction."

All this is not to claim that the composer's intent assumes an absolute primacy over reception. There is no reason why intent is *inherently* superior in deciding what makes a work nationalist. Composition, reception, and performance are all part of a social process of understanding. They are by no means mutually exclusive. However, we have to think in terms of the historical process by which the theses of national characteristics (in art as in politics) had to be propagated *before* a public could then apply these theses to their reception of works. So, reception of a work as national by a mass public has to come after that public has to some extent imbibed the ideas of what the national characteristics are. Of course, composers do not start from scratch: even they depend somewhat on preexisting ideas about elements of the national culture. They rely on certain "building blocks" often already conceived (if only by other nationalist intellectuals) as "national" in creating their larger structure of a national art. Perhaps the best example is again with folk music, as I discuss in the third chapter.

In any event, a nationalist composer's acceptance of the theses about what elements make up the national culture typically predates the mass public's. That is so because the composer, as a nationalist intellectual, belongs to the vanguard in terms of subscribing to a nationalist ideology and helping to create the discourse of the nation. Since he is a member of the activist vanguard, then, the nationalist composer's intent merits a historically prior focus over that of public reception. Reception's role in the establishment of a pantheon of nationalist music is indisputably important—so important, in fact, that it deserves its own book. For that very reason, and those aforementioned, I deal with reception only sporadically, since my focus is elsewhere.

Finally, there are also other reasons why national elements and tropes appear in music besides the intention to create a national art. Exoticism and originality are two additional motivations, often so closely bound up with nationalistic intent that only this whole complex of ideas can help explain why nationalism so thoroughly penetrated aesthetics in the nineteenth century. For instance, the notion of artistic worth in Wagner's, Smetana's, and Grieg's day was predicated partly on an artist producing something that was "original," that would make some kind of new or different contribution to musical style. Nationality became a vehicle for this goal. Indeed, as Dahlhaus writes, "One of the characteristic claims of the nineteenth century is that for individuality to be truly original it must be rooted in the 'national spirit.'…A composer was expected to be original, to bring forth the new in a manner which, at the same time, manifested the 'origins' of his existence."[17] Incorporating regional peasant dance forms, for example, or seasoning one's music with harmonies derived from folk music and hence unusual in the French-Italian-German traditions of "classical" music, would be attempts to satisfy the artistic calling for a composer to be original.

Similarly, by referring to these inspirations that were regarded as *outside* the art-music traditions, music could gain a whiff of the "exotic." Places like Norway or Andalucía seemed far-off and maybe a bit strange to the average educated person in London, Paris, Vienna, or St. Petersburg. Thus, music inspired or influenced by those lands might seem similarly striking and new. Even at home, depictions of "the folk" in music could appeal to urban audiences on these same grounds. Peasant traditions, while to some extent familiar, were at the same time "foreign," given the social divisions between rural and urban peoples. From a burgher's standpoint, a peasant doing a country dance (or someone pretending to be a peasant, or for that matter, a composer merely incorporating the dance form into a piece) could indeed appear somewhat exotic in comparison with the culture of the city.[18] One eyebrow-raising example of how "the national" and "the exotic" really did go hand in hand is worth mentioning: in 1857 in Norway, an exhibition of a dwarf wearing one of the "national" peasant costumes enjoyed enormous popularity.[19]

Closely related to exoticism is the usage of folk sources for "local color." Composers follow the local color usage to give a piece of music a "characteristic" flavor in depicting a certain land or people. This distinction Walter Wiora has described as that between "national self-portrayal" and "musical travel pictures."[20] These two modes are not necessarily mutually exclusive. However, the critical difference between when, for example, Manuel de Falla incorporates Spanish folk elements into a piece and when Glinka does the same, is that the former has a nationalist intent behind his music while the latter does not. In pieces like the *Jota aragonesa*, Glinka used the Spanish melodies and rhythms, above all, for their exotic value, and not because he was looking to create a "Spanish music" based on any sort of patriotic feelings about Spain. Obviously, not all music based on folk traditions is nationalistic. It is unfortunately impossible to say with any certainty to what extent the national elements in Wagner's, Smetana's, and Grieg's works are there for their "colorful" value, though all three were undoubtedly influenced by these widely held aesthetic conceptions.

One question that is left to address is how the ideas of nationality in music in the nineteenth century are different from those in the eighteenth century or earlier. For example, did not Bach have some idea that he was writing "German" music, or likewise Rameau with "French" music, and does that not make them nationalists? The answer is no, and it is related in part to the previous discussion about exoticism, since Bach's and Rameau's ideas of the national in music are fundamentally different from Wagner's, Smetana's, or Grieg's. As I mentioned earlier, nationalism as a social, political, and cultural force is profoundly shaped by the French Revolution, and it impacts societies on a much deeper level in the nineteenth century than it did in previous centuries.

What composers such as Wagner, Smetana, Grieg, and their nationalist contemporaries share—which a Bach or a Rameau lacks—is, first, an idea that the nationality in their music expresses a unified culture that transcends all social boundaries of the national community. This is an issue I address in more detail in the chapter on folk inspirations. Suffice it to say for now that nineteenth-century nationalists embrace the "folk"—the peasants—as culturally equal members of the community in a way that is simply not found in the Germany or France of Bach's and Rameau's time. Though in these earlier composers' understanding there may have been some notion of Germanness or Frenchness that could be expressed stylistically in their music, they assuredly did not understand that style as the outgrowth of a national spirit—a Volksgeist—that was shared equally by everyone from the king on down to the most humble peasant. They lacked such an understanding because such ideas were simply not current in their times; those ideas, again, spread only later, in the last decades of the eighteenth century with Herder, and then on into the subsequent century.

Second, what differentiates Bach's "German music" from Wagner's "German music" is the idea common to nineteenth-century nationalist composers that national music could actually help *create* the nation. This is a topic, again, that I deal with in the chapters that follow, but we must be clear that Bach was not a nationalist composer as was Wagner. Wagner, as we shall see, stated repeatedly that his music was designed to create a German culture, to help elaborate an identity for the German people. Throughout his career, Wagner undertook many nationalistic endeavors, even outside of his own composition and writing, to promote German nationalism—from reburying Carl Maria von Weber's remains in German soil to attempting to build a German national theater. Bach undertook no such activities with the understanding that he could create a unified German national culture that would be congruent with a unified and sovereign German polity. Bach predates the German nationalist movement, and does not subscribe to that movement's goals and ideology for the simple reason that those goals and ideology depend on a set of assumptions and ideas that spread only after Bach's death.

Nineteenth-century nationalism in music is thus different from earlier ideas of nationality in music, because nineteenth-century nationalist composers believed that their music expressed, constituted, and unified their putative nation in a cultural and political way that earlier composers did not share. Precisely *how* composers such as Wagner, Smetana, and Grieg believed their music was supposed to fulfill these goals is the subject of the chapters that follow.

## Endnotes

1. The classic statement of the perennialist view is Anthony Smith, *The Ethnic Origins of Nations* (Oxford: Blackwell, 1986).
2. One of the best exponents of the modernist view is Ernest Gellner, *Nations and Nationalism* (Oxford: Blackwell, 1983).
3. Ernest Gellner, "Nationalism," in *Thought and Change*, ed. Ernest Gellner (London: Weidenfeld and Nicholson, 1964), 147–178. *See esp.* p. 169.
4. See Benedict Anderson, *Imagined Communities: Reflections on the Origin and Spread of Nationalism* (London: Verso, 1991).
5. Cited in Ronald Grigor Suny and Michael D. Kennedy, eds., *Intellectuals and the Articulation of the Nation* (Ann Arbor: University of Michigan Press, 1999), 2.
6. Ibid., 3.
7. Cited in *Becoming National*, ed. Geoff Eley and Ronald Grigor Suny (New York: Oxford University Press, 1996), 21.
8. Anthony Smith, "The Origins of Nations," in ibid., 119.
9. See Gellner, "Nationalism."
10. Gellner, *Nations and Nationalism*, 36.
11. I will often refer to a "high" culture because that is the specific field in which my three composers were engaged. I do not wish thereby to reinforce the inaccurate hierarchy of cultural production by which some is "low" while other is "high" and hence superior. Nonetheless, as a commonly understood term it is easiest just to continue to use it. Nationalist composers' "high national culture" (i.e., their music) is high because it involves the products of self-conscious intellectual activity resulting from a long, institutionalized and codified tradition that requires a great degree of training to be able to produce and reproduce.
12. Richard Taruskin, "Nationalism," in *The New Grove Dictionary of Music and Musicians*, ed. Stanley Sadie (New York: Grove's Dictionaries, 2001), 689–706. *See esp.* p. 689.
13. Carl Dahlhaus, *Between Romanticism and Modernism* (Berkeley: University of California Press, 1980), 95.
14. Ralph Vaughan Williams, *National Music and Other Essays* (Oxford: Clarendon Press, 1934), 9.
15. Otto Brusatti, *Nationalismus und Ideologie in der Musik* (Tutzing: Hans Schneider, 1978), 73.

16. See Leo Treitler, *Music and the Historical Imagination* (Cambridge: Harvard University Press, 1989).

17. Carl Dahlhaus, *Nineteenth-Century Music* (Berkeley: University of California Press, 1989), 37.

18. Märta Ramsten, "'Ur forntida djup stige svenskmanna sång,'" in *"Hjemländsk Hundraårig Sång": 1800-talets musik och det nationella* ed. Henrik Karlsson (Göteborg: Kungliga Musikalska akademien, n.d.). See *esp.* p. 122.

19. Harald Herresthal, *Med spark i gulvet og quinter i bassen* (Oslo: Universitetsforlaget, 1993), 103.

20. Walter Wiora, *Europäische Volksmusik und abendländische Tonkunst* (Kassel: Johann-Philipp-Hinnenthal-Verlag, 1957), 162.

CHAPTER 2

# CREATING NATIONAL MUSIC

*Ich bin der deutsche Geist.* ("I am the German spirit.")
—Richard Wagner

*V hudbě život Čechů!* ("In music the life of the Czechs!")
—Bedřich Smetana

*Jeg tror ikke...at man går træt i det Nationale, thi kunde man det, var det ikke en Idé at kjæmpe for.* ("I don't believe one can tire of the national, since if one could, it would not be an idea worth fighting for.")

—Edvard Grieg

Wagner wrote these remarkable words in the diary he kept for his mistress Cosima while they were living apart in 1865. It was in the course of a longer, stream-of-consciousness meditation on what Germanness is that he suddenly declared that he himself, his ideas and art, embodied Germanness. Smetana's own declaration was a public utterance, triumphal words as he helped lay the foundation stone for the new Czech national theater building. On that great, festive day in 1868, Smetana delivered an epigraph to emblazon the new theater's mission. Grieg, writing a letter to a close Danish friend in 1877, was discussing modern composers' relationship to folk songs when he argued for the critical importance of the national idea. That idea, he emphasized, was fundamental to his own nature as an artist.

All three quotes express the fervor that Wagner, Smetana, and Grieg felt for their nation's culture. The prime sociopolitical concern of their lives was to translate this fervor into action in an effort to create a national art music. But, how, exactly, does an artist go about creating a national music? To answer this question, we must investigate the three composers' stated commitment to that project, the methods they employed to make their art national, and the musical works that resulted. Wagner's, Smetana's, and Grieg's plans and accomplishments constitute the first two of the three creative processes I mentioned in the Introduction, that is, the construction of nationalist music and of the national culture. The specifics of how these composers sought to create a national music—the ideas and practices involved with that goal—turn out to be nearly identical in each composer's case. And their ideas reveal how nationalist music is supposed to contribute to the establishment of a national culture.

Succinctly speaking, the program for creating a national music has three components. First, nationalist artists react against a perceived decline in the taste and artistic standards of the public. This decline prevents the public from recognizing both good art and their own true national art. Therefore, nationalist artists demand education for the populace. This is education into the standards of good art and ultimately into the values of the new national culture. The second component is institution building: it is part of the educational directive in that new, specifically national institutions such as a theater must be formed in order to enlighten the public. These institutions will also help to establish the national style and to secure glory for the national culture. Thirdly, these three composers assigned to themselves the task of producing music that would address the previous two needs—that is, they would create works of highest artistic quality that would serve as beacons of the national style.

The discourse and practice we study here also shed a preliminary light on the third creative process, that of the role of the nationalist artist. As these composers were elaborating the means of constructing the national culture, they were simultaneously also fashioning the role that nationalist artists would play in the nation-building movement. Wagner's, Smetana's, and Grieg's discourse and practice thus point to (and result from) a historical development in the social position of artists in the nineteenth century: namely, the emergence of artists as agents of social change. The potential for artists to become such social actors is very much a product of the thinking of the Romantic era. In the Romantic conception, the artist was privileged with a unique perception of the world and an almost divine creative power. With this power, he could create artworks that would communicate his unique perception and thereby change society.

What kind of change he wished to effect, of course, depended upon the individual artist. Nationalist artists, obviously, had a specifically nationalist vision of the change they wanted to bring about. They were concerned with the construction of the nation. Wagner, Smetana, and Grieg all believed that the artist had both an ability and, in a certain sense, a duty to assist in the nationalization of the public; they would accomplish this goal with their works of art. So, this *idea* of the artist's transformational role in society, and the *strategies* he developed for achieving the desired transformation, are central to the construction of a national culture. They are also integral to the formation of what we understand as the category of practice of the nationalist artist.

However, the nationalist artist's social mission also depends upon two other trends in the nineteenth century, trends which activist artists both respond to and help to produce. These two trends involve the change in the social place and the social function of art. The effort to create a national culture is part of a process of the democratization of art that occurred in the nineteenth century, the ideal of which was to make art accessible to people of all social classes. The change in the social function of art involves artists' aspiration for art to be something more than mere entertainment: it, too, would become a force for social change. These are fundamental assumptions behind Wagner's, Smetana's, and

Grieg's projects to create a national culture. In the chapter conclusion I will return to these two trends to consider in more detail how the program to create a national music reveals the change in the social place and function of art in the nineteenth century—a change that is closely tied to the growth of nationalism.

First, though, to Wagner's, Smetana's, and Grieg's own ideas and activities for establishing a national culture. Many of their ideas depend on common tropes and assumptions that informed the discourse of nationalist intellectuals more generally. What nationalist artists add, though, is a special emphasis on art's power in creating the nation. The trope of decline is a prime example here. A well-worn strategy of nationalist discourse, patriots virtually the world over recur to some complaint that while their nation once enjoyed a long-past "golden age" in which its nationality flowered, what followed was a dark period of decline. In this decline, so the complaint runs, the nation comes to be oppressed and the populace loses touch with its own unique national identity. Naturally, nationalist intellectuals hope to "rescue" their nation from this degenerate state. The particular perspective that the discourse on national art presents is that the nation has fallen from a previous, glorious period when the national culture thrived, into a contemporary nadir where the culture has become denationalized, beset by foreign and/or worthless art.

Wagner, Smetana, and Grieg all refer to the ideas of decline and a golden age in their own discourse. In so doing, they were strongly influenced by intellectual precedents within their respective nationalist movements. For instance, the trope of decline is a particularly powerful one for the Czech movement. Prominent figures such as František Palacký and Josef Dobrovský typically pointed to the early middle ages—a span of time stretching from the independent Czech kingdom up to the life of Jan Hus—as the pinnacle of Czech achievements, after which Czechs increasingly lost touch with their culture. Though perhaps less preoccupied with the past than the Czechs, the Norwegians also looked back, to the period of the sagas and the Vikings' zenith, as their era of greatness. The ancient mythic period of the Germanic tribes, or the glories of the German renaissance embracing Dürer, Luther, and Nürnberg's height, were German nationalists' contenders for the golden age to which the contemporary, "unnational" period contrasted. These specific golden ages each make their appearance in Wagner's, Smetana's, and Grieg's music.

The next major theme these three composers are concerned with—education—is an especially important one in the discourse on creating a national art. It is closely related to claims about what role the theater should play in society. The power of art to edify is a familiar idea with roots in ancient Greek civilization or even earlier. However, the idea that art "must also educate people, to lead them out of the raw, ignorant state and on to the sublime" was especially potent during the Romantic era.[1] What nationalists add to this conception is that art must educate on a national basis. When Fichte stressed the need for education (*Bildung*) of the populace, for example, this education was supposed to be moral, artistic, and also explicitly *national*. The people were to be educated into their own nationality.[2] While schools were of course central in that project, many writers beginning in the later 1700s also assigned the theater a major role. Schiller, for one, famously proclaimed that "the theater is a school."[3] In large part, the theater's importance is due to its status as perhaps the principal mode of mass communication in the eighteenth and nineteenth centuries, when much of the populace was still illiterate and before the establishment of nationalized school systems. Hence "national theaters" were widely viewed as essential means of propagating a national culture and nationalizing the populace.

National theater movements in the nineteenth century have received a fair amount of scholarly attention elsewhere, so my purpose here is simply to allude to the complex of ideas and forerunners that influenced my three composers. In Germany, figures such as Schiller and Lessing were some of the most important voices arguing for the power of the theater to improve the public's morals and taste. Schiller did also conceive a patriotic role here: the national theater should be the "teacher of the Volk,"[4] and through it, he wrote, "we will become a nation."[5] After Schiller, these ideas continue to be espoused by a variety of figures, such as Wagner's friend, the writer Hermann Laube, who demanded that the theater present "the nation on stage,"[6] or Carl Maria von Weber, who was concerned with creating a German opera.

František Palacký, F. L. Rieger, J. K. Tyl, and Karel Sladkovský are some of the main figures in the drive for a Czech national theater. They also subscribed to the conception of the theater as both an educational and a patriotic institution. As another important voice in the Czech movement, Smetana's friend Jan Neruda, wrote, the theater should be "the seed bed of all Czech art, the refiner of the Czech spirit, the guardian of Czech language, the crystallization of the purpose of Czech life, a symbol of our standing on a cultural level with other nations."[7] The drive for a national theater also included an attempt to create a Czech operatic style; Tyl and the composer Škroup were pioneers on that front in the 1840s and 1850s.

In Norway, the writer Henrik Wergeland and the violinist Ole Bull were two of the primary promoters of the establishment of a Norwegian theater. Bull in particular argued for the theater's power to "bring people up to a higher level of culture."[8] He also emphasized that the theater could communicate best with the public if it were presenting works based on national themes. Grieg's contemporary, the writer Bjørnstjerne Bjørnson, took over from Bull as the most vocal advocate of a national theater, and wrote many plays himself on themes from Norwegian history. The efforts to create a Norwegian national opera were in general quite scattered, though Wergeland was very enthusiastic about that project, and the composer Waldemar Thrane did produce a light opera called *Fjeldeventyret* ("The Mountain Tale") in 1824.

As we will see in the discourse that follows, opera is in many ways the crux of the educational and patriotic missions behind national music. This is again due to the theater's critical role as a method of mass communication. Additionally, though, opera was widely regarded in the nineteenth century as the fusion and pinnacle of all other art forms. It accordingly became the center of gravity of urban cultural life. Opera assumed an enormous importance for the nationalist movement because it was able to "fulfill the function of national representation," as Petr Vít suggests.[9] On the operatic stage, the nation's past, future, landscape, and folk life could all be depicted. It was also a major venue for establishing the use of the national language in public life. This, then, is how the theater's educational function is also national: the intent of nationalist artists was for the opera to configure the ideal of the nation on stage and to communicate that ideal to the envisioned national public.

With these sorts of ideas informing their plans for a national art, Wagner, Smetana, and Grieg employed four key methods to make their own art national. The first receives its own chapter: it is the reliance on a "folk" element. Incorporating features that were conceived as springing from the pure, natural sources of the relevant national *Volksgeist*, these three composers sought to elevate such sources into the status of an authentically national high art. In the present chapter, though, we examine the other three methods, namely, language, the use of themes from history and legend, and references to the national landscape. These are all fairly self-explanatory strategies, frequent throughout nationalist discourse. While they appear in various guises in these composers' works, nationalist operas like Wagner's *Die Meistersinger von Nürnberg*, Smetana's *Libuše*, and Grieg's *Olav Trygvason* perhaps best exemplify all four methods.

Nationalists, of course, typically conceive of language as one of the paramount marks of nationality. History and legend usually refer back to the golden age of national greatness, so evoking that greatness in art is supposed to remind audiences of the nation's achievements. An attachment to the national landscape is also one of the *sine qua non* of a patriot, and depicting that landscape in art is an obvious way to glorify the nation. These are all means of linking the artist to the nation through the artwork. Moreover, they also link both the nation to its art and the national citizens to each other by celebrating, in that art, what the nation and the artist have in common, namely the love of their language, history, and landscape.

A final strategy common to all three composers, and one which in turn unifies all the above means of constructing and propagating a national culture, was the creation of an institution or festival to showcase the nation's art. Wagner had his Bayreuth Festival, Smetana worked toward the establishment of the Národní divadlo (National Theater) in Prague, and Grieg organized a music festival in Bergen in 1898. The sociopolitical goals of all three projects were much the same, and as such they can be regarded as the culmination of each man's project for a national art.

Wagner, Smetana, and Grieg all left no doubt about their commitment to the project of building a national culture. They were indeed committed nationalists, and they often affirmed their desires to create a nationalist art. Interestingly, however, their statements to this effect also reveal their ideas on the role that they as individuals would play in that nation-building project. In this regard, of the three composers, Wagner most directly enunciates the theses of the artist as an agent for social change. Both Smetana and Grieg, less philosophically predisposed than Wagner, instead tend to frame their contributions more as stemming from a national duty than from a kind of semidivine creative power. Nonetheless, their discourse, too, evinces the belief that the artist's public duty is founded upon his power to transform society through his works. This claim alone is one of their most powerful, in that it establishes the position of artists within the nationalist movement.

## WAGNER

While one of the principal impulses behind Wagner's desire to create a national music is indeed his perception that the cultural situation in Germany languishes in a terrible state of decline, he actually expands this theme beyond only German culture, declaring that in fact all of modern art has degenerated. Modern art, he claims, is completely incapable "of influencing public life in the sense of its most noble strivings."[10] The fundamental problem is that modern art is no longer *natural*—it is too artificial, a "greenhouse plant" so far removed from its real roots that only the "artistic class" understands it anymore.[11]

Opera, in particular, has ceased to be an art at all and is merely a "manifestation of fashion."[12] Wagner's critique of "fashion" ties directly into his revulsion against all things French, since it is the French taste for the fashionable that has infected contemporary opera. And the French, as I discuss in the fourth chapter, are the antithesis of a "natural" Volk, hence the destructive effect of the spread of French tastes throughout Europe. So sorry is the state of the drama in Germany, so infected is it by harmful foreign influences, that the theater must be regarded as the "betrayer of German honor."[13] Rather than providing (quite literally) the stage from which the further glorious development of German culture would proceed—following the path set by Goethe and Schiller—Germany's theaters are filled with worthless plays and foreign trifles. The result is that contemporary opera falls far short of the "inner ideal" that Wagner knows it should achieve.[14]

In this gloom and doom, Wagner despairs that "Germany, in its terrible confusion, now offers the artist no prospect of a fruitful homeland."[15] This complaint exactly echoes the similar fears shared by both Grieg and Smetana, that the cultural situation in their homelands was too weak to foster them as artists. And like the other two, Wagner laments that the public in his own homeland simply has no taste for good art. French taste rules "almost all European nations" so that the Germans have no artistic taste of their own.[16] Indeed, the German public has so lost its good taste in music that it sooner falls into ecstasy over an Italian coloratura soprano than over Bach or Beethoven.[17] Besides just the dastardly French, however, Wagner reserves a few shots against what he calls the "exploitative imperative of bourgeois commerce" (*Nutzzweckgesetz des bürgerlichen Verkehrs*), which leads the theater to contribute to the "ruin of the people's best moral tendencies."[18] When it is ruled by profit, the theater cannot work to improve the people's morals and tastes, which should be its highest calling.

The ultimate effect of all these disastrous influences is that the Volk is distanced from its own spirit (*Volksgeist*). And when that happens, then the chances of great art—including national art—coming out of that nation are very slim. He lambastes the contemporary cultural situation conclusively when he writes:

> It is clear to everyone that groups of so many clever minds will never be able to bring a genius or a true artwork into the world: that they, in the contemporary situation of the public intellectual

life in Germany, are not even capable of presenting to the nation the works of genius—which of course do not come from their groups—is conclusively proven in that the artistic institutions in which the works of the great masters of the German rebirth would be presented to educate the people, are entirely denied to exercise their influence and are instead left to the ruin of German artistic taste. Here on the side of art, as also on the side of politics, it is irrefutable how little the German Geist can expect from all these otherwise so thoroughly German groups.[19]

On rare occasions, such as in a letter in 1851, Wagner despairs so completely about the German public that he declares that he does not even want to try to appeal to them anymore.[20] Still, though, until late in his life, when his disappointment in the direction the German Reich had taken finally grew too great, he did retain his hope that German society could be "saved."

It would be saved through the edifying power of art. Wagner's response to the perceived decline in culture and good taste was to emphasize the power of art to educate and elevate the public. As Wagner put it, "only art is the creator of the Volk."[21] The most important vehicle, to this end, was the theater's capacity to "strengthen and ennoble...the morals and taste of the public."[22] Not merely theater alone would accomplish this, though: he thought that music was also capable of improving taste and morals.[23] This "ennobling" power should always benefit the "spiritual needs of the nation."[24]

An example of the theater working this power was in the heyday of Goethe and Schiller. Wagner credits the theater with playing a decisive role in the rebirth of the German Geist:

> The most decisive effect of the spirit of the German rebirth on the nation was in the end realized through the dramatic literature from the theater. Who would disregard or deny to the theater (as these days impotent literary figures like to do) the most decisive importance for the influence of the artistic spirit on the moral spirit of a nation proves that he stands completely outside of this true exchange of ideas, and deserves to be ignored in both literature and art.[25]

Based upon the priceless contributions that Goethe and Schiller made through their theatrical works to the development of German culture, so must the theater again assume a national burden. In the theater lies the:

> seed and nucleus of all national-poetic and national-moral spiritual education…No other branch of art can come to a truer bloom and popular-educational effectiveness until the theater's all-powerful contribution in this area is fully acknowledged and assured.[26]

Hence the means he chose for that other branch of art—music—to work its own influence on spiritual education: in the theater, through the "musicdrama," the powers of both these arts are united, for the moral and cultural benefit of the national populace. In particular, performances of quality dramatic works (i.e., not French drivel) would bring about "the perfect cultivation of a hitherto completely lacking German style in the field of living drama."[27] Through the regeneration of this most important force in the German cultural scene—the theater—the arts in turn will bring "the nation's recovery."[28]

Admittedly, at one point in his voluminous writings, Wagner did actually deny that the theater should act as an "educational institute."[29] However, this is an isolated incident, and given the much more frequent references to the theater's power and moreover *duty* to elevate the public, we can regard this denial as just another one of Wagner's occasional self-contradictions. In any event, his concerns about education in the arts were strong enough that he at least twice suggested the formation of national music schools. In 1849, as part of his plans for the organization of a German national theater in Saxony, he called also for the formation of a "German National Institute for Music" in Dresden.[30] Later, he wrote a lengthy report to Ludwig II proposing the creation of a similar institute in Munich.[31] While neither the Dresden nor the Munich plan was realized, he did regard the eventual establishment of the music school in Berlin as a "success" of his plan, even though he was not directly involved with that school.[32]

Despite the importance of schools, the real target of Wagner's reforms was of course the theater, and more particularly opera. Opera would be the key to the creation of the national culture. Though geniuses such as Goethe, Schiller, and Lessing had produced noble, specifically *German* plays, no one had come along to complete their project through the means of opera. Instead of the frivolous French and Italian opera that dominated Germany's stages, Wagner called for the "reconstruction of the German theater in the sense of the German spirit."[33] His envisioned reform of the theater would thereby bring about "the formation of a life that would truly bring the appearance of the German spirit,"[34] "the national atonement for the national crime of the current effectiveness of the German theater."[35]

So, the German nation could not be truly German without a German theater. For this reason, a national theater was essential for the life of the nation. They needed to honor the achievements of their own national culture. The national theater as Wagner conceived it would present "model performances of noble German original works," displaying "to the German nation the best and noblest works."[36] After all, in Wagner's conception, "art is according to its meaning nothing else than the fulfillment of the desire to recognize oneself in an admiringly represented or loved object."[37] Thus the Germans had to see themselves on stage as a nation in order to grasp their own nationality. The particular power of the musician here is that he is able to show the nation "what it in truth is."[38] In other words, Wagner, through his privileged perception of Germanness (see the following for more on that), would be able to present the German public with its true, *national* essence.

This idea of the theater's representative function—depicting the idealized vision of the nation back to the nation itself—is the kernel of Wagner's entire conception of the national theater. Wagner says explicitly, "In the drama transfigured by music the Volk will find both *itself* and every art ennobled and improved."[39] A specifically national theater is necessary, though, because at present there are few stages upon which the composer can "show a nation to itself."[40] Moreover, a national theater would be open to the whole nation, to all classes in society. Wagner explicitly criticizes the earlier period in history when opera was the preserve of nobility.[41] He wants the *Gesamtvolk* in the theaters—the nation's totality, as I will demonstrate later in my treatment of Bayreuth.

Wagner was explicit about the role he assigned himself in the battle to improve the arts in Germany and to make them genuinely national. He wrote in 1872 that he was going to "dedicate my activity completely to the carrying out of an undertaking that first of all will realize almost solely a national intention. Should my work be completely successful," he continued, "then this success would consist in large part in that I can lead the same seed of a German-national art, whose fostering and cultivation in the field of the musical drama has until now been most damagingly arrested by the influence of Italian opera, to an independent development."[42] The role the artist should play in fostering a German national culture is further suggested by a passage from *Oper und Drama*, where Wagner describes the artist's creative power. "The artist," he writes, "manages to see in advance the formation of an as yet unformed world, to enjoy in advance through the power of his desire to create [*Werdeverlangen*] a world not yet created [*noch ungewordene*]."[43] With this special perception, the artist is then able to create the image of this "as yet unformed world" in his art, to present it to the Volk so that they at last recognize themselves and can then truly embark upon the path to self-realization. Art must "express itself most definitely after place, time, and circumstances." Only in that way would it achieve its "most lively effectiveness."[44]

Thus, art, in Wagner's thought, must communicate the nature of its origin. However, given the artist's capability of seeing a world that does not yet exist, art can also communicate the ideal toward which society must move. Music, especially, is "an idea of the world that directly presents to the world its own essence."[45] Music's special power in this regard means that the musician himself has a capability greater than that of other artists; the other arts cannot present so immediate a picture of the world as can music. The specific "idea of the world" that Wagner had in his mind came to him while living in Paris in the 1840s. His feelings there of homelessness wakened in him a longing for Germany. However, he adds, "this longing referred not to an old, familiar, regained land, but rather to one foreseen and wished-for, new, unknown, and yet to be attained."[46] In short, he began to long for the unrealized Germany of his imagination—his vision of the nation and its culture.

The problem, as the aforementioned quote indicates, was that this ideal Germany did not exist. There was no German national culture as Wagner envisioned it. Rather, as we have seen previously, German cultural life was in a dire state, dominated by foreign influences. In *Das Braune Buch*, he alleges that the decline of German arts since Goethe and Schiller showed that no one since them understood the German spirit. "But I have understood it," he declared in this 1865 entry. "I am the most German person, I am the German spirit."[47] Even twenty years earlier, though, he had already stated that he had "now set myself the lovely task to continue [Carl Maria von] Weber's work," to help emancipate Dresden and Germany musically, "to develop the public's taste for the noble," to reform dramatic music.[48]

His works would constitute the "starting point for a genuine German style in musical-dramatic performances," a style of which at present "no trace is extant," he commented.[49] Despite all the hindrances that had prevented the appearance of "a great national music work,"[50] Wagner believed that with the performances of the *Ring* at the first Bayreuth Festival, he had indeed created such a work. At the end of the first *Götterdämmerung* at Bayreuth in 1876, he addressed the audience, telling them: "You have now seen what we can do; now it is up to you to *want* it. And if you want it, then we will have an art!" What he meant by this address, he later explained, was that the Germans were lacking a national art, but that they could have one—it was there on the stage of Bayreuth for them—if only they would acknowledge it, take it to their hearts, so that the *Ring* would truly belong to the nation.[51] So, there the German art was on the stage of Bayreuth, and it had been created, of course, by Wagner, through his unique artistic capacities—the unique capacities that allowed him as an artist to reform German culture and society in a national direction.

Perhaps the best example of Wagner's nationalist intent behind his works was his insistence that with the *Ring* he had given a gift to the nation. To this "popular-national"[52] work, the "chief work of my life," he gave the dedication, "Devised in confidence of the German spirit."[53] He even claimed that he would never have conceived of the

*Ring* without the German nationalist movement.[54] With characteristic modesty, Wagner also once asked rhetorically: "Regard the incomparable magic of *my* works…You can now say nothing else but—they are *German*."[55] The *Ring*, along with Wagner's other works, displays the common tropes of nationalist discourse that were intended to make them uniquely "German."

To begin with, like virtually all nationalists, Wagner attributes an enormous power to language as a talisman of nationality. When composing *Der fliegende Holländer*, Wagner recalled, he realized that for the utterances of the dramatic characters, he could not utilize the folk melody style which he used elsewhere in the opera's music. Instead, "here the speech itself, according to its most full of feeling content, had to be reproduced, so that not the melodic expression, but rather the expressed feelings would arouse the sympathy of the listener. The melody must thus entirely of itself arise out of speech."[56] This statement expresses the technique that Wagner claimed to employ throughout his mature operas when setting to music the speech of his characters. The patterns of language were to be the starting point for dramatic music. In order for that dramatic music to attain the ideals Wagner set out for it, however, it had to be grounded on a language that was still true to its roots and "natural."[57] This language, of course, is German: "the perfect dramatic artwork," and so the reform of opera could only be realized through the German language.[58]

All of Wagner's mature operas are drawn from mythical subjects, and Wagner was usually attracted (though not exclusively) to myths that he perceived as German in origin. The *Nibelungenlied*, for example, on which the *Ring* is based, was already established as a kind of "German Iliad" or "national poetry" by the time Wagner took it as inspiration.[59] Wagner claimed that it was through his investigations of the mythical past, such as reading Grimm's *Deutsche Mythologie* in the 1840s, that he found both himself and the future course of his career. Grimm's *Mythologie* spoke "from the primeval homeland" to him, "and soon my entire sensory existence was seized by imaginings that ever more clearly formed themselves in me of the idea of regaining a long lost but continually searched-for consciousness." He calls this effect nothing less than a "rebirth."[60] This long-sought consciousness was that of a purely and self-consciously German culture. A passage from *Eine Mitteilung an meine Freunde* further explains the power and role of Wagner's mythic subjects:

> In the effort to give the desires of my heart an artistic shape, and in the zeal to investigate what impelled me so irresistibly to the ancient saga sources, I reached step by step deeper into antiquity, where I then finally to my delight precisely there in the highest antiquity, encountered the youthfully beautiful human in the most sumptuous freshness of his strength. My studies brought me thus through the literature of the middle ages back to the foundation of the old German myths; from these myths I managed to remove one guise after the other that later writings had thrown deformingly upon them so as finally to glimpse them in their most chaste beauty.[61]

A major appeal of these "old German" myths was that they were in a sense authentically and purely German, stemming from before the time that German culture began to be polluted by foreign influences. In the next chapter I will examine Wagner's use of myth more extensively, particularly the way he conceived it as a kind of folk expression.

Wagner also evokes a specifically national landscape in his works, though he does so much less than Smetana. Actually, a number of Wagner's opera plots are not even set in Germany: *Der fliegende Holländer* in Norway, *Tristan und Isolde* in Cornwall and Brittany, and *Parsifal* nominally in Spain, for example. Regardless, other works do refer to the German landscape. Most of *Tannhäuser* is set at the Wartburg in Thuringia, a medieval castle that was one of the high temples of nineteenth-century German nationalism. *Tannhäuser* and the *Ring* both make references to deep, dark German forests. *Götterdämmerung* also features the famous music of "Siegfried's Rhine Journey," which is as close as Wagner comes to Smetana's glorification of the quintessential Czech river the Vltava.

*Die Meistersinger von Nürnberg* fuses all of these tropes and thus in a sense may be Wagner's "most national" opera, not only in terms of how it has been received, but also, most importantly, according to the composer's intentions. He relied on texts by Grimm and Wagenseil as historical sources in writing the libretto.[62] Set during Nürnberg's Renaissance peak, Wagner is obviously evoking a golden age. The link to Nürnberg is also a reference to the landscape of Germany, to one of its most beautiful and formerly culturally important cities. Wagner even had the idea of premiering the work in Nürnberg, though in the end it was first given in Munich.[63] The figure of Hans Sachs, "the last appearance of the artistically productive Volksgeist," also steps forward from the halcyon days of German culture.[64] Wagner's identification of Sachs as a uniquely and genuinely German artist is even more interesting given that, during the time he was composing *Meistersinger*, Wagner took to signing his own letters "Hans Sachs."[65]

Wagner said that with this work he wanted "to present the German public with an image of their own true nature."[66] In this sense, *Meistersinger* corresponds to the idea of representing to the nation its own national self. Particularly the first scene of the third act—the Festwiese ("festival meadow") scene—presents a cavalcade of burghers, peasants, and artists all assembling to hail German art. A classic parallel to other such Volk displays from operas like *A Life for the Tsar*, *The Bartered Bride*, or *Halka*, Wagner loads the Festwiese with light-hearted choruses, dancing, and pompous processions. In this scene, he said, "resides the entire relationship of German art."[67] Wagner in fact praised *Die Meistersinger* as his "actual masterpiece."[68] The opera's premiere attracted a lot of attention throughout Europe as the appearance of a new German national opera, Martin Gregor-Dellin reports.[69] Wagner himself was convinced that the German public would cheer the work—and his perception that this did not happen was the source of much bitterness for him in his last years.[70]

The founding of the Bayreuth Festival could be considered the climax of Wagner's nationalist project. Bayreuth was the ultimate expression of his goals as a nationalist artist. There can be no doubt about the national intent behind the festival, even if there were other motivations (pecuniary, egotistical) at work as well. In a letter to Ludwig II in 1871,

Wagner suggested that the foundation of a Festspiel could be a "German national enterprise."[71] His wife Cosima also reports that Wagner referred to his Bayreuth plans as "his German undertaking."[72] Then, laying the foundation stone for his theater in 1873, Wagner proclaimed "I trust the German spirit" and "the spirit of German music."[73]

He explained the idea behind the Bayreuth Festival as follows:

> It would correspond superbly to the organism of German exis-tence, which presently it is the idea to develop politically in the newly arisen German Reich, since the active powers in it would belong as parts to the whole. It will first of all offer nothing else but the periodic, place-specific meeting point of the best theatri-cal powers of Germany for the practice and execution in a higher German original style of its art.[74]

This "national artistic" institution[75] would thus realize its nationality by presenting works (Wagner's works, of course) of "distinct German originality."[76] Such model performances would serve as beacons of a "German style." The Bayreuth theater would also benefit Germany by producing the "ennobling of taste" that was so important to Wagner.[77] Even ten years prior to the construction of the Bayreuth theater, Wagner was talking about this plan and how it would present "that which is most typical and successful of the German spirit" so that "at least in a highly significant branch of art, the German would thereby begin to be national."[78] This project would lead to "the development of a genuine, not arrogant national spirit."[79]

Bayreuth also embodies his idea of the onstage representing of the nation to the nation. An essential element of this aim is thus to ensure that the public who attended the Bayreuth Festival would be a wide one—the Festival would not be exclusive. "Not belonging to a particular social class," Wagner wrote, "but rather penetrating all levels of society, the new totality will in my eyes represent the actively realized receptivity of German feeling for the original demonstration of the German spirit in the same areas which until now have been left to the neglect of the most un-German cultivation."[80] He insisted that the whole German public, "far and near," should be invited to the Festival.[81] Bayreuth was the bearer of his "most noble German hopes" that it would bring about the realization of a German nation that as yet was only "provisional."[82] So he called the foundation stone a "magical stone" with the power to make these dreams come true. And for good measure, he even expressed his hope that the new building would serve as a monument for a "German architectural style."[83] Though it eventually ended up being built on a hill in Oberfranken, Wagner's earliest idea in fact was that his national theater would stand on the banks of the Rhine—and the geographic symbolism of that idea is obvious.[84] The vicissitudes of Wagner's thought and career notwithstanding, his plan remained essentially the same throughout: with this theater, Wagner would give people the meaning of his revolution. It would display the ultimate, instructive spectacle of German national art.

## SMETANA

Smetana's view on the perilous situation of Czech cultural life is first enunciated publicly in his article "Regarding our concerts," in the periodical *Slavoj* from October 1862. The Prague concert scene was dismal in part because so few concerts were given—but more damagingly, because the music that tended to predominate was of negligible artistic worth.[85] The dearth of public performances of music of true artistic quality had caused a serious crisis in Czech cultural life. Gloomily surveying this wasteland, Smetana wrote,

> If we examine with an impartial but keen eye our current musical conditions, comparing them with the life developing in this direction in the great cities abroad, we must acknowledge—even though it is unfortunate—that all the activity up to now in the musical field is deplorable, effectively zero. The art of which we speak declines day by day, and all the more so as floozies tend to use it for diversion and entertainment.[86]

Art itself was suffering because the public was more interested in entertainment than in an edifying culture. According to Smetana, this was especially shameful given the Czechs' reputation as one of the most musically talented peoples in Europe. The public's poor musical taste and its mal-education through bad pieces had the further negative result that even when a good, truly Czech artist or work came along, the public did not recognize it. When high-quality concerts were offered, attendance was typically poor, as Smetana found on more than one occasion. To his chagrin, such was the case with one of his first Prague concerts, shortly after he returned from his years in Sweden.[87]

The problem was not just with concerts, however. Opera was also seriously infected. Smetana's article in the *Národní listy* of June 24, 1864, lays out the principal complaints against the serious deficiencies of Prague's Czech opera. Looking objectively at Czech opera as it currently stands, Smetana declared,

> we must recognize that it is incapable of arousing the confidence that it will finally set out on the path assigned to it: that it will justly manifest the heights of our national artistic activities and our artistic efforts, that it should become the central focus of the entire domestic artistic world—that is that it should fulfill its foremost and most exalted role.

Unfortunately, the opera in its present state was completely inadequate for this momentous task. Instead, its function remained the same as in decades past. It served "merely the amusement of the public, with the sole difference that now it resides in its own home [the Provisional Theater]. The repertoire itself consists mostly of works only few of which have any worth in the musical literature."[88]

The Provisional Theater was the building the Czechs were using to put on their Czech-language opera and theatrical performances. While it was something of a coup just to have a viable, Czech-language alternative to the predominantly German theaters in Prague, Smetana believed that merely possessing a separate theater building did not make it a genuinely *Czech* theater. The operas given were almost entirely French or Italian, and they rarely met Smetana's standards for artistic quality. The few ostensibly Czech operas were mostly just translations from the

French or Italian, and poor translations at that. He remarks additionally that quite often these operas were not even well performed.

All this bad, nonnational music, Smetana protested, "ruinously impacts the public so long that it [the opera] falls victim to its own faulty direction. If our Czech people can only poorly distinguish good music from bad, the public musical production bears the blame, above all the opera and then concerts."[89] Presented with so few examples of a quality national art, the public's taste languished in its predilection for trifles. The institutions that did exist to elevate and educate the public simply failed in that goal, and so the public remained "poorly educated" artistically.[90] Another example of this failure was the conservatory, about which Smetana commented that "our conservatory firmly holds to its meaning; it remains *conservative*."[91]

The thrust of Smetana's complaint here is that the conservatory was not educating students in the best modern music, instead remaining steeped in styles that were already outmoded. This complaint manifests Smetana's commitment to the most recent international trends in music of the day, the trends represented by Berlioz, Liszt, or Wagner. Smetana's idea is that if Czech musicians were not educated in the most "progressive" music (for that is the way Smetana viewed it), then the entire nation would stagnate artistically. For all his interest in "national music," Smetana always insisted that such music must correspond to the most advanced compositional styles of the day. Thus when he reviewed works of a "national" character in the *Národní listy* of December 5, 1863, though doubtless he was sympathetic to their national aims, he found them generally of low musical worth.[92] If a piece was national but weak musically, then it was ultimately of little worth in uplifting the national culture.

As with Wagner, Smetana's response to this perceived rot in the public's artistic taste was to provide opportunities to educate people in what was good, truly national art. In fact, Smetana went even further than Wagner in organizing groups and institutions to this end. His earliest effort was the music school he founded in Prague in 1848. While the main intent behind the school may have been to help Smetana pay his bills, it also served a social function in that he organized evenings of chamber music to which the public was invited.[93] His idea was not just to give Czech musicians good training, but to have them perform good music for the Czech public. Given his poor opinion of the concerts already on offer in Prague, he in fact explicitly assigned to himself the "role of bringing in concerts that according to the composition of their program and their performance…would meet the highest standards of art."[94] So, at various points in his career, he organized concerts to showcase what he regarded as the best and highest musical works. In the 1860s, for example, he directed several concerts of the philharmonic society. These concerts were also designed to advance specifically Czech music. "Being a Czech, I will organize Czech concerts," he explained.[95] Obviously, his idea was that these concerts would be uniquely Czech in a way that concerts sponsored by the Prague Germans, or concerts featuring French and Italian music, could never be.

Smetana's educational plans even once included the idea of giving public lectures to teach other musicians what he had learned throughout his career.[96] This idea went unrealized, however, because of his deafness. Nonetheless, Smetana did achieve the major goal he set for himself in terms of edifying the public. This goal was becoming the director of the Czech opera. His view of the importance of this job is clear:

> From the national point of view the post of conductor at the Czech Theater is no doubt most important. From here one really has a direct influence on the public in the broadest sense and would be able to influence to the greatest possible extent the refinement of artistic taste as well as, above all, the trend of art. It is therefore understandable that this post would suit me best.[97]

In this letter he added that "the director of the Conservatoire, if he is a Czech artist, can also do great things for art at home."

The function that Smetana ascribed to the theater in creating a national culture is thus both readily apparent and immense. He wrote that "the theater must be a school," in an obvious echo of Schiller.[98] And like Wagner, Smetana stressed the paramount importance of opera in particular for the national cause. First, however, Prague opera itself had to be reformed. From the amateurish, purely entertainment-oriented institution that Smetana derided, he insisted that it must become truly artistic, focused on the:

> execution of works in a *conscientious, faithful, pure artistic spirit.* To that end it is necessary for the material to become more sophisticated. Operas cannot be a musical production that one merely sings just to sing, where it suffices that everything follows the same tempo and nothing gets mixed up...Operas must be uplifted on the basis of *drama.*[99]

As a quotation cited earlier indicates, opera should teach the public to distinguish good from bad music. By presenting works of the highest artistic quality, and performing them in a true dramatic spirit, opera would be capable not just of edifying the public, but in fact of "lifting up" all of music.[100] The emphasis here on the fusion between music and drama, and the social mission the opera could accomplish thereby, points to Smetana's knowledge of Wagner's writings.

With the reform of the theater, however, the Czechs would be able to concentrate on the "first and most beautiful role of our opera" which is the "cultivation of our domestic art...for that is its role and even duty. About that there can be no doubt and one could hardly find anybody who would want to dispute it."[101] The opera, in Smetana's plan, would present many more works by Czech composers than it did under its current administration. This would include new works by Czech composers, of course, as well as neglected works from earlier composers such as Škroup and Kittl. Additionally, Smetana calls for the opera to present the works of other Slavic composers, "our tribal brothers," mentioning specifically Glinka, Moniuszko, and Rubinstein.[102] Improving the standards of the opera would also necessitate a new building. Smetana devoted an entire article in 1864 to complaining that the Provisional Theater was too small to do opera properly: there was not enough room for the orchestra, they could only use a reduced chorus, and so on. These limitations prevented them from mounting many operas as they should be seen, and rendered some operas, such as Wagner's, all but impossible to perform in that theater.[103]

Voices such as Smetana's, calling for a fitting building in which to house Czech opera, were vital impulses for the campaign to construct the National Theater, which I will discuss more extensively later. Smetana's ultimate conception for Czech opera was that it should "represent the artistic heights of the whole nation."[104] We see here again the idea of the opera's representative power. Indeed, Petr Vít reports that this idea was often discussed in Czech nationalist circles in the 1860s, including in the group Umělecká beseda (literally, "artistic discussion group"), of which Smetana was a founding member.[105] The Umělecká beseda was, in fact, another of Smetana's efforts to improve Czech cultural life; the group's stated purpose was to further the " 'blossom of our national art.' "[106]

As in the purpose of the Umělecká beseda, Smetana boldly proclaimed the patriotic goals of his artistic activities. He declared in a diary entry of 1843 that "I am the instrument of a higher power."[107] In his conception, the higher power he would serve was the Czech nation. He would serve it by creating a genuinely Czech music that would represent his nation at the highest levels of international art. He insisted that "the blossoming of national art takes precedence over everything, in that I have dedicated all my energies, all my knowledge and abilities to the Czech stage."[108] His desire to create a national art was a matter of pride to Smetana; his goal was:

> to prove that we Czechs are not mere practising musicians as other nations nickname us, saying that our talent lies only in our fingers but not in our brains, but that we are also endowed with creative force, yes, that we have our own and characteristic music. How far I have succeeded in this hitherto, not I but the world will judge. To judge from the great ovations which I have experienced so many times I have at least the consolation that my efforts are being recognised and rewarded and that I am on the right way. I also see how my example draws young and hopeful talents to continue along my path, and how these talents grow, so to speak, out of our earth, to the glory of our dear country![109] I was the first who had the courage to step onto the battlefield, but I was not defeated and let that be my reward![110]

This statement of Smetana's is reminiscent of an argument he once had in Franz Liszt's circle in Weimar with a German musician who accused the Czechs of being nothing more than mere "fiddlers," that is, of lacking a genuinely creative musical talent.[111] That argument, and Smetana's desire to defend the Czechs' artistic honor, reportedly played a major role in spurring him on to his career as a nationalist artist. The Czech composer Vaclav Juda Novotný claimed that Smetana once told him the story of that argument in connection with "how the idea of creating an independent Czech musical style began to mature in him [Smetana] for the first time."[112] At the end of that evening in Weimar, according to Novotný, "Smetana turned moist eyes to the starry heaven, raised his hand, and deeply moved, swore in his heart the greatest oath: that he would dedicate his entire life to his nation, to the tireless service of his country's art."[113]

Though Novotný's anecdote is evidently romanticized, we know at least that the sentiments he reports Smetana as expressing were genuine. In his own words, Smetana once declared that he would "sacrifice everything to his homeland."[114] Late in his life, he also summed up his career this way: "I am according to my merits and according to my efforts as a composer a Czech and the creator of the Czech style in the branches of dramatic and symphonic music—exclusively Czech."[115] The social role of the artist is clear from this statement. Smetana saw himself as the man who created for the nation a whole, thoroughly national art form. He gave the Czechs an essential part of their culture—their own music, transfigured into a high art. Smetana's conception of his achievement is parallel and virtually identical to Wagner's.

Influenced again in part by Wagner, Smetana placed the same emphasis on language's role in dramatic music. "It is the correct declamation that makes the music Czech," Smetana wrote of his work.[116] The rhythm and character of the Czech language determined the nature of the music. Hence Czech style comes not just from Czech songs and dances but more importantly from "the characteristic declamation of Czech words." In fact, Czech music of "a higher style…hangs only on the declamation of the words," making it unnecessary to rely slavishly on folk songs.[117] In this way, regardless of the subject matter or ostensible stylistic influences (such as from non-Czech composers like Liszt or Wagner), music based on a Czech text would inevitably be thoroughly Czech.

Smetana also admitted to preferring libretti based on Czech history, since they would contribute most to the establishment of a national operatic style.[118] Most of his operas are in fact based on historical and legendary material. *The Brandenburgers in Bohemia* deals with peasant resistance against a German occupation in the thirteenth century, *Dalibor* is the story of a great tragic hero from Czech history who was imprisoned in Prague Castle, and *The Devil's Wall* incorporates an old legend about the devil trying to trick a couple of Czech peasants— for three examples. Outside of opera, several sections of the cycle of symphonic poems *Má vlast* evoke prominent legends. The first poem, *Vyšehrad*, depicts the golden age of the independent Czech kingdom and its castle on a promontory overlooking the Vltava river. Three later poems, *Šarka*, *Tábor*, and *Blaník*, are also inspired by legends—the last one is about a prophecy that Hussite warriors would one day rise again out of Blaník mountain to defend the Czechs in their hour of need.

*Blaník* thus also makes reference to a specific point of the Czech landscape. *Má vlast* is in fact rich in its landscape evocations, above all in Smetana's famous symphonic poem about the Vltava river and also in the poem entitled *Z českých luhů a hájů*, or "From the Czech Woods and Meadows." The *Vltava* poem is almost a travelogue, beginning in the springs that form the Vltava's headwaters, passing through the St. John's rapids, and continuing all the way to the end of the piece where the Vltava flows into the Elbe. *Z českých luhů a hájů* Smetana described as "a general description of the feelings which the sight of the Czech countryside conjures up…*everything* is remembered in a hymn of praise."[119] *Má vlast* as a whole is, in fact, dedicated to an important place of Czech geography: the city of Prague itself. The operas also deal with distinct places in the Czech lands, such as *Dalibor* with Prague Castle, *Libuše* with Vyšehrad, and *The Devil's Wall* with a rock formation known by the same name on the Vltava.

Aside from his operatic and symphonic output, Smetana's works in other fields often express a strong nationalist sentiment as well. Some of this music is occasional, such as the *Jubel-Ouvertüre* inspired by the events of 1848, or the men's chorus composed for the dedication of the memorial to fellow nationalist Karel Havlíček Borovský in 1870.[120] Many of his choruses have patriotic themes, and often they were written specifically for the Prague men's choir known as the Hlahol, which itself was founded to promote singing in the Czech language. A striking demonstration of the importance of nationalism to Smetana is his first string quartet, the biographical "From My Life," which contains a movement portraying "the joy upon the recognition of the path of national art."[121]

Smetana regarded his opera *Libuše* as his "most perfect work in the field of higher drama."[122] The story is taken from an incident documented by Palacký's history of the Czech lands, and the librettist Josef Wenzig even consulted Palacký on historical details.[123] The legendary queen Libuše is a golden age trope, an evocation of the nation's "prehistory" analogous to Wagner's characterizations of figures from old Germanic myths. This legend had actually been used before by a variety of artists: there was an opera in Italian about Libuše in the 1700s, and the Czech composer Škroup also wrote an opera called *Libušin sňatek* ("Libuše's Marriage") in the1840s.[124] Smetana's version is the most overtly nationalistic, however, integrating the typical panoply of themes of nationalist art. He has a section of dancing peasants to fulfill the folk requirement, for example, and the end of the opera features a stirring "prophecy," where Libuše foretells the future greatness (and decline!) of the Czech nation. Thanks to her powers as an oracle, she sees a parade of great Czech figures such as Jaroslav ze Šternberku, the supposed defender of the Czechs against the Mongol attacks; legendary kings such as Karel IV, the founder of Charles University; and Jiří z Poděbrad, the one-eyed general of the Hussite movement.[125]

The Hussite reference also provides the musical material for the opera's boisterous conclusion. Despite her foreboding about an eventual decline for her nation, Libuše proclaims in her final lines that "the Czech nation will not perish!" As the full chorus joins her to assert the Czech nation's immortality, Smetana brings in the Hussite hymn "Kdož jsu boží bojovníci," typically translated as "Ye Warriors of God." This hymn had already attained associations of resistance by the time Smetana used it,[126] but Jiránek credits Smetana with transforming its symbolism into a statement about how the Czech nation would fight forever against oppression in order to stay alive and rise again to greatness.[127] Smetana also used this hymn in *Tábor* and *Blaník* of *Má vlast*, influencing many subsequent Czech composers who would take up the melody with much the same symbolic purpose. Fittingly for such a solemn but triumphal festival opera, *Libuše* was intended specifically for "the celebrations of the whole Czech nation."[128] Smetana decided that it should have its premiere once the Czechs finally had their own national theater. So, though he completed the score in 1872, he had to wait until 1881 for it first to be performed—and at that point, sadly, he was already deaf.

Nonetheless, *Libuše* was indeed the first opera performed in the new national theater. The Národní divadlo, or National Theater, which opened in Prague in 1883 was what Smetana had always hoped for. By the time the theater was finally rebuilt after it burned down in 1881, Smetana had only a few months left to live, so he was far enough gone that he could not enjoy the realization of his dream. Nonetheless, he did lay the foundation for the theater, both literally and figuratively. On April 16, 1868, a ceremony took place in Prague on the banks of the Vltava for the placement of the foundation stone of the Národní divadlo. At this ceremony, Smetana was the third speaker, following Palacký and Rieger, the two most prominent Czech nationalists of their day. Smetana was wearing a national costume with the three Slavic colors (i.e., blue, white, and red), and in laying the foundation stone he declared, "In music the life of the Czechs!"[129] He uttered these words apparently as both a proclamation of his goal—to express in music the life of the Czechs—and as a statement of the centrality of music to Czech culture. The same night as the laying of the foundation stone, also as part of the celebrations, *Dalibor* had its premiere in the Provisional Theater.

Smetana also figuratively laid the theater's foundation. His operatic creations were designed to create a "wide and diverse foundational standard for the further development of Czech musical-dramatic work," as Séquardtová writes.[130] For instance, Smetana composed an opera for every genre he could: *The Brandenburgers in Bohemia* is grand opera, *The Bartered Bride* is the paragon of the folk opera, *Dalibor* is a "heroic-romantic" opera, *Libuše* is a "solemn festival tableau," *The Two Widows* is a salon comedy, and so on.[131] His evident intent was to create a varied repertoire of Czech operas for the new Czech theater. And though some of Smetana's operas never attained wide popularity (*The Devil's Wall*, for one), nonetheless his operas even today make up the core of the Národní divadlo's offerings. At least until 1945, Smetana's operas amounted to a quarter of the theater's total performances. *The Bartered Bride*, in particular, has become far and away the most performed opera at the Národní divadlo, reaching 1,000 performances only sixty years after its premiere.[132] As a venue for displaying the spectacle of Czech nationality to the entire Czech nation, Smetana's wildest dreams for the theater have been fulfilled. Indeed, so firmly implanted is this nationalist conception of the institution that its programs today continue to insist that "the historical building of the National Theatre in Prague is the embodiment of the will of the Czech nation for national independence."[133]

## GRIEG

Grieg's complaints about the cultural situation in Norway differ somewhat from Smetana's and Wagner's in that he is not primarily lamenting the insufficiencies of Norwegian music, or that Norwegian cultural life is dominated by vacuous foreign forms such as French opera. Grieg's repeated complaint is rather that there is simply no artistic life at all in Norway. He said that in Norway is "frost and roughness, in nature as in temperaments,"[134] where "to be an individual was the same as to be a criminal."[135] Norway was just not a place where a creative artist could find his way. In various letters, he wrote of the isolation he felt in Christiania in the later 1860s especially, and about the "mess of pettiness and misunderstanding [an artist has to] wade in daily."[136] In the 1880s, during his stint directing the Bergen orchestra, he maintained the same grievances.

Here in Norway no man of intellect can stand it much longer than a short while. A kick from this side and then another kick from that side. But the unfortunate thing is that a Norwegian artist's creative activity also becomes spasmodic and unharmonious because of the inept conditions here. So I can in a way understand those who still have the clarity to turn their backs on Norway and become Europeans. But I couldn't do that. No, never! Unfortunately I have a heart![137]

A few years later he repeated this theme—and it was one that he obviously felt throughout his life as a mature artist—that "your soul gets as heavy as lead here at home," such that he had to go out into the world for artistic stimulation. Nonetheless, while abroad, he was always wanting to be home, "where the sense of beauty is."[138]

The heart of the problem with the cultural life in Norway, Grieg suggests, is that most people just don't care how bad it is. In 1881 he wrote, "only with bitterness can I think back to the indifference, even disdain and scorn, that met Norwegian art music. I could tell things…that would sound unbelievable. But there was a complete lack of anything resembling artistic morals."[139] He said that people were more interested in "dilettantism" than in "Norwegian art." The public did not seem to appreciate his and fellow composer Johan Svendsen's efforts to create a "real artistic life" by giving concerts of Norwegian music. Following one of those concerts at which turnout was especially poor, he remarked, "It's a dismal thought, but it should nonetheless be said that if the public continues to act, as it has here begun to, in relation to the best of our own, then in very little time Norwegian art music at home will be only a joke, while abroad, and particularly in enlightened Germany, it will find the recognition it deserves."[140] Grieg was also exasperated by the attacks that artists working to improve the cultural situation suffered at the hands of the newspaper critics, who were all "Philistines."[141] Given that (at least early in his career) "most hate my compositions, even musicians," it was perhaps not surprising that Grieg began looking at receiving recognition abroad as the practical way for building his career.[142] Nonetheless, he hoped for the "possibility that the time might come while we're still alive that a Norwegian artist won't become homeless in his own country."[143]

Though often frustrated and discouraged by Norway's cultural climate, Grieg was thereby also motivated to improve it. As with Wagner and Smetana, Grieg believed that presenting the best musical works to the public would educate them and teach them the value of true art. Grieg's efforts in this realm included stints leading orchestras in both Christiania and Bergen. In the later 1860s, he and his colleague Johan Svendsen organized a series of philharmonic concerts in Christiania, often featuring Norwegian composers' latest works. Looking back on those concerts, Grieg estimated that they had given "the musical sense a powerful impetus, indeed even brought many honorable people who otherwise had no interest in art, to think that good music in a society could actually be something more than a necessary evil."[144] It was important to him that even the less educated classes would attend these concerts. As he said, art provides "spiritual nourishment," and as such should be everyone's art, shared across all classes, to benefit the whole of society.[145] Thus he was glad when "in a musical respect by no means enlightened public" nonetheless enthusiastically enjoyed one of Johan Svendsen's concerts in 1867. That concert, Grieg wrote, was a "great triumph" for "Norwegian art." It was a triumph because even the unenlightened public learned to enjoy a symphony, "the arty music," which they tended otherwise to avoid.[146] However, Grieg expressly opposed the idea of performing "popular" or "more accessible" music for the masses. He stressed that art should never "go down" to the people. "No and a thousand times no! The people shall go *up* to art!"[147]

Another significant element in Grieg's educational designs was the music academy he cofounded in Christiania in 1866. With his partner Otto Winter-Hjelm, Grieg coauthored the announcement of the academy's founding, which explicitly advances both the need to educate the public musically and to do so on a *national* basis. They wrote:

> The obvious development—increasing with every day—in our musical life, and the highly legitimate struggle to stand also in this area upon a national basis, makes it constantly more and more

evident that we are no longer obliged to defer to foreign countries and their conservatories.

...We have said above that such an academy is necessary to support the struggle for nationality in art that has also in a musical direction been awakened. When we wish to have the national element respected, we do not thereby mean any one-sided desire for isolation. We only desire that the music student shall also come to know our own, that which is closest to him and possibly is first and best suited to work fruitfully upon his fantasy. When all that is great and powerful in foreign music is presented to him, it will not so overwhelm that the domestic music's impression is supplanted, as unfortunately is now often the case.[148]

Their theory was to base the education on melodies that the student knew already "from the cradle," such as pieces from L. M. Lindeman's collection of Norwegian folk songs. This method of preserving the "national impression" would allow a more rapid development of the pupil.[149] The historical importance of this music academy, Herresthal comments, is that it was the first in Norway to have "a clearly national objective" and a group of musicians who worked together "in a joint pedagogical environment."[150]

Grieg was less obsessed than Wagner or Smetana by the role of the theater in the national project. That may be because he was never as much a "man of the theater" as were the other two, whose careers were so deeply bound up in the opera house. The relatively weaker tradition of theater in Norway may also explain why Grieg was never ensnared by this art form in the same way that Wagner and Smetana were. Still, though, Grieg did consider the theater important. He lamented that Norwegian cultural life lacked the "foundation that resides in a national opera with an orchestra and chorus corresponding to art's and our time's requirements."[151] Even two years before his death, Grieg saw it as a "shame" that still so little progress had been made toward creating a Norwegian national theater and a Norwegian musicdrama. The main hindrance, he thought, was "our economic misery," which prevented the establishment of a state-supported national opera house.[152] So, though Norway did not have a national theater, Grieg fervently believed they needed one, and in his fervor he had always hoped to be able to produce a national opera, as he told his friend Frants Beyer in a letter of 1886: "Now you can understand why I so many times have gone staring up into the heavens, as if I could find there the Norwegian drama in Norwegian music that I have dreamed of, that I always believed I could someday create, but which I am now beginning to believe is destined by Fortune's wheel to come from another. But—it will come."[153]

With little prospect for establishing a national opera, Grieg instead tended to focus on the role that national music more broadly had to play in both educating the public and thereby contributing to the nationalist movement. This role is clear in an article from the newspaper *Morgenbladet* of 1866:

> In a time such as ours, when nationality in all regards plays such a prominent role, one can quickly comprehend the great significance of the efforts in our country to seek to develop the national element in language, poetry, and art. And as we seek it along different paths, we are all nonetheless working toward the same goal—the nation's independence, development and improvement. Music, too, is here a battlefield.[154]

The artist's duty on this "battlefield" was "to hold national sentiment up," as he said on another occasion.[155] He stressed that art can serve politics—and more particularly, that a *national* art serves *nationalist* politics, as Grieg wrote in 1880.[156] Since "every art that has remained vital has been national,"[157] then the most lasting contribution an artist can make is to produce national art, an art of and for his nation. The artist should bring the public nearer to their "domestic art."[158] Grieg wrote in an 1896 letter of the importance of "improved communications" in bringing together the many "small nations" of Norway, to produce a unified society.[159] For him, music was one element of such communication, to show Norwegians their common cultural heritage. A national art, in Grieg's as well as Smetana's and Wagner's views, teaches the public what is theirs, and teaches them to love it.

Grieg's intent to create an art that the Norwegians could consider their own was motivated by his sense that Norwegian culture was an essential part of his own being. "Norwegian folk life, Norwegian sagas and history and above all Norwegian nature have since my youth had a great influence on my works," Grieg stated, succinctly, in a letter to Henry T. Finck.[160] "The spirit of my fatherland," he told Finck, "hovers over my entire output." As he says, he felt a special bond to Norway's mountains and fjords, and in particular to the western part of the country, where he was born and raised. "Western Norway gave me life, enthusiasm for life, and the goal to reproduce it in tones."[161] Grieg evidently believed in the Herderian idea of national spirits, and that this spirit mystically expresses itself through the individual. Indeed, nationality was not something one could escape, as he suggests in a diary entry: "the national you bear with yourself like your joys and sorrows, but you never leave it!"[162] However, why would a person *want* to escape his or her nationality? Grieg remarked that "I don't understand why *everyone in his own way* doesn't lay hold of his fatherland, its nature, history, and folk life."[163] Nationality was a worthy basis for one's art, and it is apparent that he could imagine no better.

With such a font of inspiration, Grieg made plain his intention to render Norwegian nationality into music. A famous quote has him saying in a letter to Bjørnson, "To paint Norwegian nature, Norwegian folk life, Norwegian history and Norwegian folk poetry in sounds stands for me as the area where I believe I can achieve something."[164] In fact, he admitted that after his conservatory education in Germany, he felt that the only way he could really "develop myself further" was "on a national basis."[165] He would create national music, and he promised "to work and strive such for our home's art, that one day it may be said I have been worthy of it."[166] Grieg "found himself" and was spurred on to his nationalist cultural goals through meeting another young Norwegian nationalist composer, Rikard Nordraak.[167] After Nordraak died only in his early twenties, in a letter to Nordraak's father Grieg assured him that he, Grieg, would continue down the path Nordraak had set out on:

> We both hoped to be able to work together for the advancement of our national art. Since that was not granted to us, I can merely hold faithfully to the promise I gave him, that his cause would be my cause, his goal mine. Don't believe that what he aspired to

will be forgotten. I have the great calling to bring his few genial works before the people, our Norwegian people, to fight for their recognition, and to build further upon that great foundation.[168]

Or, as Grieg put it much later in his life, on the occasion of his sixtieth birthday celebrations, "what I have strived for up until now is indeed nothing else than what every good Norwegian does: to lay a little stone to the building called Norway."[169] The particular stone he laid was to "introduce national music" into Norway.[170]

It is evident from these sorts of statements that Grieg believed that he had a kind of mission to fulfill as a nationalist artist. The ultimate goal Grieg envisioned for his art was actually expressed most concisely by Ferdinand Rojahn, who, in an autobiographical sketch of Grieg, wrote: "it belongs to Grieg's own quiet dreams that with his music he might become known in every Norwegian nook, and that the people could be entirely incorporated into a better understanding of our own uniqueness, with a richer love for a land that possesses all the requirements to sustain every person who loves it enough."[171]

Though these words are not Grieg's own, he said explicitly that he agreed with Rojahn's article, so we can take this description as accurate.[172] Two notable incidents show Grieg enacting the role of the nationalist artist in a most public fashion. The first was in 1891, during a debate in the Student Society over whether to fly the Norwegian-Swedish Union flag or just the Norwegian tricolor. Grieg stood up on the stage and spoke in favor of keeping the tricolor flying, and he closed his impromptu speech by encouraging the gathering to sing the national anthem, which they all did, beginning with Grieg's cue.[173] The second was Grieg's plan to assemble all of western Norway's singers in Bergen for the rebuilding of Håkon's Hall, a structure dating from the Middle Ages and a reminder of Norway's past independence. His idea was for the singers to perform a cantata on a theme from the sagas, to which Bjørnson would write the text.[174] This gathering would be a mass assembly to commemorate Norwegian history, and to celebrate the nation through music.

The Håkon's Hall idea in itself encapsulates many of the most powerful tropes of nationalist music: the fascination with a past golden age, a mass performance/celebration, and an artwork to express and stimulate national feeling. Grieg wrote some works, such as his "Valgsang" ("Election Song"), with the specific intent "to stimulate love of the fatherland."[175] Interestingly, such works were not necessarily conceived for mass gatherings or even the concert hall. He said of his "Fædrelandssalme" ("Fatherland's Psalm") that it was "absolutely for school and home and not for the concert hall."[176] Thus national music could work on a variety of levels, publicly as with the national anthem in the gathering in the Student Society, or privately just in an individual home, for a family to sing and enjoy.

Historical or mythical subjects figure prominently in Grieg's work. He composed incidental music to Bjørnson's play *Sigurd Jorsalfar*, a story of the crusader Sigurd in twelfth-century Norway. Two sections in particular of Grieg's music for this work, the chorus "Norrøna folket det vil fare" ("The Northland folk are born to travel") and the "Hyldningsmarsj" ("Homage March"), are bombastic showpieces of patriotism. This music was particularly good for "national days of celebration," as Grieg found when it was given a gala performance shortly after the coronation of the new Norwegian king Haakon VII in 1905.[177] Grieg also composed a cantata called *Land-sighting*—about Olav Trygvason, the king who Christianized Norway—as well as the "melodrama for orchestra" *Bergliot*, set to saga-based texts by Bjørnson. Two of Grieg's compositions pay respect to more recent Norwegian history, specifically to two figures from the Norwegian nationalist movement. His song "Henrik Wergeland" honors that early patriot, and his *Funeral March in Memory of Rikard Nordraak* was written for his close nationalist composer friend. In addition to these historical subjects, Grieg often made use of elements from Norwegian myths and folk tales, such as his famous "March of the Trolls" from the *Lyric Pieces*, or the lesser-known *Den bergtekne* (typically called "The Mountain Thrall" in English), for baritone and orchestra, which tells the story of a man led astray by a troll's daughter.

Given Grieg's professed love of the Norwegian landscape, it is perhaps surprising that he never wrote a grand symphonic piece extolling the Hardangerfjord or something similar. Instead, his references to the Norwegian landscape are limited to brief passages in smaller works.

The aforementioned *Den bergtekne*, for example, takes place in a "dark wood" where the singer was seduced by the troll. The song "Langs ei Å" ("Along a Stream") also addresses the mysterious Norwegian forests—directly, in fact, since the song opens and closes with the line, "You forest!" More common in Grieg's output are references to the Norwegian landscape through evocations of rural life. "Cow Call" from the *Lyric Pieces* simulates the distinctive cries employed by Norwegian shepherds to gather their herds. The song cycle *Haugtussa* ("The Mountain Maid") also makes reference to cow calls and other features of the Norwegian countryside, such as slopes covered in blueberries.

One way by which Grieg's works (like *Haugtussa*) evoke a specifically Norwegian, and rural, milieu is through language. The text of *Haugtussa*, by the poet A. O. Vinje, is written in the form of Norwegian today called "Nynorsk," or "New Norwegian." This is a variant originating in the rural areas of Norway, distinct from the Norwegian spoken in the cities, which is much closer to Danish. Grieg composed equally to texts in both Nynorsk and Dano-Norwegian. In fact, Grieg was never doctrinaire about what language he would compose music to. Many of his songs are to German texts. So, though Grieg did believe in the idea of languages as emblems of nationality,[178] he was never as strict as Wagner or Smetana about the necessity to use only his national language in his music. There is no obvious reason to explain his flexibility on this issue, though it may have to do with Grieg's cosmopolitan outlook (his connections to Denmark and Germany, for instance), his recognition that Norwegian was a relatively minor language, or the simple fact that his personality was inherently undogmatic.

Grieg's unfinished national opera is called *Olav Trygvason*, based on the same story as his cantata *Land-sighting*, about the king who brought Christianity to Norway. The text is also by Bjørnstjerne Bjørnson, marking another collaboration by two of the most important Norwegian nationalist artists of their day. The story of the legendary king is taken from the sagas written by the ancient Icelandic poet Snorri Sturluson, and the opera is positively awash in both history and myth. It is set near the town of Trondheim, where Olav supposedly founded the first

Christian church in Norway. The completed scenes portray the reaction of the pagan hordes to the prophesied coming of the Christian king, and with it, the downfall of the gods from Old Norse mythology. Following a solemn rite in which a panoply of Norse deities are invoked, the pagans erupt in dances around a sacred flame, which corresponds to a typical portrayal of "the folk." The opera fragment ends at that scene, though according to Bjørnson's plan the conclusion was to feature Olav as victorious, surrounded by throngs desperate to be baptized. It is interesting that the opera embraces both the pagan, Old Norse mythology as well as the achievements of the Christian king as elements of a total Norwegian national culture.

Grieg said that his music to *Olav Trygvason* was inspired by this "saga enthusiasm," which he defined in parentheses as "the national."[179] With the dark tonal colors he brings out of the orchestra, Grieg is quite successful in evoking a days-of-yore epic mood. What he was aiming for in this music is suggested by his comments about Wagner's *Ring*. While he admired Wagner's use of saga subjects, he thought that if a Scandinavian had composed to such subjects, then "we would have gotten to hear a bit more of the Edda-sound," the "Old Norse tone."[180] *Olav Trygvason* was left incomplete because after a few complications and misunderstandings, he and Bjørnson had a falling out, and the text was never finished. The reasons Grieg never attempted another national opera are various. One reason he gave was that he could never get a text that satisfied him. And, rather than compose to a bad text, he would just not compose an opera at all.[181] Another reason is likely his poor health as he got older, which generally prevented him from being able to concentrate sufficiently on such a large-scale work as an opera. In any event, Grieg returned to the music in the late 1880s and revised it before the opera fragment was first performed in Christiania in 1889, where audiences received it rapturously.[182] So, though Grieg's opera was never finished, it was obviously designed to fulfill a similar national function as were Wagner's and Smetana's dramatic works.

The themes of creating a national music and elevating the public come together in the music festival that Grieg organized in Bergen in 1898.

As a summation of his career, it is not too much of a stretch to think of this festival as "Grieg's Bayreuth." Grieg wanted to call the festival a "Norsk Musikfest"; it would feature exclusively works by Norwegian composers.[183] His intention was to showcase modern Norwegian music, to show Norwegians that they own a "national art music…capable of speaking to *everyone*"—that is, to all members of Norwegian society, and presumably to people from all nations.[184] In this way, Norwegian music would come "nearer to the people's heart"—indeed, he said, this was a "national responsibility" that the festival would fulfill.[185] The festival was not only an artistic experience, though, for it was also "a link in our people's education."[186]

The way to achieve these goals, Grieg thought, was through the "most ideal possible" performance of the music.[187] To that end, he engaged Amsterdam's Concertgebouw Orchestra to come to Bergen. That act set off a storm of protest from "chauvinists" (Grieg's term) who thought it an insult that a "foreign" orchestra would be performing these Norwegian works. However, Grieg countered that even the alternative, the Christiania orchestra, was made up of many German musicians, so that it was not "truly" Norwegian. And in any event, it was also an ensemble far inferior to the Concertgebouw.[188] Grieg's insistence on hiring the Amsterdam orchestra shows how he could put the goals of art over more narrowly nationalistic concerns. Beyond that, according to Grieg, one additional benefit of engaging the Concertgebouw was that it would then have these Norwegian pieces in its repertoire, and so Norwegian composers (especially the lesser-known ones) could make greater inroads into European musical life.[189]

Finally, by inviting all "decent" Norwegian composers to be performed at the festival, Grieg did his own part to bring together the network of nationalist artists.[190] Besides Grieg's music, that of Johan Svendsen, Christian Sinding, Johan Halvorsen, Catharinus Elling, Iver Holter, Johan Selmer, and Gerhard Schjelderup was also performed.[191] Many of these composers already knew one another before the festival; Grieg and Svendsen, at least, were good friends. But, as an opportunity to bring them all together (minus Selmer, who could not attend) and for them to hear each other's music actually performed, the festival was unique. Here they had the chance to see how other national composers were writing, to learn from one another. In this sort of setting they could personally trade ideas about what Norwegian national music could and should be. The festival did turn out to be a resounding success, with extremely enthusiastic audiences. Grieg seems to have regarded those two weeks in Bergen as some of the most rewarding and happy of his life.

## CONCLUSION

This, then, is the formula for creating nationalist music: in response to a perceived decline in their respective nation's cultures, Wagner, Smetana, and Grieg all demanded that the populace be educated in the values of high art. This art would be superior not only because of its aesthetic standards but also because it would be national. It would simultaneously grow from the nation and help construct that nation. These three composers set themselves the task both of founding the educational institutions to enlighten the people and of creating the artworks that would make the people national. The strategies for creating national artworks are effectively identical in all three cases, comprising incorporation of the national language and aspects from myth or history and the national landscape.

It is in the process of creating this art that nationalist composers simultaneously fashioned a role for themselves within the nation-building movement. This role dealt, of course, with the creation of the national music, and it involved the educational and artistic strategies mentioned previously. They made this role *for themselves* in that they identified certain spheres where they perceived their populace as insufficiently "national" and then set about correcting that deficiency with the educational and creative strategies they devised. In this way, they elaborated the practice of the nationalist composer, and showed that artists could play a critical role in effecting social change.

This emergence of artists as agents for social change is further bound up with two phenomena I mentioned in the introduction: the change in the social place and the social function of art. First, beginning principally in the later eighteenth century, art gradually moved away from being the preserve solely of the higher classes (the nobility, in particular) and became "democratized"—that is, open as well to those outside the aristocracy, from the middle classes all the way to (in theory) the workers and peasants.[192] There were naturally several contributing causes to this democratization of art. The decline of noble patronage for the arts is especially important. The heyday of noble patronage expired with the French Revolution, and increasingly artists supported themselves through other means—selling their commodities to a much larger public. Hence the progressive embourgeoisement of the populace is also responsible for increasing the potential audience for art. There are certain self-preservation motives to the artist's seeking support from the middle classes, then, in that the river of aristocratic largesse flowed ever more feebly as the nineteenth century proceeded.[193]

There were ideological motives as well, however, particularly for nationalist artists. We have seen how Wagner, Smetana, and Grieg all insist that their music is for the broad mass of people equally. In these artists' conception, the audience for their artworks is not a select circle of aristocrats but rather the entire nation. Even if the middle and upper classes continued to be those who most frequented the theater and the concert hall, the nationalists' rhetorical appeal is to all classes, to the *Gesamtnation*. It is worth noting that the actual, historically observable expansion in the audience for high art occurred at much the same time as nationalism was becoming a mass movement. There is a striking degree of coincidence between the growth of middle-class support for the arts and increased support for the nationalist movement among the wider populace. This dynamic applies in all three countries of my study, at slightly different periods of course, with Germany earliest and Norway latest. Without wishing to oversimplify the picture, one can nonetheless observe that as these nationalist movements took on a mass character, simultaneously, audiences and public support for the high arts such as music were also expanding.

Through their discourse and practice, activist artists were partly responsible for this democratization of art. Wagner, Smetana, and Grieg made art that they intended to speak to everyone. They wanted all kinds of people in the opera house or concert hall to hear their music. Part of the purpose beyond their avowedly democratic approach was that their art would effectuate the fusion of the different classes into one people; we will examine this unifying power of art more closely in the next chapter.

However, their discourse also reveals that part of the democratization of art entails the move away from aristocracy as the artist's patron toward *the nation* becoming the patron. The nation is in fact the patron, audience, and subject of the nationalist artist's work. The nation is the patron because all members of the national society are supposed to support the artist in his work; it is the audience because the artist intends all members of the national society to appreciate his work; and it is the subject because, of course, in his work the artist is celebrating (and constructing) the nation's culture. Interestingly, then, nationalist artists were concerned with creating their own patrons, since their project was to create the national populace.

Nationalist artists were also critically involved in the second phenomenon I mentioned previously—the change in the social function of art. In the nineteenth century, art becomes viewed increasingly as something not solely for entertainment or decoration. Instead, artists such as Schiller argued for art as a force for social change. Again, this conceptualization is not wholly without precedent, nor do I wish to suggest that it is ineluctably associated with the rise of nationalism. However, there can be no question that the work of men like Wagner, Smetana, and Grieg to utilize art precisely for this purpose of social change played a role in altering the conceptualization of art's function more broadly. These three composers all deride the idea that art's purpose is mere amusement. They insist that art must be edifying, and they append to this edification a specific nationalist goal. As we have seen, in addition to improving a people's morals and tastes, art is supposed to educate them in the values of their own nationality. In the nationalist artist's conception, art can thereby help create national citizens. Artists first create a national high culture, and through propagation and performance of their work, they educate the populace into that culture.

We should regard this idea of art's power to edify and nationalize as a supplement to the "classical model" of nationalism, which stresses the educative role of schools in producing national citizens. Clearly, there are more institutions for national education than just the school; the opera house and the concert hall played a part as well. Moreover, in nationalist artists' vision, art was actually able to *physically* constitute the nation: the national populace is brought together by assembling in the theater or concert hall to view or hear the expression of their nationality in art. When they are all sitting there to participate in the spectacle of the nation's culture, the members of the public are themselves becoming national in the process. In this way, the *Gesamtnation* is forged by representing it through art, and art thus becomes a force for social change.

## ENDNOTES

1. Bernhard Giesen, *Die Intelektuellen und die Nation* (Frankfurt am Mein: Suhrkamp, 1993), 156.
2. See Jörg Echternkamp, *Der Aufstieg des deutschen Nationalismus (1770–1840)* (Frankfurt: Campus Verlag, 1998), 239.
3. Cited in Jiří Rak, "Divadlo jako postředek politické propagandy v první polovině 19. století," in *Divadlo v české kultuře 19. století* (Praha: Národní galerie, 1985). *See esp.* p. 45.
4. Cited in Horst Steinmetz, "Idee und Wirklichkeit des Nationaltheaters. Enttäuschte Hoffnungen und falsche Erwartungen," in *Volk—Nation—Vaterland*, ed. Ulrich Herrmann (Hamburg: Felix Meiner Verlag, 1996), 141–150. *See esp.* p. 149.
5. Cited in Friedrich Tomberg, "Das Theater als politische Anstalt betrachtet," in *Philosophie und Kunst: Kultur und Ästhetik im Denken der deutschen Klassik* (Weimar: Hermann Böhlaus Nachfolger, 1987). *See esp.* p. 166.
6. Heinrich Laube, *Kritiken*. Ed. S. D. Stirk (Breslau: Verlag Priebatsch's Buchhandlung, 1934), 21.
7. Cited in Stanley Buchholz Kimball, *Czech Nationalism: A Study of the National Theater Movement, 1845–1883* (Urbana: University of Illinois Press, 1964), 141.
8. Herresthal, *Med spark i gulvet og quinter i bassen*, 94.
9. Petr Vít, "Hudba v programu českého národního hnutí doby předbřeznové a po Říjnovém diplomu," in *Povědomí tradice v novodobé české kultuře (doba Bedřicha Smetany)* (Praha: Národní galerie, 1988), 54–64. *See esp.* p. 56. Tomberg also discusses this idea.
10. Wagner, *Kunstwerk der Zukunft*, 148.
11. Ibid.
12. Wagner, *Oper und Drama* Part I, 308.
13. Wagner, *Über die Bestimmung der Oper*, 155.
14. Wagner, *Zukunftsmusik*, 97.
15. Wagner, *Briefe* Band II, 667.
16. Wagner, *Bericht an Ludwig II*, 5.
17. Wagner, *Deutsche Kunst und deutsche Politik*, 94.
18. Ibid., 116–117.
19. Ibid., 51.
20. Wagner, *Briefe* Band IV, 76.

21. Wagner, *Deutsche Kunst und deutsche Politik*, 58.
22. Wagner, *Über Devrients Geschichte*, 231.
23. Wagner, *Entwurf zur Organisation eines deutschen National-theaters für das Königreich Sachsen*, 269.
24. Ibid., 235.
25. Wagner, *Deutsche Kunst und deutsche Politik*, 42–43.
26. Ibid., 60.
27. Ibid., 122.
28. Cited in Martin Gregor-Dellin, *Richard Wagner* (Munich: Piper, 1991), 246.
29. Wagner, *Ein Theater in Zürich*, 36.
30. Wagner, *Entwurf zur Organisation*, 273.
31. See Wagner, *Bericht an Ludwig II*.
32. Wagner, "Zur Einführung (*Bayreuther Blätter*, Erstes Stück)," 20.
33. Wagner, *Deutsche Kunst und deutsche Politik*, 117.
34. Wagner, *Über die Bestimmung der Oper*, 123.
35. Ibid., 156.
36. Wagner, *Bericht and Ludwig II*, 47.
37. Wagner, *Oper und Drama* Parts II and III, 32–33.
38. Wagner, *Das Braune Buch*, 210.
39. Wagner, "Vorwort zur Gesamtherausgabe," vii. Italics mine.
40. Wagner, *Über deutsches Musikwesen*, 85.
41. Ibid., 94.
42. Wagner, *Schreiben an das Bürgermeister von Bologna*, 292.
43. Wagner, *Oper und Drama* Parts II and III, 227.
44. Ibid., 237.
45. Wagner, *Beethoven*, 72.
46. Wagner, *Eine Mitteilung an meine Freunde*, 268.
47. Wagner, *Das Braune Buch*, 86.
48. Wagner, *Briefe* Band II, 431.
49. Wagner, "Vorwort zur Herausgabe der Dichtung des Bühnenfestspiels," 278.
50. Wagner, *Über deutsches Musikwesen*, 86.
51. See Gregor-Dellin, *Richard Wagner*, 723.
52. Wagner, *Briefe* Band VIII, 85.
53. Cosima Wagner, *Tagebücher* Volume II, 649.
54. Ibid., 814.
55. Wagner, *Das Braune Buch*, 86. Italics in the original.
56. Wagner, *Eine Mitteilung an meine Freunde*, 324.
57. Wagner, *Oper und Drama* Parts II and III, 211.
58. Ibid., 212.

59. Hagen Schulze, *Der Weg zum Nationalstaat* (München: Deutscher Taschen-buch Verlag, 1985), 74.
60. Wagner, *Mein Leben*, 273.
61. Wagner, *Eine Mitteilung an meine Freunde*, 311–312.
62. Wagner, *Mein Leben*, 684.
63. John Warrack, *Richard Wagner: Die Meistersinger von Nürnberg* (Cambridge: Cambridge University Press, 1994), 136.
64. Wagner, *Eine Mitteilung an meine Freunde*, 284.
65. Hannu Salmi, *Imagined Germany: Richard Wagner's National Utopia* (New York: Peter Lang, 1999), 136.
66. Wagner, "Wollen wir hoffen?," 119.
67. Cosima Wagner, *Tagebücher 1881–1883*, 692.
68. Ibid., 910.
69. Gregor-Dellin, *Richard Wagner*, 584.
70. Cosima Wagner, *Tagebücher 1881–1883*, 692.
71. Gregor-Dellin, *Richard Wagner*, 641.
72. Cosima Wagner, *Tagebücher 1869–1872*, 519.
73. Wagner, "Das Bühnenfestspielhaus in Bayreuth," 327.
74. Wagner, "Schlußbericht über die Umstände und Schicksale, welche die Ausführung des Bühnenfestspiels 'der Ring des Nibelungen' bis zur Gründung von Wagner-Vereine begleiteten," 316.
75. Ibid., 317.
76. Wagner, *Bericht an Ludwig II*, 10.
77. Wagner, "Schlußbericht," 318.
78. Wagner, "Vorwort zur Herausgabe der Dichtung," 279–280.
79. Ibid., 281.
80. Wagner, "Schlußbericht," 322.
81. Wagner, "Vorwort zur Herausgabe der Dichtung," 273.
82. Wagner, "Das Bühnenfestspielhaus in Bayreuth," 329.
83. Ibid., 343.
84. Wagner, *Briefe* Band IV, 176.
85. Smetana, *Kritické dílo Bedřicha Smetany 1858–1865*, ed. V. H. Jarka (Praha: Nakladatelství Pražské akciové tiskárny, 1948), 38.
86. Ibid., 37.
87. *Bedřich Smetana: Letters and Reminiscences*, ed. František Bartoš (Prague: Artia, 1955), 65.
88. Smetana, *Kritické dílo*, 77–78.
89. Ibid., 69.
90. Smetana, Letter to Otakar Hostinský, apparently from January 9, 1879, in *Z dopisů Bedřicha Smetany* (Praha: Pourova edice, 1947).

91. Ibid., 165.
92. Ibid., 46.
93. Hana Séquardtová, *Bedřich Smetana*. (Praha: Editio Supraphon, 1988), 51.
94. Smetana, *Kritické dílo*, 38.
95. Ibid., 39.
96. Bartoš, *Bedřich Smetana*, 182.
97. Ibid., 88–89.
98. Smetana, *Kritické dílo*, 108.
99. Ibid., 89. Italics in the original.
100. Ibid., 38.
101. Ibid., 87.
102. Ibid., 88.
103. See ibid., 93.
104. Ibid., 78.
105. Vít, "Hudba v programu českého národního hnutí doby předbřeznové a po Říjnovém diplomu," 59.
106. Cited in Jan Racek, *Idea vlasti, národa a slavy v díle Bedřicha Smetany* (Praha: Nákladem Hudební matice Umělecké besedy, 1947), 69.
107. *Smetana ve vzpomínkách a dopisech*, ed. František Bartoš (Praha: Topičova Edice, 1948), 16.
108. BS: Rudolf Wirsing, September 22, 1876. MČH #2140.
109. Bartoš, *Bedřich Smetana*, 210.
110. This last line from the same letter is cited in Séquardtová, *Bedřich Smetana*, 264.
111. This incident is cited in full in the fourth chapter.
112. Bartoš, *Bedřich Smetana*, 45.
113. Ibid., 47.
114. Cited in Séquardtová, *Bedřich Smetana*, 117.
115. Bartoš, *Bedřich Smetana*, 250.
116. Bartoš, *Bedřich Smetana*, 249.
117. Ibid., 220.
118. Ibid., 202.
119. Ibid., 264.
120. Séquardtová, *Bedřich Smetana*, 46 and 168.
121. Séquardtová, *Bedřich Smetana*, 236.
122. Bartoš, *Bedřich Smetana*, 130.
123. Jaroslav Jiránek, *Dílo a život Bedřicha Smetany: Smetanova operní tvorba I* (Praha: Editio Supraphon, 1984), 322.
124. See ibid., 321.
125. See ibid., 323.

126. Brian Large, *Smetana*. (New York: Praeger Publishers, 1970), 218.
127. Jiránek, *Dílo a život Bedřicha Smetany*, 420.
128. Bartoš, *Bedřich Smetana*, 273.
129. See Josef Jiránek, *Vzpomínky a korespondence s Bedřichem Smetanou* (Praha: Statní nakladatelství krásné literatury, hudby a umění, 1957), 42; and Bartoš, *Smetana ve vzpomínkách a dopisech*, 88.
130. Séquardtová, *Bedřich Smetana*, 179.
131. Jaroslav Střítecký, "Tradice a obrození. Bedřich Smetana," in *Povědomí tradice v novodobé české kultuře (doba Bedřicha Smetany)* (Praha: Národní galerie, 1988), 65–76. *See esp.* p. 66.
132. Vladimír Lebl and Jitka Ludvová, "Nová doba (1860–1938)," in *Hudba v českých dějinách: od středověku do nové doby* (Praha: Editio Supraphon, 1988). *See esp.* p. 372.
133. So it read in the Národní divadlo's ballet program from 1999.
134. Finn Benestad and Dag Schjelderup-Ebbe, *Edvard Grieg: mennesket og kunstneren* (Oslo: Aschehoug, 1980), 118.
135. Ibid., 136.
136. Grieg, *Brev* Bind II, 135; Grieg, *Letters*, Volume I, 463.
137. Finn Benestad and Dag Schjelderup-Ebbe, *Edvard Grieg: mennesket og kunstneren*, 2nd edition (Oslo: Aschehoug, 1990), 251.
138. Ibid., 259.
139. Grieg, *Brev* Bind I, 247.
140. *Edvard Grieg: artikler og taler*, ed. Øystein Gaukstad (Oslo: Gyldendal Norsk Forlag, 1957), 71.
141. Benestad and Schjelderup-Ebbe, *Edvard Grieg*, 135.
142. Ibid., 122.
143. Grieg, *Brev* Bind I, 136.
144. Gaukstad, *Edvard Grieg*, 36.
145. Ibid., 173 and 180.
146. Ibid., 69.
147. Ibid., 173.
148. Ibid., 222 and 225.
149. Ibid., 225.
150. Herresthal, *Med spark i gulvet og quinter i bassen*, 187.
151. Benestad and Schjelderup-Ebbe, *Edvard Grieg*, 143.
152. Grieg, *Brev* Bind I, 626.
153. Edvard Grieg, *Breve til Frants Beyer 1872–1907*, ed. Finn Benestad and Bjarne Kortsen (Oslo: Universitetsforlaget, 1993), 98.
154. Cited in Dag Bredal and Terje Strøm-Olsen, *Edvard Grieg: «Musikken er en kampplass»* (Oslo: Aventura Forlag, 1992), 45. Some confusion

actually exists over the true author of this article; Bredal and Strøm-Olsen attribute it to Grieg, while others, such as David Monrad-Johansen, credit Otto Winter-Hjelm. Whatever the case, the ideas expressed in the quotation are congruent enough with Grieg's views as we see them throughout this chapter, that we can assume Grieg's agreement, even if he was not the author.

155. Grieg, *Brev* Bind I, 485.
156. Gaukstad, *Edvard Grieg*, 101.
157. Ibid., 50.
158. Grieg, *Breve til Frants Beyer*, 223.
159. Grieg, *Brev* Bind I, 31.
160. Gaukstad, *Edvard Grieg*, 49.
161. Edvard Grieg, *Dagbøker* (Bergen: Bergen Offentlige Bibliotek, 1993), 152.
162. Ibid., 119.
163. *Breve til Frants Beyer*, 153.
164. Grieg, *Brev* Bind I, 57.
165. Benestad and Schjelderup-Ebbe, *Edvard Grieg: mennesket og kunstneren* (1990), 338.
166. Grieg, *Brev* Bind I, 26.
167. See the Grønvold letter in ibid., 246.
168. Ibid., 537.
169. Gaukstad, *Edvard Grieg*, 197.
170. Ibid., 196.
171. Ferdinand Rojahn, "Edvard Grieg som national tonedigter," *Nordisk Musik-Revue*, 3, no. 12 (June 15, 1903): 94.
172. See the letter to Olav Anton Thommessen of June 21, 1901, in *Brev* Bind I, where Grieg approves of Rojahn's article.
173. Gaukstad, *Edvard Grieg*, 122.
174. Grieg, *Brev* Bind I, 147.
175. Ibid., 296.
176. Ibid., 300.
177. Grieg, *Brev* Bind II, 410.
178. He says in his letters that while one must love one's language (*Brev* Bind I, 177), nationality ultimately lies deeper (*Brev* Bind II, 324).
179. Grieg, *Brev* Bind I, 103.
180. Gaukstad, *Edvard Grieg*, 86–87.
181. See Grieg, *Breve til Frants Beyer*, 98.
182. Finn Benestad and Dag Schjelderup-Ebbe, *Edvard Grieg: The Man and the Artist*. William H. Halverson and Leland B. Sateren, translators (Lincoln: University of Nebraska Press, 1988), 166.

183. Grieg, *Brev* Bind I, 202.
184. Gaukstad, *Edvard Grieg*, 171.
185. Grieg, *Brev* Bind I, 486.
186. Gaukstad, *Edvard Grieg*, 172.
187. Grieg, *Brev* Bind I, 486.
188. Ibid., 202.
189. Ibid., 315.
190. Uses the term "decent" in ibid., 204.
191. Ibid., 315.
192. See, for example, Conrad L. Donakowski, *A Muse for the Masses* (Chicago: University of Chicago Press, 1977).
193. However, that river by no means dried up completely; Wagner and Tchaikovsky, for instance, both relied on aristocratic support at some point in their careers—Wagner from King Ludwig II, and Tchaikovsky from the Countess von Meck.

CHAPTER 3

# THE ROLE OF FOLK SOURCES
# IN CREATING A NATIONAL MUSIC

Where would nationalists be without "the folk"? Without this envisioned group of people to mythologize, romanticize, idealize, and extol, the entire nationalist project would perhaps be like a house built without a foundation. Some idea of the folk serves as a central subject in virtually all European nationalist discourse. Music, in this case, is no different. But, the example of music is especially illuminating in terms of how nationalist intellectuals attempted to construct the relationship between the folk and the putative nation—in so doing, constructing not just that nation but the folk as well. The folk is constructed in two ways: most obviously, nationalist intellectuals are trying to create a nationalized populace, a *Gesamtvolk* that shares a unified national culture. Secondly, however, nationalists are constructing an image of the "original" folk— that is, the peasants who are conceived as the purest bearers of nationality. Yet this romanticized image of the peasants occasionally comes into conflict with the harsh reality of peasant life; the dichotomy between the ideal and the actual is something nationalist intellectuals grapple with in their discourse.

The relationship between "the folk" and the national high culture is something that had to be negotiated in any historical nation-building movement. The key first phase in this relationship is conceiving of folk sources as "national." This conception is a result of a contingent historical process, contrary to what nationalists (and even some later scholars) have claimed. Rather than accepting an idea of the inherent nationality of folk sources, we must first see how such sources were "nationalized." Nationalists' fundamental claim is that folk culture is a kind of inheritance on which the national culture would be built. As the discourse shows, however, the utility of folk culture is actually somewhat limited. Folk inspirations are building blocks for the national culture, but in and of themselves they cannot constitute that culture. They must be refashioned into an artistically worthy high culture. In this way, the effort to create a national music exposes the social tensions between the ostensibly "low" and "high" cultures that exist within the envisioned national populace.

Nonetheless, the entire nationalist project is one that attempts to bridge these divisions, to produce the unified national culture. Music itself fulfilled this function of a bridge, in the nationalists' vision: it was a product of the "natural," "folk" inspirations that would become "refined" into high art forms. Wagner's, Smetana's, and Grieg's treatment of folk sources is unthinkable without the historical and philosophical precedents of their nation building movements' embrace of peasant culture. However, while all three do obviously rely on these precedents, they also take a few further rhetorical and practical steps toward the incorporation of the folk into their own artistic creations.

## NATIONALIZING FOLK TRADITIONS

To understand how nationalist artists employed folk sources in their works, we first have to understand how these sources came to be viewed as national. There are several identifiable steps in this nationalization of peasant culture. To begin with, a growing interest in the folk was inspired in large part by Herder's researches. Subsequently, efforts to preserve the folk's culture—folk song and folk tale collections, for example—began to code this culture as inherently national. Even once the products of peasant culture were identified as national, however, a divide between this "low" culture and the "high" culture of art continued to persist. The focus of nationalist artists' embrace of folk sources, then, was to raise these low forms up into the realm of high art. The building of this bridge to create a unified national populace is, in fact, one of the key tenets in the theory of nationalism.

Before plunging into the topic of the peasantry, however, we should ask: To *whom*, exactly, were nineteenth-century nationalist intellectuals referring when they invoked "the folk"? An answer to this question is complicated by the fact that the English version of the word "folk" does not convey the full range of meaning behind the German term *Volk*— whose range of meaning I do nonetheless wish to imply. "Folk" in English, with its most frequent connotations of "old folks" or "folksiness" simply misses out on the significance of "the people," a community of shared history, culture, and values, found in the German term. Often in a consideration of these ideas, the German term is indispensable, particularly with regard to such specific concepts as the *Volksgeist*, which have no real equivalent in English. The Czechs refer to the *národ*, a term that fuses a variety of ideas such as "folk," "people," and "nation," making translation also quite complicated. The Norwegian word, though, is *folk*, and fewer translation problems arise with it.

When Herder, one of the ultimate prophets of the *Volk*, uses that term, he often means the "wild, lively, free, sensual [*sinnlicher*]," "unpolished" "people of nature," that is, the supposedly uncivilized peoples like the North American Indians.[1] Also, however, he suggests that it can refer to rural people or even to the ancient Greeks, who had their own "folk poets," such as Homer.[2] Subsequent writers take up these various strands, using the term *Volk* to refer alternately to the "vulgus in populo" or also to the entire populace, the *Gesamtvolk*. The term that best expresses the typical nationalist use of *Volk*, though, is Albert Dietrich's phrase, "soil of the culture-nation."[3] This conception suggests the change in meaning from merely the lower classes (such as the peasants) to an idea of *Volk* as nation. The work of the folk-song researcher Carl Engel provides a perfect example of how the peasants came to be associated with the nation as a whole. "In most European countries," Engel wrote in 1866, "it is…among the working classes, the artisans, the field labourers, and the country people in general, that we must look out for genuine specimens of National music."[4]

Here, it is the lower classes who automatically produce—naturally and inevitably—the truly "national." As we shall see, this idea is carried throughout the discourse on national music and on the role that folk inspirations should play in the national culture. How, though, is the folk "national"? The move to understand folk sources as inherently national in character involves several steps, historically speaking. Collection efforts form the first step. These collections are then presented as kind of cultural inheritance of the whole nation. The idea is that the *Volksgeist*—the ethereal, eternal font of the nation's identity—endures in peasant traditions long after city dwellers have become denationalized. I will discuss these steps in greater detail later.

With the example of folk music, however, what were fundamentally rural, local, or regional forms came to be reinterpreted (by nationalist intellectuals and eventually by nationalized publics) as national. Oftentimes, folk dances or tunes are associated with a particular region. In this sense, they are originally subnational. And as Walter Wiora has pointed out, folk traditions can also be supranational.[5] Before the nineteenth-century nationalist movements, folk traditions not infrequently consisted of "international" elements, in that some traditions are common across wider territorial boundaries. Hence, certain musical features, like perhaps the bagpipe drone common to a number of peasant traditions, appear in the folk musics of more than one "nation." The nationalist understanding of folk musics conceptually binds the local peasants and their traditions to an artificial "whole" in the territory that would eventually become the nation. In actual fact, however, folk musics did not develop as individual, autochthonous traditions unique to a particular plot of land and hence completely distinguishable from one another. Rather, these traditions interacted, cross-pollinating, often spreading across what would come to be national or nation-state borders.

The incorporation of folk elements into high art is admittedly not new with nationalism. Colorfully costumed "peasants" were tramping around opera stages long before such peasants came to be regarded as expressions of the *Volksgeist*. Indeed, the national treatment of folk sources builds in some ways upon previous artistic practice of the eighteenth and nineteenth centuries. For example, an idealized depiction of rural life is a popular trope in French comic opera as well as north-German Singspiels prior to 1800. The use of peasant choruses, dances, and songs are common elements in many operas of this period. Nationalists take up this presentation of traditional peasant life as a kind of "dreamland." They portray the peasants as living in a "cozy idyll."[6] However, this idyll, in the nationalist conception, is a state of nature in which the springs of nationality flow freely and purely.

Only after about 1800, however, with the emergence of nationalism as a political and cultural force, would the peasant forms be invested with a national meaning. Hence, when we find a peasant dance in an opera of Grétry from, say, 1784, we can be sure there was no nationalist intent behind its use—instead, it was most likely meant to evoke a pastoral mood of the countryside. In Smetana, however, the peasant dance becomes a symbol evoking the entire nation. There is both a continuity and a divergence in these two uses of peasant material, then: the continuity is that both the nationalist and the non-nationalist recur to peasant forms to express an idyllic rural life. The divergence is that, for nationalists, this idyll is like a time warp back to the uncorrupted sources of the national culture, and the peasants are not just peasants but are rather the consummate preservers of that culture. Nationalists *identify* with the peasants, whereas in earlier historical depictions of the peasantry in opera, there is no assumed unity between the rural people and the spectators in the theater.

Complicating this question, though, is the fact that peasant dances were sometimes, even before nationalist movements gathered steam, called "national." For example, in Norway in 1815, Lars Roverud wrote of the peasants' "national dances."[7] Indeed, musicology has generally accepted that musical production in different countries had already taken on certain "national" characteristics in the seventeenth century. Whether Italian madrigals, French courtly dances, or English lute music, certain styles are admittedly identifiable. Nonetheless, these traditions are not truly "national" in the same way as music that was created *after* the rise of nationalism.

These earlier descriptions of "national" music simply depend upon an idea of nationality as a more-or-less apolitical indicator of provenance— "German" music, for instance, may come from the German-speaking lands, and perhaps betray certain idiosyncracies unique to those lands (whether features of musical form, or recognizable character traits ostensibly attributable to the Germans), but the idea of a German nation is not at all the same as what it would later come to mean. What nationalism adds, conceptually, to preexistent understandings of "nation" is the idea of common duties and a shared culture across social divisions. Given this shared culture, so nationalism would have it, peasant dances belong just as much to, say, middle-class, urban Norwegians as to the rural dwellers in their isolated hamlets. It seems likely that when Roverud used the term "national," it was a reference to group distinctiveness, predicated on evident differences between Norwegian and German peasant dances (for example), rather than as a reference to the deeper commonalities uniting a people on the basis of nationality. In contrast, when the folk musician Knut Dahle wrote to Grieg in 1901 about the need to preserve the "national" tunes he knew, Dahle was evidently relying on this "nationalized" conception of peasant traditions as belonging to all of Norwegian society. He therefore argued that those tunes had to be preserved as an inheritance of *all* Norwegians, not just of Norwegian peasants.

Allied to this new understanding of what "national" means, folk traditions themselves underwent a process of *becoming* national. One of the first ways that folk traditions become national is simply through the labeling of them as such. For instance, in *Stimmen der Völker in*

*Liedern,* Herder identifies the songs he presents as "Italian," "Spanish," "German," "Danish," and so on. Very rarely does a song receive any sort of designation of a regional or local provenance. This was the typical practice of the folk song collectors: they went looking for specifically "German" or "Czech" or "Russian" songs, and when they published them, they identified them as such. Admittedly, such songs occasionally also received regional identifications, such as specifying where exactly in Norway a particular dance was practiced, or whether a given tune was "discovered" in Moravia versus Bohemia. However, even in such cases, the emphasis is on such objects as national rather than local. They are Norwegian first, and only secondly from, for example, the Gudbrandsdal region.

The fact that these songs were not in any way "originally" national has been too often misunderstood, however. George Herzog reminds us that "[t]he main danger in classification is that it leads to assuming that objects in a storeroom were originally created and deposited in that order."[8] Of course, the mere labeling of songs as national is not sufficient for a shared belief in their nationality to take root in the populace. However, these classification schemes help *establish* the idea of a particular tune or text as "German" or "Czech." Subsequently, nationally-minded thinkers continue to configure such sources as national, reinforcing this conception both through their discourse and, in the case of artists, through their own works.

This initial, classificatory process is very much akin to Benedict Anderson's discussion of censuses, maps, and museums in *Imagined Communities.* Print capitalism, censuses, maps, and museums all help fix ideas of national cultural patrimony and of national boundaries. The latter can be boundaries in the territorial sense, as in a map, or in a more purely conceptual one, such as by packaging an exhibit of "Indonesian" cultural treasures in a museum. Folk song editions similarly help produce a *conception* of nationality and national cultural patrimony through the classification of folk songs according to the criteria of national provenance. Print capitalism even plays a role here, too: folk song collection was a movement that penetrated virtually all the corners of the European continent, and the publication and dissemination of these collections was a similarly widespread phenomenon. Different, though, from Anderson's examples, at least early on in European history, the state was not involved in promoting or supporting folk song collection (though in Norway, Lars Roverud thought there should be government funding for such endeavors). Collectors were primarily independent scholars or enthusiastic amateurs interested in promoting their putative nation's culture.

Herder is generally credited with sparking the subsequent explosion of national folk song research. He is followed in Germany by figures such as Achim von Arnim, Clemens Brentano, the brothers Grimm, and later others such as Ludwig Christian Erk. These collections were not always "folk songs," strictly speaking. Herder's collections, for example, rarely included reproductions of any actual melodies. Similarly, von Arnim and Brentano's *Des Knaben Wunderhorn* is a compendium of texts, and the Grimms' works focused primarily on folk and fairy tales. For our purposes, it is important to remember that nationalist music is not based solely on folk songs—other folk elements such as legends play an equally prominent role in Wagner's, Smetana's, and Grieg's efforts to produce a national music, as we will see.

Herder's influence and example were a direct inspiration for later collectors throughout Europe, and nowhere was this influence more immediate than on Czech collectors. Herder's Czech counterparts are figures such as Jan Ritter z Rittersberku, František Ladislav Čelakovský, and Karel Jaromír Erben. In Scandinavia, folk song collections by the Danes Abrahamsen, Nyerup, and Rahbek, and by the Swedes Afzelius and Geijer preceded those of the paramount figure for Norway, Ludwig Mathias Lindeman. Lindeman's collections, which he began publishing in 1840, form the bedrock of all subsequent interest in Norwegian folk music, and his compendium of melodies would be used by many subsequent composers, Grieg among them. Peter Christen Asbjørnson and Jørgen Moe's collections of folk tales (1841–1844) are the prose analog of Lindeman's work, in terms of their centrality in Norwegian culture.

A principal stated motivation for all such collections was to preserve a culture that was perceived as dying out. Herder again provides an early impulse here. He admonished the Germans, saying that "the voices of your fathers" are *not* "faded away," or "silenced in the dust." These national folk traditions are still there, "but they lie under mud, they are underestimated and despised." Hence his rallying cry: "Get to work, my brothers, and show our nation what she is and is not, how she thought and felt, or how she thinks and feels."[9] Note how Herder switches tenses here, implying the continuity between the nation's past and its present. Von Arnim later also lamented "the complete extinction of the folk song in many areas, or otherwise its fall into dirt and emptiness."[10]

This call for preservation applied to folk songs, folk tales, and even languages. The effort by men such as Josef Dobrovský or Josef Jungmann to "reconstruct" a modern Czech language out of its medieval roots not coincidentally takes place almost exactly at the same time as the investigations into folk song. Indeed, the publication of such folk songs in Czech was an essential part of the linguistic "revival," in that through such collections, nationalists hoped to encourage the use of the Czech language among urban dwellers. These collections were conceived in both a scholarly and patriotic sense, since they were supposed to serve as an archive of the nation's history and cultural values. An excellent expression of the ethos of preservation is a letter Grieg wrote to the Storting (the Norwegian parliament) in 1900, calling for state support of folk song research:

> It is absolutely essential at this time that a historical report of our folk melodies be undertaken. How often I receive from the big culture lands requests for information on source material for studies of Norwegian folk tunes (that is, folk melodies). To my shame I have to say: I don't know any such source materials. Or rather: to our nation's shame. For there aren't any.[11]

The guiding idea behind these collections is the conviction that folk songs and tales are an inheritance of the *entire* nation, and hence need to be preserved so the nation does not lose its culture. Herder calls folk songs the "archive" of the people's "science and religion, its theology and cosmology...impression of its heart, picture of its domestic life in joy and sorrow."[12] They are the "eternal hereditary and joyful song of the Volk."[13] He admits that the folk tunes may not correspond to the demands of "art" per se, but he insists that "the music of a nation, even in its least perfect developments and typical styles, shows the inner character of the same, that is, the actual disposition of its sensitivities, more deeply and truly than the longest description of its outward quirks ever could."[14] There are two key claims here. The first is the trans-historical nature of the folk traditions; they are "eternal." Secondly, Herder emphasizes that, despite any deficiencies in artistic quality, folk traditions are nonetheless the best repository of the nation's values. These claims are key because upon them Herder builds the idea that a national art must grow out of folk inspirations. He says that his collections of folk songs are not so much poetry in themselves but rather "materials for poetry."[15] He calls for a "living" German poetry to build upon this folk inheritance, so that the Germans would finally have their own, national style of poetry.[16]

Herder's bundle of ideas—eternal folk traditions as a cultural inheritance upon which a national art must be built—are of course fundamental for many subsequent thinkers on nationality, within the discourse on national music as well. Goethe, for one, though strictly speaking no nationalist, took up the conception of the "country people" as a "repository" of cultural values that could "refresh" art.[17] Thus he called for folk songs "revived and celebrated to return to the Volk and to merge into the life and culture [*Bildung*] of the nation."[18] Later German writers such as Josef von Eichendorff and W. H. Riehl similarly praise folk traditions as the "roots" of national poetry and music. Indeed, these ideas are carried over into the twentieth century by figures such as Ralph Vaughan Williams and Hubert Parry. In his essay *National Music* Vaughan Williams approvingly cites Parry:

> All things that mark the folk-music of the race also betoken the quality of the race and as a faithful reflection of ourselves we

must needs cherish it. Moreover it is worth remembering that the great composers...have concentrated upon their folk-music much attention, since style is ultimately national...The purest product [of communal-based efforts to create a style] is folk-song which...outlasts the greatest works of art and becomes a heritage to generations and in that heritage may lie the ultimate solution of characteristic national art.[19]

As regards individual cases of nationalist movements such as the German, Czech, and Norwegian, we should understand the research and exaltation of folk traditions as an attempt to establish the essential and fundamental qualities of the national identity. With respect to Germany, we have seen how Herder looked to find a uniquely German poetic art in the folk song traditions. Fichte carries on this idea of "Germanness" as residing in the Volk, and von Arnim and the Grimms similarly locate the German *Volksgeist* in the folk tales that they published.[20] Adhering to the same pattern, collectors such as Čelakovský and others in the Czech lands also regarded the peasants as the bearers of "Czechness." Folk poetry and song were the "most healthy and most sincere display of all spiritual values" for early Czech patriots.[21] Norwegian nationalists, with their claim that the rural people preserved an "untouched" or "pure" Norwegian culture, were accurate in one sense: living snugly tucked away in their remote valleys and fjords, the peasants did indeed largely escape assimilation into the Dano-centric culture that dominated Norwegian towns and elites.[22] Hence it was to those remote peasant settlements that the Norwegian violinist (and all-around nationalist activist) Ole Bull looked when he declared that "the Norwegian art stands ready and waiting in the mountains."[23]

One common idea that the Norwegian example clearly emphasizes is the connection between the folk and nature. Peasant culture, as a source of nationality "untainted" by foreign influences, acquires a certain natural, almost elemental force. Here, again, is an area where Herder's contribution has a ripple effect on subsequent thought. Herder argued that only a folk that was still close to nature really had a "living" culture: "The farther from an artificial, scientific way of thinking, speaking, and writing a Volk is, the less must its songs be made only for paper"; when they are made only "for paper," they are just "dead verses."[24] Indeed, to produce culture at all, a Volk must be "natural," and not "artificial," as he terms it.[25] Part of this natural force is a quality of timelessness, as I remarked upon previously. Folk traditions were, in Herder's and subsequent thought, "a remnant of the world gone by," preserved in peoples who dwell in cut-off corners of the world where the past still lives.[26] Being cut off in this way, the peasant traditions are true to themselves, true to their authentic nationality, expressing the "natural, universal, enduring, individual" characteristics of that nationality, as Erben declared in his *A Word about National Songs*.[27] In this article, Erben tautologically emphasizes that a people can only be truly national if the "national spirit" still lives in them. This spirit or *Volksgeist* expresses itself through a people's songs, stories, and traditions; it is what makes such cultural products uniquely national.

In order to understand better the role that folk traditions played in constructing national cultures, we need to take a step back from these nationally rooted conceptions of peasant culture. The idea of naturalness, based as it is on the perceived connections among the peasants, the Earth, "timeless traditions," and their isolation from the modern world, confers a kind of authenticity upon the peasant traditions. This authenticity is what makes the peasant traditions suitable as a foundation for the national music. When they are still "living," they have this kind of natural, national force (thanks to the *Volksgeist*) that can create a truly national music. How, though, did the traditions cease being "alive" or "vital"? Part of the answer is that the inherently national traditions could become supplanted by "foreign" practices. Also, the folk traditions could become de-natured by trivial or outright worthless artistic treatments of them. Such trivialities subvert the innate dignity of the folk's national spirit. Wagner and Smetana both rail against such trivializing treatments.

Despite nationalists' evident reverence for the folk traditions, they nonetheless considered these traditions in and of themselves an insufficient base for a national art. What came from the peasants had to be refined into something more worthy. Thus, together with all the paeans to the pristine folk culture, we also see in the nation-building discourse a troubled attempt to grapple with alternate, condescending perceptions of the peasants themselves: the mutual embrace between the peasants and the rest of the populace does not quite amount to a teary-eyed family reunion. The simultaneous exaltation of the folk combined with the rhetorical attempt to skirt the deep social divisions within the envisioned national populace is a theme that has received too little attention. It is, though, a fundamental theme, above all in the efforts to create a national culture.

The tension between ideas of "high" and "low" in the discourse is related to the problem of the multiple meanings of the term *Volk*. Though the nationalist aspiration was for a Volk as a *Gesamtvolk*—that is, a unified, culturally homogeneous national populace—there is also the legacy of the Volk as the *hoi polloi* to contend with. Thus even if the peasants, in their idealized form, embody the "soil of the culture-nation," in reality those same peasants were often rather too smelly and coarse for the intellectuals advancing the idea of nationhood. The folk, though a cultural repository of nationality, remained politically inert, at least through the early stages of the nationalist project. That project, though, is precisely an attempt to motivate the populace—across social divisions—for the theses of nationalism. The political and cultural goal, after all, is to create a *Gesamtvolk*. In a certain sense, the effort to build a national culture is an attempt to inspire these inert but inherently national peasants to live up to the nationalists' claims for them. However, just as the masses must be mobilized for the nationalist project to succeed, so the peasant traditions need to be transformed to create a national high culture.

The practice and performance of folk and nationalist musics was fundamentally affected by the processes of urbanization and embourgeoisement, which gradually accelerated throughout the nineteenth century. On the one hand, the influx into the cities hastened a decline of folk music traditions as they had long been practiced in the rural areas. This decline, as we have seen, is often described as the folk traditions becoming less "vital" or "authentic." The other side of urbanization is that a built-in audience for folk music gradually came to exist in the cities. The profile of the folk music traditions heightened as they came to be practiced in urban areas. They retained their association with rural life, of course, but now a much wider audience would be exposed to the traditions of various regions and communities, as the people from those regions, along with the more established urbanites, all rubbed shoulders in the city streets.

Hence the traditions of folk music became more familiar across society. This development would be crucial in the subsequent creation of a nationalist art music that relies partially on the incorporation of folk melodies and styles. The general public, including concertgoers, increasingly had some exposure to folk music. And that music was being configured in public discourse as national. Herder again establishes a precedent here, arguing for the appeal of folk music across society with his claim that "the way to the heart" for all people is through "national melodies"; these national melodies have a "powerful appeal."[28] Musicians of the time often relied upon such an appeal: they would bridge the gap between their artistic ideals and their public by turning to the folk song. Incorporating folk elements lent art music a "popular character," since the barriers to appreciation or understanding of folk music were perceived to be not as high as with art music. A folksy trapping could thereby provide "serious" music a wider entry into middle-class homes or informal get-togethers. In this way, folk elements really did act as a bridge, particularly between the publics to which nationalist intellectuals were trying to appeal. The folk traditions appealed to the lower classes who may have recognized those traditions as "their own," as well as to the bourgeoisie who were becoming more familiar with these rural forms of cultural expression.

Nonetheless, a divide would continue to separate not only peasant and art musics but also the treatment of the "upper" and "lower" layers of society. This tension underlies the concurrent efforts to produce a unified national culture. The fact is that, despite their attempts occasionally to be folksy by relying on some familiarity of their publics with the peasant traditions, the audience for art composers' work was still quite limited to the educated urban classes. People fresh off the family farm in the mountains were not rushing into the concert halls. Similarly, the very notion of artistic worth continued to enforce a deep divide between folk traditions and art music. The long-standing hierarchical division of composed art music over folk music would not be overcome in the space of just a few decades.

The term "composed art music" to distinguish between this form and folk music comes from Bohlman.[29] He also reminds us, importantly, not to accept automatically this dichotomous understanding of folk music versus art music. The idea that these are two rigidly stratified, noninteracting genres is simply not tenable historically: folk and art music have rarely failed to influence each other in some way. Nonetheless, in nineteenth-century thought, the stratified conception of folk versus art music *does* pertain. Acknowledging this fact allows us to examine its consequences for the society and culture of the time.

For instance, the persistent understanding of peasant music as "low" coexists, contradictorily, with the idealization of the rural people. Perhaps, in fact, the dichotomy obtains precisely because of the contradiction between the idealization of the peasants, on the one hand, with the way they actually lived, on the other. Engel amusingly expressed this dichotomous perception when he wrote, "The inhabitants of Kamtschatka possess music far more expressive and beautiful than their ignorance, and their wretched life in a most ungenial climate, would lead us to expect."[30] However, even the rhetorical exaltation of peasants as a cultural repository sometimes collided with the actual judgments of those same peasants' culture. Liszt, for one, regarded "the Hungarian songs we encounter in our villages" as too "poor and incomplete" ever to "win general respect."[31] Similarly, Lars Roverud, who took an early interest in the folk songs of Norway, thought that the peasant music as it was performed was uncultured and of little actual worth, dismissing the peasant musicians with epithets such as, they "do not know even the slightest bit about harmony."[32]

Most commonly, peasant sources were considered valuable principally as raw materials for a "legitimate" art. I have mentioned earlier

Herder's idea that the folk song texts he published were not so much art as "materials for art." Despite the beauty of such sources, in themselves they were valuable as inspiration but not really as art per se. These ideas are predictably carried on in the Czech and Norwegian movements. F. L. Čelakovský inscribed on his second volume of folk songs the motto that "popular poetry" should serve "today's poet" much as the "ancient chronicles" underlie the historian's writings.[33] Again showing the influence of Herder, Čelakovský believed that folk songs should be "adapted" so as to provide the most perfect model for poets to use.[34] Erben published his own collections partly with the hope that they would serve as a launching point for higher forms of art, particularly a Czech opera. Folk song collectors virtually never recorded *verbatim* the texts or melodies they encountered. Instead, they considered it necessary "to tame and improve" these folk sources "in order to make them edifying to the singer or reader."[35] The improvement or elevation of folk materials could be accomplished partly through arrangement: by smoothing off the raw edges of the folk songs, for example, they would conform more nearly to the standards of art music. Smetana even admits explicitly to "idealizing" his folk sources.

The insistence on the necessity of "elevating" in no way implies that these writers disdained folk materials. Indeed, they very often loved them, and that is precisely why they wanted to present the products of folk culture in the best light possible. As one Norwegian writer put it, through "artistically suitable patchwork," these folk sources could be given "a worthy and appropriate appearance."[36] The poet A. O. Vinje, a great admirer of Norwegian folk culture, nonetheless also thought that "without scientific development the ingenuity [of folk songs] is an uncut diamond."[37] Lindeman, the godfather of Norwegian folk melody collection, in fact expressed this bundle of ideas on "elevating" and "adapting" with an amazing directness and clarity:

> Norwegian folk music is rich; in its abundance and characteristicness it is second to none. But unless it is artistically arranged and thereby developed into a national art music that can become the

property of all social classes, it will lose its richness with each passing year. Foreign music that the educated classes cultivate will inexorably sink deeper in the populace and either corrupt or supplant the national melodies. Therefore, it is of great importance that our folk melodies be collected and published as soon as possible, in order to foster the development of a Norwegian art music and to bring forth a musical life that can become an effective means of education for the masses, since they will find it easy to become familiar with this music. Thereby Norway will also contribute to musical development more generally, in that a large part of modern music's task is to transfer folk music into the educated art forms.[38]

The aim, as Lindeman claims, is to produce, from the example and inspiration of folk music, a "modern" music to fulfill its educational role for all classes. Clearly, the uncultured peasant forms cannot attain such an end, according to Lindeman. The call for folk sources to be "created anew" in order to become an "artistic culture" was one that explicitly motivated the work of several generations of nationalist artists, including Smetana and Grieg.

For the artists who relied in one way or another on folk sources, the integration of these sources into art music was a way not just of expressing the idealized unity of the nation, but of actually *creating* that unity. To begin with, the nationalist use of folk sources expresses unity through the process of collecting folk tunes. Folk tunes that are presented as "German" or "Czech," and so on, actually come from a variety of sources within society. They are collections of church songs, shepherds' songs, school songs, and farmers' songs, for example.[39] However, by labelling them as "German" or "Czech," they come to belong to the whole envisioned nation, and not just to one of its component parts. Beyond just songs and folk tales coming from different groups in society, they also come from different time periods. But, again, by fusing sources from different periods into a single national inheritance, nationalists produce a shared history for the entire nation.[40] In particular, the use of legends and historical figures in nationalist works of art unifies the nation's present with its past in the artwork: the past is alive in the contemporary nationalist culture being fashioned, and that past, no matter how remote, belongs to all present living members of the nation precisely because of their nationality. One might even say that the artwork ties the past to the future as well, since nationalist artists usually dreamed of their works lasting forever.

The incorporation of folk materials into high art also has a creative power: it actually creates unity by assembling a unified body of national cultural inheritance. The national culture, by definition, is assumed to be shared equally across all classes of the society. Art thereby belongs as much to the peasants as to the upper classes, just as the peasant sources are assumed to be part of the common property of the bourgeoisie. Even if folk sources are not perceived as equally valuable as high art within the national culture, these elements are nonetheless assumed to have an equal right or necessity of being included. Ralph Vaughan Williams expressed succinctly the equality and unity inherent in the national culture when he wrote: "The greatest artist belongs inevitably to his country as much as the humblest singer in a remote village—they and all those who come between them are links in the same chain, manifestations on their different levels of the same desire for artistic expression, and, moreover, the same nature of artistic expression."[41] So, the incorporation of folk sources into high art works as a kind of bridge over social divisions, from the greatest artist to the village singer and everyone in between. The national culture itself is this bridge, incorporating elements from both the "high" and "low" of society. It thereby effects a symbolic unity of the different classes within the envisioned national populace.

The national culture's unifying power goes beyond symbolism, however. In fact, the very idea of "the nation" is based on such a goal of bridging social cleavages to unite people around a common culture. The common metaphor of the nation as family assumes this deep, basic shared identity and kinship. However, what the nation adds above the mere notion of a kinship or descent group is the equality (at least in theory) of all members. All the members of the national body are assumed to have, again at least rhetorically, equal and fundamental entitlements to be equal bearers of the national identity. But, much as with the folk sources needing to be elevated into a worthy art, the national populace itself must be *made*—work is required to fashion the people into a nation. For nationalist intellectuals, an essential element of nationalizing the masses is the propagation and inculcation of the national culture, first constructing it and then ensuring that it is shared across the populace. One common example of the propagation of a national culture is with language: historically, as nation-states were constructed, a single national language was inculcated through national schooling to which everyone had a right. The use of a single language was supposed also to eliminate social divisions by giving every member of the nation equal access to communicating within the society. Similarly, other institutions such as a national parliament or a national theater were designed to implement a single, unified national administration and culture to which all citizens would be equally entitled.

In terms of the nation-building project, then, the use of folk sources in constructing a national music actually attempts to effect communication across the rural/urban and class divides. Just as nationalist artists incorporate these folk traditions into their cultural production to create a unified national art, so this art is supposed to unify the national populace by being mutually shared. Since the national art as a unification process is often far ahead of any such unification within the society, the presence of folk traditions in high art is largely a symbolic integration. Still, though, by incorporating elements of peasant culture—however idealized—into high art forms, the peasants are in a sense incorporated into the broader society as well. Given that in practice these high art forms communicate primarily to the educated, urban dwellers, the national art thus becomes a means of imparting to these urbanites some of the cultural traditions of the rural people. As one example, Derry credits Asbjørnson and Moe's folk tale collections with introducing "the upper classes and the town population in general to a fascinating achievement of the peasant mind."[42]

This cultural bridging of social divides is critical because the emergence of modern nations is a process defined in part by the growth of social groups integrated in terms of their economic, political, linguistic, cultural, religious, geographical, and historical relationships.[43] Indeed, the meaning of "nationalization" is largely the move away from the rigidly segmented, isolated social strata of the preindustrial period, when high culture was exclusively the preserve of elites, toward a homogeneous, integrated populace where all members have a claim to the high culture. Gellner reminds us, though, that this national culture must not be exclusively high.[44] It *is* high to an extent, but in order to communicate across the various social classes, the national culture has to have some kind of fundament recognizable by all, some characteristics that every member of the nation—whether pig farmer or prime minister—can identify with. Folk sources' unification across historical periods is also related to Anderson's notion of "homogeneous time." At the root of homogeneous time is the idea of shared activity with other members of the nation whom you may not actually know, but whom you can comfortably imagine to be doing things not unlike what you are doing at any given moment.[45] Sharing time presumes sharing a history, such that in a certain sense, the modern members of a nation even share time with their national kin of the past. Nationalism, in sum, encourages a belief in culture as a widely shared social space or possession that unifies across social divisions by belonging equally to every member of the national community.

So, thanks to the rhetoric and practice of nationalist artists, the peasants obtain a role and place in society, perhaps before they are truly "integrated" in a political or economic sense. The national culture, by integrating peasant influences, fulfills an expressive function because it is supposed to express the nationality allegedly inherent in the populace. Moreover, the national culture is an expression of the idealized unity of this populace, across the various social divides. Simultaneously, the national culture performs a creative function of actually trying to construct this unity. The vehicle for unifying the national populace is the broadly shared culture. The national culture, as the ostensible possession of *all* the nation's members, thus both represents and effects the social unity that is the very basis of the concept of the nation.

## Folk Sources in Wagner, Smetana, and Grieg

With this philosophical and theoretical understanding of folk music's role in nationalist art as our springboard, we can now turn to how our three nationalist composers in particular treated folk sources. To begin with, those who know Wagner's career and thought only superficially might raise their eyebrows at the claim that he was a composer deeply inspired by folk sources. Particularly in comparison with Smetana or Grieg, he doesn't seem "folksy." Wagner never wrote a suite of German dances à la Smetana's Czech or Grieg's Norwegian ones, for example. However, to reduce our understanding of folk sources' role in creating a national music to merely the reliance on folk tunes would be a mistake. In fact, as we shall see, Wagner looks to the folk as the ultimate source of *all* art, including his own.

Wagner actually emphasizes the creative and inspirational power of the folk to an even greater degree than do Smetana or Grieg. He follows very much in the tradition of Herder, von Arnim, et al. in conceiving of the Volk "in the sense of the incomparable productivity of the prehistorical, original community [*Urgemeinschaft*]."[46] This idea of the "community" is paramount in Wagner's conception of the nature of the Volk. In *Das Kunstwerk der Zukunft*, he returns again and again to "necessity" ("Not" in the German) as the motivating force behind the Volk, and in fact behind effectively every worthwhile action. The Volk "is the embodiment of all those who feel a communal necessity."[47] Only the Volk acts according to this "communal necessity," so only the Volk is "irresistible, triumphant, and uniquely true."[48] Thus it is to the Volk we must look to find "our great benefactor and savior, the representative of necessity in flesh and blood"—the actor that will unite everyone through the artwork.[49]

It is the Volk that acts to bring about "the new";[50] in fact, "the actual discoverer has always been only the Volk."[51] Since only the Volk acts "exclusively correctly," we can thus understand Wagner to mean that it is similarly "exclusively correct"[52] that the Volk only makes its own that which perfectly "native [*heimisch*]."[53] In this way, then—its fully natural, irresistible, and inherently "native" action—the Volk becomes the artist of the future.[54] However, he also finds that in the Volk's art from the past—"in the times of racial-national communality"—the Volk was already "the sole poet and artist."[55] As such, "all material and all form, if they are to have some healthy life, can only be taken from this poetry- and art-discovering Volk."[56] This is how Wagner maneuvers to the claim that true art can only come about through "national communality," stemming from the ultimately national source of the Volk.

As the aforementioned quotations indicate, though, Wagner thinks that the Volk has already created art. His firm belief in the Volk as an "artist" is suggested by the parallel he draws between the work of art and religion. "The artwork is the living, represented religion," he says. "But artists do not discover religions—they emerge from the Volk."[57] The great artwork that the Volk has produced is myth: in myth "the Volk becomes the creator of art."[58] Myth "constitutes the communal poetic energy of the Volk."[59] The Volk integrates through myth "the diverse natural phenomena into god, and from god finally into the hero." In this hero, Wagner says, "the Volk recognizes itself through the composite image of its own being, it celebrates its own deeds in the epos, and in the drama the Volk represents itself to itself."[60] Myth, then, is the most characteristic artistic expression of the Volk.[61] Wagner here also explicitly references the expressive power of the national culture: the Volk, through its art, presents its own image to itself.

Though it is not clear whether Wagner ever actually read Herder, their ideas in this area correspond almost exactly. The "most characteristic artwork" Wagner refers to, the highest achievement of the Volk's art, comes about through the theater. Theater is "a product of the Volk and its *Geist*… to a greater degree than any other art."[62] This link among the Volk, myth, and drama is direct kin to Herder's idea that, historically, the drama has grown from the "folk tale, romance, and song."[63] The theater, as a product of the Volk's culture, is the kernel of Wagner's inspiration for making his own art *völkisch*—roughly translated, "folky" or possibly "national."

Indeed, as the consummate representation of the Volk to itself, the theater is the ultimate sphere in which to pursue an art inspired by the Volk's own creativity. "Only in the sense of the Volk can one truly compose," Wagner declares.[64] Theater's supremacy, in his view, stems from the way it unites all the Volk's arts: poetry, dance, and music.[65]

These are the philosophical underpinnings of Volk inspiration for Wagner, or (in his view) for any other artist. There is a more metaphysical element of inspiration as well, however. With his ideas on how an artist's "Volk origins" are expressed in his creativity, Wagner relies on the common idea of the national cultural inheritance. Every artist should take joy in the cultural inheritance of his "fatherland"; Wagner praises the "immeasurable pleasure…to recognize one's own self through the mother-tongue of one's forefathers."[66] This source of inspiration is readily apparent in the poet or the visual artist. For the poet, the language in which he writes is an obvious indication of his origins. For the visual artist, in turn, "the nature of his land and Volk" is decisive "for the form and colors" of his art.[67] For the musician, however, this origin is less obvious. While to some extent a musician's nationality is evident in the kind of music he composes (such as the Italian's gift for song), the real expression of his nationality lies deeper—Wagner suggests it lies in the *Geist*.

Wagner credits the German Geist with bringing about the rebirth of German culture, in the form of Schiller's plays and Beethoven's music.[68] A particularly miraculous feature of the German Geist is that it was able to absorb beneficial foreign influences (such as rediscovering the Greeks), but then it was also able to develop itself further "out of its own inner riches."[69] Wagner implies that Goethe, Schiller, Beethoven, and Bach were both German and great precisely because their art proceeded so directly from "German-ness." Admittedly, this is a tautology, but such is allowable in Wagner's metaphysics. But, in this formula (great art = Germanness + greatness) we find his recipe for the art he himself hoped to produce. "Only that which the Volk, which nature has itself produced," he writes, "can serve as material for the poet; through him, though, the unconscious in the Volk's product achieves consciousness, and it is he [the artist], who imparts this consciousness to the Volk. Thus in art the unconscious life of the Volk achieves consciousness."[70] Notice how he equates the Volk with nature here. Also, he states once again that the role of the artist is to represent to the Volk its own, unknown life. Nonetheless, the artist is in a sense only a means, because as he says, "the poet cannot create…only the Volk can, or the poet can, only insofar as he takes the creation of the Volk and gives voice to it."[71]

There can be no question that Wagner was conscious of using "the Volk's art" in his own art. In this regard, he praised the medieval *Nibelungenlied* as "folk poetry."[72] He similarly explains his own decision to employ Stabreim (an alliterative rhyme scheme) instead of end-rhyme in his poem of *Siegfried*. He praises Stabreim as being the most authentic and natural verse form, and declares moreover that it was with Stabreim that the Volk itself once composed, "when it was still a poet and myth-maker."[73] Dahlhaus suggests that Wagner's evocation of myth and "German pre-history" corresponds to the "exoticism" appeal of folk motives.[74] Such a calculation may well have played some role in Wagner's reliance on mythic sources—but such sources' real importance, as he conceived it, was as products of the Volk's own art. In this conception he actually echoes the Grimms, who regarded myth as "nature poetry," the Volk's own "unconsciously existing truth."[75]

Thus the "folksiness" in Wagner's art proceeds above all from his reliance on folk literature—that is, his extensive use of material from narratives which he perceived as products of the Volk's creativity. Wagner's relationship to the other principal basis of folk inspiration in music—namely, folk tunes—is much more complicated. On the one hand, he shares some of the same general conceptions of folk music as do Smetana and Grieg, but on the other, he takes an even stricter stance on the possibility of building a national art music out of folk music. To begin with, he does espouse the common idea on the "characteristicness" of folk music. In his extended consideration of folk music in *Das Kunstwerk der Zukunft*, he writes:

> Only that is characteristic which is produced out of itself. Nowadays only the folk or national dance is characteristic, since in an inimitable way it communicates how it came into being, its

> particular essence in gestures, rhythm, and tempo. It created
> spontaneously the laws of its own being, and these laws become
> recognizable, communicable, as its abstracted essence, when they
> appear in the work of folk art.[76]

It is the fact that folk music remains true to itself that gives it its power. This power, besides the ability to represent the genuine nature of the Volk, he somewhat surprisingly describes as "salvation" for the "musical world."[77]

This is surprising because Wagner concurrently believed that folk music had itself been largely destroyed, the principal culprit being the opera: Wagner decries the "repulsive, indescribably disgusting deformation and distortion of the folk tune" as it appears in the modern opera aria.[78] Wagner lambastes contemporary composers who have tried to prop up the form of opera, which he says was expiring as a meaningful art. Their solution, he charges, was to fall upon exotic-seeming, characterful, and colorful elements from folk music. A "great hunt" for these elements went loose, specifically outside of Germany—and the French, in particular, ransacked folk sources for "flavor" for their operas.[79] This terrible trend resulted in the complete "pillaging" of folk traditions, "sucking the folk source dry."[80] So, now, when the *volkstümliche* is used in opera, it is not truly *völkisch* (that is, not a genuine representation of the Volk and its art), but is rather just a "colorless," "artificially revived" "imitation" of the Volk.[81] Modern opera composers failed to discover or tap into the true sources of the Volk; instead, they merely paraded around on stage an eye-catching, exotic particularity. This shallow, exploitative use of folk sources is what Wagner sometimes terms "the national."

How can he here criticize "the national" when throughout much of the rest of his writing he extols its virtues? Part of the reason may be an unresolved contradiction in his thought, or merely hypocrisy: he praises legitimate depictions of nationality in art (such as his own) while attacking nationality in art where it is only exploitation, proceeding from no genuine national feeling. Music where the use of national elements amounts merely to trendy "decoration" is worthless, and this applies to most French operatic music. His criticism is also based on the view that modern opera is artistically degraded, aiming more to be entertainment than art. National "decoration" is just another attempt at entertainment. Wagner's own national music, however, is legitimate because it returns to and grows out of the Volk. And the Volk is the source of "true" nationality, which, he suggests, ultimately transcends itself in the "purely human," thus rising above the narrowly "particular" as found in the cynical French exploitation of folk-national sources.[82]

Distinctions between French and Italian versus German composers illustrate the contrast between the acceptable and the deplorable uses of folk songs. As I mentioned, it is French and Italian composers above all who bear the blame for destroying the folk tune. Wagner not surprisingly praises how German composers (principally Weber) used the folk tune, though he uncharacteristically even reserves some criticism for Weber in this regard. Wagner regarded Weber's *Freischütz* as the ultimate incarnation of German *Volkstümlichkeit* in music. He saw in it the expression of all that he loved about the German character:

> How must I love the German Volk that loves the *Freischütz*, that even today believes in the wonder of the naïvest sagas, that even today, in its manhood, feels the sweet, mysterious shudders that ran through its heart in its youth! Ah, you charming German reverie! You rapture of the forest, of evening, of the stars, of the moon, of the village clocktower when it strikes seven! How he is happy, who understands you, who can believe, feel, dream, and fall into raptures with you! How glad I am, that I am a German![83]

In this opera, Weber brought the aria back to the "original style of the folk song," after Rossini had sacrificed the aria completely to melody.[84] Weber, as a German, was able to hear the "true source" of melody in the folk song. He found that source "on the forest meadow": it was the flower that still grew there on the banks of the "cheerily trickling brook, amongst fragrant forest grass," and so on.[85] With this little flower, Weber wanted to heal humanity, to deliver it from its insanity, and so he plucked the flower out from its forest meadow and placed it in a "precious vase," "up in a magnificent chamber," by which Wagner presumably means an artistically worthy setting.[86] However, in so doing, Wagner says, Weber *broke* the flower—though its brief bloom lent itself to his last operas, it soon expired, and upon the forest meadow no more flowers would grow.

Wagner uses this enraptured allegory to explain why all reliance on folk music in opera since Weber has been "artificial" and disgusting. Part of his complaint rests on the distinction he draws between folk songs as originally natural with what happened to them subsequently. The fad-ish and destructive hunt for folk tunes in opera, of which French composers were guilty, Wagner poses as an unnatural distortion of these sources.[87] One motivation for his uncharacteristic criticism of Weber (given how much Wagner revered him otherwise) may be that he regarded Weber as launching this hunt as a result of the success of *Der Freischütz*. Such criticism of Weber seems to indicate that Wagner thinks no possible future could lie in the incorporation of folk melodies into opera. The flower did die, after all, he says. Nonetheless, on a few instances he backpedaled, opining that there was still some future in the folk melody. For instance, he remarked that the folk dance could be developed further into a "richer, entirely capable art" by means of associating it with music and poetry.[88]

Here comes to the fore the idea that folk sources must be elevated into the higher forms in order to meet the demands of true art. Wagner also referenced it in the previous excerpt from *Das Kunstwerk der Zukunft* when he mentioned the "abstracted essence" of the "folk artwork." So, regardless of the extent to which the folk melody might have been destroyed, Wagner held fast to his conviction that "the *Volkstümliche* has always been the fertilizing source of all art," as long as it is "lifted up" into an artwork.[89] He even claimed, though, that "the opera composer never managed to touch the truly *Volkstümliche*." In order to do that, Wagner wrote in *Oper und Drama*, the composer "would have to have created out of the Geist and ideas of the Volk."[90] So, what is this "truly *Volkstümliche*"? Wagner suggests that it is a complete understanding of the Volk and its Geist—that is, not just a convenient cherry-picking of the fruits of the Volk's creativity, which is what French composers did. This kind of cherry-picking amounted, ultimately, only to a parade of "the particular," a mannered striving after effect.[91]

Beethoven, Wagner thinks, knew how to use folk music legitimately. Beethoven used folk tunes not for mere entertainment but for a nobler goal—"he played them in an ideal sense to the Volk itself." Indeed, he played the folk tune not just for the Volk to dance to, but for all nature to dance, as in his Seventh Symphony.[92] Wagner enthuses that Beethoven "takes up the folk tune and gives it transfigured back to the Volk."[93] So, Beethoven presents a "transfigured" or idealized version of the folk melody. For Wagner, the purpose of idealizing folk songs is not just to elevate them to an artistic level, but also to a level of universality. Thus the legitimate use of the folk tune is when the composer transports it beyond the mere particularity that Wagner criticizes and instead reaches back to the "purely human" nature of the Volk. In the chapter on universality, I discuss in detail how the Volk—and particularly the German Volk—is in fact universal in its essence.

Though it may not seem readily apparent at first, Wagner did claim to have used folk music elements quite extensively in his operas. From his own statements, and an examination of a few moments from his work, we will see how he put into practice his ideas on the role of folk elements in producing high art music. Wagner said that when writing *Der fliegende Holländer*, he found a "compensating nourishment" for the disease of the modern opera aria in the folk song. In Senta's "quite vividly *volkstümlich*"[94] ballad, he says, "the spontaneous content of the characteristicness of the national folk melismus guided me; even more so in the spinning song and also namely in the sailors' song."[95] Wagner wrote in his "Eine Mitteilung an meine Freunde" that, "in *Der fliegende Holländer* I drew upon the rhythmic folk melody, but only when the material brought me into contact with the folk elements where they more-or-less revealed themselves in a national sense."[96] Admittedly, the folk elements in *Holländer* are nominally Norwegian, given the opera's setting. But, the important point is that Wagner stresses the "folksiness" of his own work. Interestingly, in the aforementioned quote we also witness Wagner attaching a positive valuation to "the national," contradicting his criticism of it from *Oper und Drama* that we examined earlier.

Wagner also avows that he relied on folk elements in *Lohengrin*. With the chorus in the second act of this opera, he said that he wanted to show "how a folk song arises."[97] His wife Cosima also relates another, analogous anecdote:

> We were talking about *Lohengrin*, and [Richard] told me that in 1848 [his friend] Röckel told him, "Now we need this kind of Volk hymn." "Well," said Richard, "I have that theme," and he sang him the motive from the march in the third act of *Lohengrin*. Röckel, though, found it too arty, which Richard acknowledged and said, that's how you can tell that this piece belongs in an artwork.[98]

Wagner's suggestion here, that a folk song belongs in an opera only when that song is treated in an "artistic" manner, is an idea espoused identically by Smetana and Grieg. Rather than *Der fliegende Holländer* or *Lohengrin*, though, probably Wagner's most "folky" opera is *Die Meistersinger*. This opera, in fact, is as close as Wagner came to writing something like a folk opera along the lines of *The Bartered Bride*. The third act of *Die Meistersinger*, in particular, features the spectacular setpiece of the town gathering, in which the villagers of Nürnberg sing, dance, and (the women, at least) wear peasant costume, as Wagner indicates in the libretto. However, since we examined *Die Meistersinger* in the previous chapter, let me instead focus now on *Tannhäuser*.

This may seem a strange choice, but, in fact, *Tannhäuser* is an excellent illustration of how Wagner used the folk sources of myth and legend as material for his art. The plot of the opera is actually made up of three separate, semilegendary stories all taken from German myth, which Wagner wove together. The first is the story of Tannhäuser himself, the medieval German poet and musician. Wagner interpolates this figure into the second source, the stories of the singing competitions at the Wartburg castle. Finally, the idea of Venus in her Venusberg seducing knights errant is another mythic element that Wagner adds to the mix.[99]

The immediate inspirations for the story he fashioned also came from several directions, including Ludwig Tieck, Heinrich Heine, E. T. A. Hoffmann's story "Die Bergwerke zu Falun," Jakob Grimm's folk tales, and *Des Knaben Wunderhorn*. In the case of the last two, then, Wagner clearly draws from folk traditions. And, in fact, he himself referred to the story of Tannhäuser as a "folk poem."[100] In his account of the genesis of the opera's text in "Eine Mitteilung an meine Freunde," however, Wagner attempts to downplay the impact of "modern" sources such as the Tieck story on his own conception of Tannhäuser. Marion Bless explains this by referencing Wagner's insistence that the music-drama should be inspired exclusively by folk sources—so, he diminishes Tieck's role and emphasizes that his real inspiration was the old sagas.[101] In this way, he tried to configure his opera as more truly *völkisch*.

He also sought to emphasize the specifically *German* character of the work. He indeed declared that *Tannhäuser* was a "German from head to toe."[102] Certainly the setting of the opera in the courtly milieu of the Wartburg, that fervent symbol of German nationalism for nineteenth-century patriots, is intended to evoke a past era of German greatness, when the Minnesänger such as Wolfram von Eschenbach enjoyed their heyday. The pilgrims' choruses are also supposed to evoke an "old German" folk tone, according to Dahlhaus.[103] The shepherd boy in the first act, playing his shawm as the sheep bells tinkle around him, is obviously a common representation of the rural idyll. However, the fact that the shepherd sings a folklike song about Holda, a goddess from Teutonic mythology, emphasizes the specifically German rustic atmosphere.

If we recur to a quote cited earlier, where Wagner swoons over the "charming German reverie" and enumerates the things that the German Volk supposedly loves, we can see that a number of these elements make their appearance in this opera. For example, we see the "rapture of the forest" in the first act, when the Landgraf and his hunting party emerge from the woods around the Hörselberg, with the horns blaring in the orchestra. The "rapture of evening [and] the stars" appears (metaphorically) in Wolfram's famous third act aria "Wie Todesahnung, Dämmerung deckt die Lande / O du mein holder Abendstern," where he serenades

Elisabeth in the darkness as she goes off to die. The incorporation of stories from German myth, along with the reference to these elements Wagner conceived as particular to the German Volksgeist, all place this work within a national framework. But, of course, Wagner's goal was also to produce a work of art, and thus into this framework he built his plot of Tannhäuser's relationship to Elisabeth. This typically Wagnerian spiral of damnation, redemption, impossible love, and the martyrdom of a woman reflects the human and spiritual preoccupations that he explores in so many of his dramas. The ostensibly national features of *Tannhäuser* are thereby intertwined with the thematic and artistic ambitions of his work.

Not unlike Wagner's, Smetana's artistic career takes an occasionally difficult position regarding folk inspirations. While he did appreciate the national-cultural value of folk sources, he also resisted what he saw as an undue obsession with them. In part, he was reacting against the "cult" of folk music that developed in the Czech lands in the first half of the nineteenth century. After the work of the collectors, folk songs became genuinely popular throughout Czech society, including among the bourgeoisie. National dance gatherings attracted a significant following. Concurrently, figures such as Rittersberk were calling for national music to be built upon these folk foundations. The enthusiasm for folk songs, including among nationalist intellectuals, came to the detriment of interest in developing other musical forms, however. Folk music took on such a privileged place within the Czech nation-building movement that relatively few people—though Smetana was one—expressed reservations about the value of that music for a national art.

Smetana's early exposure to folk music, though, very much fits into the pattern of middle-class Czechs encountering the rural traditions. Growing up in a small town where his father's brewery served as a center for social life, Smetana often had the opportunity to hear "living" folk music. Hana Séquardtová suggests that in this environment, Smetana was exposed to "folk life in all its colorfulness: he heard folk songs and dances, and his (still unconscious) sense and feeling for Czech folk-musical expression would have developed early on."[104] So, this rural upbringing set the stage for Smetana's interest in folk music. And indeed, most of his earliest compositions are dances that he probably performed for parties and other gatherings around the brewery. Later, his experience of the patriotic balls of the 1840s, where "national" dances were performed, directly inspired works such as his *Jiřinková polka*.[105] The polka from *The Bartered Bride* was reportedly inspired, at least in part, by Smetana's experience of a big dance gathering in Prague in 1864.

Eventually he also began working with some of the material gathered in the most famous collections of Czech folk songs. In the early 1860s, while director of the choir *Hlahol*, he performed songs from Karel Křížkovský's collection. He also owned a copy of Erben's *Nápěvy prostonárodních písní*, which he relied on while composing his *Czech Dances* as well as the operas *The Two Widows* and *The Kiss*.[106] In fact, prior to composing the *Czech Dances*, Smetana himself investigated some "original" sources. His son-in-law Josef Schwarz reports that after Smetana's deafness had forced him to retire from active musical life and leave Prague, he discovered in the rural area he moved to an old man who was a kind of living compendium of Czech folk traditions. According to Schwarz, Smetana learned some old Czech dances from this musician.[107]

A quick glance at his compositional output emphasizes the importance Smetana assigned to forms broadly conceived as rooted in Czech folk music traditions. He wrote dozens of pieces based on dance forms, especially for the piano. Of these, the polka occupies a particularly prominent place in his output: polkas even appear in his most "serious" compositions such as *Libuše* and *Má vlast*. In fact, a letter to his friend Dr. Ludevít Procházka in regard to the latter piece suggests what such dances represented for Smetana. Smetana says that in planning the third section of *Má vlast*, he wanted to add a part "that depicts Czech life in songs and dances, like what the Germans call 'Volksweisen' or 'Tanzweisen.'"[108] Interestingly, however, we also gain an idea of the limits of Smetana's knowledge of such traditions, since in this letter he is in fact asking Procházka for advice as to such dances. He requests from him a book by Max Waldau called *Böhmische Nationaltänze*.

Smetana regarded these folk traditions, above all the polka, as an element representative of Czech life, as the above quotation shows. In addition, this quotation fairly explicitly refers to the expressive function of national music, since Smetana is interested in "depicting" Czech life through these ostensibly national traditions. He used these dances as a form or tool within his compositions to refer to something else, namely the rural sources of Czech culture. He was probably relying to some extent on the notion of the popularity of such forms, that is, that the polka would be familiar to a wide segment of the Czech populace as something already coded "characteristically Czech." Karel Jaromír Erben, for example, in the 1840s propounded the idea that the polka was inherently Czech in origin and hence a "national dance."[109] However, Jaroslav Jiránek actually credits Smetana with being the one who transformed this "artificial societal dance of the 1830s" into a widely accepted "symbol of the Czech people and nation."[110] Indeed, for Smetana, the polka's "characteristicness" went even deeper, as Hana Séquardtová argues:

> [the polka was] characteristic as an original manifestation of the developing Czech society. From the beginning Smetana regarded the polka—at first perhaps instinctively—as a specific reflection of Czech life, in which the elements of popular songs and dances...of a Czech folk pastorale were remarkably projected. Later, this genre crystallized in Smetana's conception as a form that was the most faithful reflection of Czech national life, and in that sense Smetana used it in all his work as the bearer of a distinct meaning and content.[111]

However, when we examine Smetana's ideas on how a national music should be constructed, we see the limits he imposed on the usefulness of folk sources. Contrary to many of his contemporaries in Czech nationalist circles, Smetana did not see the future of a national musical culture as residing solely in the reliance on folk tunes. For Smetana, such a reliance was only a first step; as such, operas like František Škroup's *Dratenik* ("The Tinker," of 1826) while having some value in contributing to Czech culture, did relatively little to further Czech *art*. Škroup's work is for the most part based on folk songs, evinces a rather sentimental tone, and does not strive for lofty dramatic goals.[112] Smetana's wariness of the folk-song route was doubtlessly conditioned by the relatively weak quality of earlier attempts to express Czechness in opera. The earliest attempts, the "popular" or "folk" musicals/operas ("lidové zpěvohry" in the Czech) of the last decades of the 1700s, were very modest productions whose folk character proceeded mostly from a plot set in the countryside. These were entertainments evincing no real musical ambition: they featured perhaps only three solo parts, a small orchestra, and arias confined to the three-section song form.[113] By the time of *Dratenik*, these "popular operas" had developed to the point where most of the forms and musical style were Italian, but the text was in Czech.

Nonetheless, for many Czech nationalists pieces like *Dratenik* provided a template for how Czech opera should be developed, though Smetana disagreed. The conflict within the Czech nationalist movement over the attitude toward folk sources is well illustrated by an anecdote that, because of its importance to the present topic, is worth quoting in full. This anecdote comes from the memoirs of Smetana's friend Josef Srb-Debrnov, who, along with Smetana, used to attend the gatherings of Czech nationalists in Prague in the 1860s. At one such gathering, Smetana got into an argument with Dr. František Ladislav Rieger, one of the paramount figures of the Czech nationalist movement, who exercised a great deal of influence in journalism, politics, as well as the theater. Srb-Debrnov recalls:

> At such evenings the question of Czech opera, music, drama etc. was also discussed by the prominent personalities. Smetana was then preparing to write the opera *The Brandenburgers in Bohemia* to words by Sabina. During a discussion on this, Dr. Rieger proffered the opinion that it was easy to write a serious opera on a historic theme, but that to write an opera of a lighter kind dealing with the life of the (Czech) was a thing no one would easily succeed in doing. Smetana took him up on this and said that he intended to do something about that and that he thought that he could make a success of it. Rieger objected that the basis for such an opera would have to be Czech folk songs; Smetana again opposed this,

saying that in this way a medley of various songs, a kind of quod-libet would come into being, but not an artistic work of any continuity. The dispute was quite heated until Smetana finally told Rieger that he did not know what he was talking about, but that he, as a musician, would see this thing through. Thus Smetana started work on *The Bartered Bride* immediately after having finished *The Brandenburgers in Bohemia*. But that was the end of Smetana's friendship with Dr. Rieger.[114]

Rieger's conviction was that the "national spirit" could only be expressed in opera through folk songs; thus he insisted to another composer, Karel Šebor, that such songs "must be the soil, from which our new art music shall grow."[115] Rieger specifically rejected a reliance on what he saw as foreign models—which is essentially code for rejecting anything that he would consider a German influence on Czech music. The "Othering" of German culture in the Czech nationalist discourse is a topic I deal with in the next chapter, but it is important here to note that these anti-German feelings were part of what motivated Rieger and his followers in their fixation on folk songs.

Smetana's attitude toward this cult of folk music in the Czech lands is demonstrated by another anecdote, this one from Aleš Heller, who relates an incident from his father, Ferdinand Heller, a longtime friend of Smetana's:

> [Jan] Neruda taught them [the Smetanas and the Hellers] all to dance the "Beseda" and Smetana danced gaily…After the "rehearsal" however, Smetana laughed at the "jig-jogs" as he called the national songs and dances used in the "Beseda"…My father [i.e., Ferdinand Heller] argued that they were treasures, pointing out their characteristic expression, their spirit, the rhythm of the Furiant and so on. His opinions found an advocate in Neruda who enthusiastically defended and described Czech national songs and dances, on which, above all, he was an expert.
>
> Smetana brought his Polka *To Our Girls* and wanted to know "whether it was any good for dancing"…He played it himself. When they had danced it, the unanimous verdict was "no good"!

> Smetana could not understand why. My father pointed out to him that the dance rhythm was lacking here and there. Smetana became "angry" and said: "All right, see to the rhythm yourself, but I'm going to dance!"[116]

This quotation shows that Smetana was definitely interested in and aware of the "national songs and dances," but equally that he maintained a certain distance from them. This distance means that even when Smetana was composing polkas such as *To Our Girls*, he was not writing popular dance music—he was writing an art music that one would be hard put to dance to. In the same way, it is hard to imagine actually dancing to the third movement of a Haydn symphony. Smetana obviously assigned strict limits to the value of "the popular" in realizing his social and artistic goals. He seems to harbor a suspicion that popular forms can be too "cheap" to constitute, in and of themselves, a national art. Smetana's reaction to some Hungarian "national musicians" (i.e., folk musicians) he heard in Prague in 1861 points to his view on the limitations of folk music: he found that some of the pieces performed lacked "refinement and understanding."[117] This apparent snobbery is something we will find also in Grieg.

Smetana's fear about basing music on actual folk tunes is that the resulting composition would be no more than a pastiche, as his dispute with Rieger demonstrates. Apart from quoting actual folk tunes, he even cautions against too slavish an adherence merely to folk "styles" or forms. According to Otakar Hostinský, Smetana declared that "the imitation of the melodic cadence and rhythm of our folk songs will not create a national style, but at the most a weak imitation of those very same songs."[118] What is more, Smetana added, there would be no way to create "dramatic truth" with such imitations. The danger in limiting a national music just to folk songs—and this is a danger not just for the artist, but by extension for the envisioned national culture—becomes clear in the reminiscence of one of Smetana's librettists, Ervín Špindler, who reports the composer as saying,

> Perhaps now that idle talk about it being possible to write Czech operas of purely national kind only on the basis, i.e. in imitation of

folk songs, will cease. I have already written two quite different operas of this kind [referring to the "folk operas" *The Bartered Bride* and *The Kiss*], but in neither of them will you find a trace anywhere of an imitation of folk motives. Yes, for the sake of proving that, I have used one real folk lullaby and immediately following it my own [in *The Kiss*]. I hope that in time every Czech will love it just as dearly as the folk lullaby and yet not a single bar has been borrowed from folksongs, let alone whole motives, a thing which would go against the creative originality of a real artist.[119]

It is in his ideas for dramatic art that Smetana's resistance to folk tunes is expressed most clearly. Much like Wagner, Smetana intended that the theater should become the "central focus of the entire domestic artistic world."[120] Finkelstein insightfully explains Smetana's position on the incorporation of folk elements into opera: "he rejected 'folk style' if it were only to be a light divertissement, contrasted to 'serious music.' If Czech folk music were to be used for creative composition, it had to show itself as material fit for great emotions, for sensitive character portrayal and organic form."[121] A true national artist—that is, an artist who really aimed at producing works of lasting value for his nation—would not be content with mere pastiche or imitation. Smetana obviously sided with the "high art" imperative vis-à-vis folk culture. And thanks to an 1879 letter to his publisher, we need be in no doubt about Smetana's own manner of treating folk sources. He wrote, "my efforts are directed towards *idealising* the polka in particular, as Chopin did with the mazurka."[122] His music is not a mere imitation of the polka but a *transfiguration* of it, elevating it so that it could serve as a plank in the national high culture. The evolution in Smetana's conception and treatment of folk forms such as the polka is actually easily traceable: from his earliest efforts in this genre, which generally aspire to no more than entertainment pieces, his technique develops on to the 1843 composition *Memories of Plzeň*, which becomes a kind of "scherzo-polka" meant as a "vehicle for virtuoso display and not for dancing."[123]

His late *Czech Dances*, then, represent the culminating achievement where he transposes the "national dance to the highest artistic levels."[124]

This work comprises ten individual sections, some of which are titled after established dance forms (like the furiant and the skočná), while others bear more abstract titles ("Oats," "Little Onion") and are based on particular folk songs. However, though in several of these pieces he does incorporate folk melodies (from Erben's collection, for example), he quotes them not note for note, but rather uses them in a theme and variations style, or as the basis for a kind of fantasy.[125] Thus he shapes the folk inspirations into larger formal units, creating subsidiary sections, preludes, interludes, codas, and developmental sections. The technical demands are of a virtuoso order, and Vladimír Tichý argues that in terms of their formal composition, these dances are as comparably "serious" as a classical sonata.[126] There can be no doubt that Smetana wanted with these pieces to demonstrate definitively how "simple" folk sources could and should be elevated into a consummate "artwork." His other stated intention behind this work is as a kind of response to Dvořák's *Slavonic Dances*: Smetana wrote to his publisher that "every Czech, at least who loves music, should know these remarkable original dances... Where Dvořák calls his pieces by the general name *Slavonic Dances*—without anybody knowing what those are, or even if such a thing exists—we will show what specifically named dances we Czechs have!"[127]

Beyond just the individual musical forms, though, Smetana's project is one of idealizing entire genres, such as the "popular opera." *The Bartered Bride* is the prime example in this regard; it perfectly represents how Smetana fuses folk sources with his own, invented, folk-styled material into an organic, sophisticated, dramatic work. Smetana purposefully set out to write a folk opera after critics accused his first opera, *The Brandenburgers in Bohemia*, of being too heavy and portentous in style. The work that emerged in 1866 (though after a series of revisions it attained its final form in 1870) can indeed be regarded as the very epitome of the folk opera: *The Bartered Bride* managed to achieve the status of both a great work of art and an immensely popular entertainment. The dance and choral numbers not surprisingly are the central element in effecting the fusion among folk inspirations, the representation of the folk itself, and Smetana's own artistic ideals.

In fact, the only time in the opera that Smetana quotes an actual folk melody is in the furiant dance number—yet he arranges this tune with chord structures and dissonances in such a way that, as Brian Large writes, "it is unlikely the folk of Smetana's day had ever heard [this traditional tune] harmonized quite as chromatically as this."[128]

Elsewhere, Smetana was able to create a folk "flavor" without actually quoting folk songs, as in Mařenka's first aria, where the irregular three-bar phrase lengths are typical of Czech folk music.[129] In his instrumentation, such as the strings and woodwinds in the polka, he also evoked a folk sound without relying on a folk tune per se. The opening of the second act shows how Smetana could transform a genre convention of popular opera into a dramatically effective scene. Through a drinking song, his scene plays off the Czechs' fabled love of beer. However, the scene is not just a setpiece, since Smetana also uses it to deepen the characters and motivations of Jeník and Kecal. Indeed, the entire opera is not merely an excuse for some "local color," but rather presents a drama about individual characters and their particular social situations. In turn, Smetana gave each of the major characters a differentiated, personalized musical expression—including the "folk" itself, who indeed is one of the main actors in the work.[130] Both musically and dramatically, the opera aspires to and attains a level of sophistication greater than that of any of the popular Czech musical theater pieces prior to that time.

*The Bartered Bride* exemplifies Smetana's design to create a work of art out of the more modest sources that inspired it. Folk sources, in Smetana's conception, were limiting to the kind of "high art" music that he wanted to compose. As a committed adherent of the stylistic directions trailblazed by Liszt, Wagner, and Berlioz, Smetana aspired to a "progressive" music for which a slavish reliance on folk sources could only be too conservative. Thus he was open to the sort of "foreign" influences that the likes of F. L. Rieger rejected. In evident contrast to Rieger, Smetana thought that the best possible national art could only proceed from the most advanced or progressive trends of the day, and he saw no impossibility in building an authentically Czech music on European-wide trends. Folk music, albeit thoroughly "Czech," needed to be transformed according to sophisticated artistic precepts into musical forms that would establish a Czech high culture.

Grieg is unquestionably the most obviously "folksy" of these three composers. An enormous proportion of his compositional output is based in one way or another on folk sources. Also, while he subscribed to the idea of elevating folk music into high art forms, he did not harbor the same kind of reservations about less ambitious, "popular" folk music that Wagner and Smetana did. Despite his deep embrace of folk forms, though, Grieg actually waffled a bit in his own professions of how well he really knew Norwegian folk music. In his expansive letter to Henry Finck of February 2, 1900, Grieg claims that when he wrote his Opp.3 and 6, he knew Norwegian folk tunes "hardly at all."[131] In his diaries, however, Grieg reports that in 1865 he was already playing Danish and Swedish folk songs—and if he was playing these, then assuredly he was also familiar with Norwegian folk music as well.[132] His demurral was likely motivated by his concern (which we see repeatedly in this letter to Finck) to refute the accusations of some German critics that he was "nothing more than a copy machine for Norwegian folk tunes."[133]

In any event, it is clear that Grieg's interest and exposure to folk music began quite early in his artistic career. He eventually came to know the major source of Norwegian folk music, Ludvig Mathias Lindeman's collection. Grieg would use melodies from Lindeman's collection in many works, including the *Symphonic Dances* and his *Four Psalms*. Like the folk song collectors, Grieg also shared the preservation ethos. During his trips to the mountains, he copied down the tunes he would hear from local peasants—though this was really more for his own personal use than to be included in some kind of larger collection.[134] Probably the most notable example of Grieg's attempts to assure the survival of the rural musical traditions is his edition of the *slåtter* (originally a kind of peasant dance form) that was published in 1903.

The story behind this project reveals both Grieg's interest in and respect for folk traditions. Knut Dahle, a musician who played what is known as a Hardanger fiddle, wrote Grieg a letter suggesting that Grieg, as the most famous and influential Norwegian musician, should publish the *slåtter* tunes that Dahle knew. Dahle convinced Grieg that these tunes would soon be lost as rural traditions faded. Grieg eventually agreed and got his friend Johan Halvorsen—who, as a violin player, could transcribe for string instruments better than Grieg, whose instrument was the piano—to do the transcriptions. In letters to Halvorsen from around this time, Grieg stresses that the most important thing in producing the transcriptions must be "the stamp of authenticity."[135] When Grieg's piano version of the *slåtter* was published, he insisted (despite reluctance from his publisher) that the violin transcriptions be published along with the piano version. Grieg stressed both the musicological and cultural-historical interest behind these pieces as a valuable artifact of Norwegian folk culture.[136] Grieg's piano version, however, had somewhat different aims, as I will demonstrate later.

Grieg's ideas on the role folk sources should play in creating a national culture are very closely connected to the common intellectual trends I discussed in the first part of this chapter. First of all, Grieg clearly espouses the Herder-derived idea of the relationship between the composer and his nation's music. This is the idea of a "national spirit" that speaks through each individual and imbues his creative production. Grieg refers to the "folkesjæl," (folk-soul), which can never be wiped out of a person or a people; "it goes together with the people's temperament and nature," he says.[137] And this "folk-soul" is inevitably expressed through a people's art: "the folk song reflects musically the inner life of the people."[138] Grieg marveled at (fellow Norwegian nationalist composer) Rikard Nordraak's "intuitive feeling for the soul in our folk music," suggesting in a sense that what a Norwegian composer has to do to produce Norwegian music is just to look inside himself.[139]

This common idea of the time could be stretched to lengths that today seem absurd. So it was that the Norwegian composer and writer Gerhard Schjelderup describes the "natural" connection between a composer and his nation's music: "In Norway, where in many places the cows are called in the morning through the repetition of the major seventh, it is thus entirely natural that sevenths, ninths and augmented triads sometimes appear where they would seem mannered in a German or

French composer."[140] According to this conception, Norwegian nature comes out "naturally" in a Norwegian composer. As Schjelderup suggests, a Frenchman cannot produce truly Norwegian music, and vice versa, of course. A national spirit will always speak through the music, inescapably. Schjelderup even claimed, "In Grieg's music I occasionally hear a certain Scottish tone, which can be explained by his Scottish descent."[141] Grieg's great-grandfather was Scottish, but luckily that Scottish folk-soul didn't speak too loudly, otherwise Grieg would have been the founder of the Scottish national music, and not the Norwegian.

For Grieg, predictably, the Norwegian "folk-soul" expressed itself most clearly through folk music. Folk music is therefore an inheritance of the entire Norwegian nation, and he wanted to see this inheritance preserved and propagated in the national culture. He wrote of the "heaped-up treasures of unused material"[142] and the "treasures in our folk music"[143] that would form the basis of the national music. However, like his compatriots Lindeman and Vinje, Grieg thought that folk music *in itself* did not constitute the basis for a national art. Rather, folk music must be "lifted up to Art's level," as Grieg suggested to Percy Grainger so that the latter could thereby create an "independent" English music.[144] Just as Grainger learned from Grieg in this regard, so Grieg was influenced by his forebears. Waldemar Thrane wrote a Norwegian Singspiel in 1824 that incorporated folk tunes, Herman de Løvenskiold in the 1840s worked in a similar way, and particularly Halfdan Kjerulf was "the first who emphasized the Norwegian folk-life melody's great significance for the national music," as Grieg put it in an 1879 article.[145]

Grieg claimed that without a basis in folk music, "all forms of art music [are] impossible."[146] Indeed, even Mozart and Beethoven based their compositions on "the elevated German folk tune," according to Grieg.[147] However, the folk forms are only a starting point: thus, as he wrote in his obituary to Kjerulf, "Every nation's art has in the course of time progressed from the folk song through the small forms on to the larger, richer, the more integrated."[148] Fittingly, then, Grieg's objective was to artistically elevate folk songs, as he said in his introduction to his *Slåtter*.[149] This was how the national music must be created—a

Norwegian composer must "get into the spirit of the Norwegian folk music…[he must] make use of its outer features, of course idealized and made manifold."[150] So, here again we see the call to "idealize" the original folk sources into a true art.

Grieg's treatment of folk elements, he insisted, was never a "planned imitation" of folk models. His intent was to use folk tunes in a *motivic* fashion.[151] In turn, the influence of folk elements in a piece—most particularly in his songs—comes to the fore when the subject matter so dictates: "Where the Norwegian poets do not describe nature, folk life, or sagas, but rather merely universal human-spiritual events, a national coloring has never entered my mind."[152] Similarly, Benestad and Schjelderup-Ebbe describe Grieg's style in his second violin sonata as not based on a direct loan from folk sources, but rather as being "inspired" by rhythmic-melodic impulses.[153] Also, one of the most notable characteristics of Grieg's style, his harmonic originality, was inspired by folk music. "I have found," he wrote Finck, "that the dark depths of our songs, in all their richness, are grounded on undreamt-of harmonic possibilities."[154]

While seeking to distance himself from the "copy machine" accusation, Grieg nonetheless does admit that he used folk elements extensively and in a variety of ways. In a letter to Gerhard Schjelderup, he commented favorably on the former's intent to write a composition treating folk tunes in a manner suitable for use in a concert. Grieg says that this is what he and his friend and colleague Johan Svendsen aimed for in various of their own compositions. In this way, he suggests,

> the folk tune will meld with your own individuality and, through that process, contribute to the artwork. I have also published folk songs in their original form, but harmonized them after my own inclinations. This kind of treatment, however, is only for "gourmets" and shouldn't count on a wider dissemination. On the other hand, if you want to harmonize or in general treat folk tunes with the goal of getting them spread amongst the folk, then the best idea is to hold off on the "oysters and caviar" and instead to go with the "rye bread and butter." One has to let go of heaven and remain on the earth.[155]

In a sense, this quotation is the summation of Grieg's ideas on the role of folk tunes in the national music. He does maintain that the real value of such tunes lies in their contribution to the artwork. However, he also recognizes that tastes differ, and that a too "artful" treatment of folk material will fail to appeal to the masses. Thus he reserves a place even for less ambitious treatments of folk music—they too have their part in the national culture.

Grieg himself said that "the spirit of the fatherland, which has always found expression in the folk song, hovers over all my creations."[156] He unquestionably loved the cultural inheritance of Norwegian folk traditions. His ideal was always the "fairy tale in music," even if he never realized his ambition of writing one like Engelbert Humperdinck's *Hänsel und Gretel*, which he said lived up to that ideal.[157] And not surprisingly, just as he idealized the Norwegian folk tunes, like nationalists before and after him, Grieg also idealized the "beautiful" and "noble" peasants themselves.[158] However, in Grieg we also see the opposite side of the coin present in this discourse, where the idealized peasants do not quite correspond to their incarnations in reality. During the time of the transcription of the *slåtter*, Grieg wrote to Halvorsen snide comments, such as that he was surprised Knut Dahle was not drunk all the time.[159] Likewise, the story Grieg told of getting a band of peasants to help him move his composing hut from one part of his property to another displays a condescending tone, with its descriptions of the peasants' uncouth and drunken behavior.[160]

So much of Grieg's compositional output is based in one way or another on folk sources that almost any individual work can demonstrate how he put into practice his goals of expressing the Norwegian "folk-soul" in an artistic form. The *Slåtter* are among his most adventurous compositions musically speaking, in terms of their forward-looking harmonization. These "stylized harmonics" Grieg specifically pointed to as elevating the *slåtter* to an artistic level.[161] After they were published, young French composers in Paris swooned over "le nouveau Grieg," and Bartók's later dissonant treatments of folk music were also influenced by the *Slåtter*.[162] While based on folk melodies, Grieg often departs from them, adding preludes, interludes, and postludes, as well as thematically developing the material. His use of the piano was also quite unusual for the time, exploring the percussive possibilities of the instrument and experimenting with other ways of approximating the sound of the Hardanger fiddle.[163]

Grieg's second violin sonata, which was first performed in 1867, is also an important work for demonstrating his treatment of folk sources. Benestad and Schjelderup-Ebbe write that "in no other piece of chamber music did he make use of elements drawn from Norwegian folk music to the extent that he did in this work."[164] These elements, however, do not include any quotations from actual folk songs. Rather, the folk music character of the piece proceeds above all from rhythmic and melodic features, such as in the outer movements, which recall the traditional dance known as the *springar*. This sonata is also perhaps Grieg's highest achievement in translating folk inspirations into the classical forms; as such, it is the actual realization of his stated goal (mentioned previously) for folk music to move into the "large forms." In a related way, his four *Symphonic Dances* present folk material (using melodies from the Lindeman collection) in a version for large orchestra. Hella Brock suggests that Grieg was inspired to orchestrate these dances after his experiences in 1898, conducting some of the world's leading ensembles such as the Berlin and Vienna Philharmonics.[165] This work was thus conceived symphonically, in that he wanted all four sections to be played in order by a large orchestra, thereby transmuting folk sources into the realm of the symphony.

## CONCLUSION

While both Grieg and Haydn wrote symphonic versions of folk dances, the treatment of folk materials in art actually betrays a clearly traceable evolution in the nineteenth century. From earlier conceptions of the folk as merely peasants, charming rustics with an exotically antiquated cultural expression, by the end of the century nationalist composers have equated the peasants with the city dwellers through the vehicle of nationality, such that all of them are actually *one* folk. This process of reconceptualization was effected through the works and discourse of men like Wagner, Smetana, and Grieg, and these three all shared a similar ethos on how folk sources should inspire art, even if typical musical forms like dances and folk song quotes are largely lacking in Wagner's output. In fact, Wagner's insistence that the *völkisch* and the *volkstümlich* are ultimately the *only* legitimate sources for art is perhaps even more strict than Smetana's or Grieg's claims for folk inspirations. Wagner located the essence of the folk primarily in the mystical, ill-defined conception of *Geist*. For him, these inspirations were more metaphysical and less "actual," while for Smetana and Grieg the actual inspirations of peasant tunes and dances were more significant, even though the metaphysical side is not absent in their discourse either. Moreover, we have to acknowledge that Smetana and Grieg also looked to myths and legends as a kind of folk source, just as Wagner did. Smetana's *Libuše*, *Dalibor*, and *Má vlast* are all inspired by episodes from Czech history and myth. Similarly, Grieg composed a number of works—such as *Bergliot*, *Landkjenning*, and his opera fragment *Olav Trygvason*—to texts by Bjørnstjerne Bjørnson that were based on the old Norse sagas.

Wagner, Smetana, and Grieg also all agreed that folk sources need to be elevated to constitute a worthy base for the national art. Hence they all engage in some degree of "idealizing" of their folk inspirations. This idealizing treatment of folk sources is a common trend in European art of this period. We see it, for example, in E. T. A. Hoffman's retellings of German legends; in Moritz von Schwind's illustrations evoking a sort of timeless German mythic history; in Božena Němcová's and Jan Neruda's tales of Czech peasant life; and in Hans Gude and Adolph Tidemand's famous painting of a Norwegian bridal procession through the Hardangerfjord. Interestingly, however, it is perhaps in music that the actual practice of fusing peasant elements with high-art forms is the most clearly traceable, in that we can analyze how a composer actually integrates a given folk melody into, say, a violin sonata. The discourse and practice of creating a national music is uniquely illuminating of nationalist intellectuals' somewhat ambivalent embrace of the peasant classes into the national movement. The goal, of course, was to create a fully unified nation across social boundaries, but there was a condition of admission for peasants into that national whole: they had to be uplifted, fully "nationalized" into modern, educated citizens.

Thus the discourse on creating a national music points to a useful conclusion about the periodization of nation building movements. This is the evolution of the movement from what might be called a "research" phase into an "institution-building" phase. The research phase is when nationalist intellectuals undertake their investigations of the "national character," collecting folk songs and tales, writing histories, and reconstructing the "national language." This phase aims at generating a basic conception of the values and attributes of the national identity. Miroslav Hroch calls this "Phase A" in his schema of national movements.[166] Phase B, for Hroch, is agitation to "awaken" the national consciousness among the populace. However, I stipulate that nationalist intellectuals' understanding of the envisioned national culture actually undergoes a change in the transition from Phase A to B. The institution-building phase attempts to construct not just a universally shared culture but a *high* culture. The founding of museums, theaters, musical and literary societies, and schools all correspond to the overriding goal of educating the populace. The motives behind institution building thus go beyond the more limited cultural ideals of the research phase, where preservation of the national cultural inheritance is the chief concern.

As the discourse of Wagner, Smetana, and Grieg shows, nationalist intellectuals from later stages of the movement do not merely want to preserve the national cultural inheritance. They do not approach the Volk's culture uncritically, but rather seek to elevate it, to make it art. Assuredly, this goal fits into Hroch's conception of Phase B as the nationalist movement's transition to a mass phenomenon. The incorporation of folk elements into "higher" art forms is symbolic of nationalist intellectuals' desire to incorporate the folk into the nationalist movement. But, again, the discourse makes claims not just about incorporation but also about elevation. From the likes of von Arnim, Čelakovský, and Ole Bull, the discourse about the proper constitution of the national culture changes in Wagner, Smetana, and Grieg. In moving away from a narrower fixation on folk sources as the ultimate expression of national culture, a "high art" becomes the focus of nationalist artists' ambitions. This national high culture is supposed to be the most treasured possession of the populace at home, and the most dignified representative of the nation abroad. While not completely absent in the earliest stages of the nationalist movement, this theme becomes much more explicit later on. It marks a historically observable change within nation-building movements, and at the heart of nationalist discourse.

ENDNOTES

1. Johann Gottfried von Herder, *Stimmen der Völker in Liedern*, in *Ausgewählte Werke* (Stuttgart: J. G. Cotta'scher Verlag, 1844), 301 and 305.
2. Ibid., 306 and 312.
3. Werner Danckert, *Das Volkslied im Abendland* (Bern: Fracke Verlag, 1966), 25.
4. Carl Engel, *An Introduction to the Study of National Music* (London: Longman, Green, Reader and Dyer, 1866), 3.
5. Wiora, *Europäische Volksmusik und abendländische Tonkunst*, 163.
6. Walter Wiora, *Das echte Volkslied* (Heidelberg: Müller-Thiergarten-Verlag, 1962), 59.
7. Lars Roverud, *Et Blik paa Musikens Tilstand i Norge* (Christiania: Forfatterens Forlag hos Thr. Grøndahl, 1815), 21.
8. Cited in Philip V. Bohlman, *The Study of Folk Music in the Modern World* (Bloomington: University of Indiana Press, 1988), 50–51.
9. Herder, *Stimmen der Völker in Liedern*, in *Ausgewählte Werke*, 311.
10. Cited in Wiora, *Das echte Volkslied* (1962), 56–57.
11. Gaukstad, *Edvard Grieg*, 111.
12. Herder, *Stimmen der Völker in Liedern*, in *Ausgewählte Werke*, 311.
13. Ibid., 301.
14. Cited in Walter Wiora, "Herders Ideen zur Geschichte der Musik," in *Im Geiste Herders*, ed. Erich Keyser (Kitzingen am Main: Holzner-Verlag, 1953), 75–125. *See esp.* p. 117.
15. Herder, *Stimmen der Völker in Liedern*, in *Ausgewählte Werke*, 316.
16. Ibid., 310.
17. Cited in Wiora, *Europäische Volksmusik und abendländische Tonkunst*, 23.
18. Cited in Wiora, *Das echte Volkslied* (1962), 9.
19. Cited in Vaughan Williams, *National Music and Other Essays*, 40.
20. Wolfgang Michael Wagner, *Carl Maria von Weber und die deutsche Nationaloper* (Mainz: Schott, 1994), 35.
21. Racek, *Idea vlasti, národa a slavy v díle Bedřicha Smetany*, 28.
22. Rolf Danielsen, *Norway: A History from the Vikings to Our Own Times* (Oslo: Scandinavian University Press, 1995), 190.
23. Cited in Niels Grinde, "Grieg as a Norwegian and a European Composer," *Studia Musicologica Norvegica* 20 (1994): 125.
24. Herder, *Stimmen der Völker in Liedern*, in *Ausgewählte Werke*, 301.

25. See Wiora, "Herders Ideen zur Geschichte der Musik," 75.

26. Ibid., 91.

27. Karel Jaromír Erben, *Próza a divadlo* (Praha: Melantrich, 1939), 151.

28. Cited in Wiora, "Herders Ideen zur Geschichte der Musik," 115.

29. Bohlman, *The Study of Folk Music in the Modern World*, 47.

30. Engel, *An Introduction to the Study of National Music*, 4.

31. Cited in Jan Ling, *A History of European Folk Music* (Rochester: University of Rochester Press, 1997), 11.

32. Roverud, *Et Blik paa Musikens Tilstand i Norge*, 21–22.

33. Artur Zavodský, *František Ladislav Čelakovský* (Praha: Melantrich, 1982), 153.

34. Ibid., 158.

35. Ling, *A History of European Folk Music*, 13.

36. Cited in Herresthal, *Med spark i gulvet og quinter i bassen*, 107.

37. Ibid., 229.

38. From a stipend application to the Storting; cited in Herresthal, *Med spark i gulvet og quinter i bassen*, 150.

39. Wiora, *Das echte Volkslied* (1962), 26.

40. I am indebted to Michael Beckerman, "In Search of Czechness in Music," *19th-Century Music* X/1 (1986), for this general point.

41. Vaughan Williams, *National Music and Other Essays*, 7.

42. T. K. Derry, *A History of Modern Norway 1814–1972* (Oxford: Clarendon Press, 1973) 241.

43. Miroslav Hroch, "From National Movement to the Fully-Formed Nation: The Nation-Building Process in Europe," in Geoff Eley and Ronald Suny, eds. *Becoming National* (New York: Oxford University Press, 1996), 61.

44. Gellner, *Nations and Nationalism*, 37.

45. Benedict Anderson, *Imagined Communities*, 26.

46. Wagner, "Einleitung zum dritten und vierten Bande," 5.

47. Wagner, *Kunstwerk der Zukunft*, 48.

48. Ibid.

49. Ibid., 50.

50. Wagner, "Das Künstlertum der Zukunft," 256.

51. Ibid., 258.

52. Ibid.

53. Wagner, "Was ist deutsch?", 86.

54. Wagner, *Kunstwerk der Zukunft*, 170.

55. Ibid., 172.

56. Ibid.

57. Ibid., 63.

58. Wagner, *Oper und Drama* Parts II and III, 32.
59. Ibid., 31.
60. Wagner, *Oper und Drama*, 268.
61. Wagner, "Das Genie der Gemeinschaft," 268.
62. Wagner, "Über Eduard Devrients *Geschichte der deutschen Schauspielkunst*," 231.
63. Herder, *Stimmen der Völker in Liedern*, in *Ausgewählte Werke*, 311.
64. Wagner, *Kunstwerk der Zukunft*, 103.
65. Ibid.
66. Wagner, "Ausführungen zu 'Religion und Kunst'," 272.
67. Wagner, *Beethoven*, 62.
68. See Wagner, *Deutsche Kunst und deutsche Politik*, 78 and 42; and *Beethoven*, 106.
69. Wagner, "Was ist deutsch?," 93.
70. Wagner, "Zu *Die Kunst und die Revolution*," 259–260.
71. Ibid., 260.
72. Wagner, *Tagebücher* 1873–1877, 702.
73. Wagner, *Eine Mitteilung*, 329.
74. Dahlhaus, *Between Romanticism and Modernism*, 84.
75. Danckert, *Das Volkslied im Abendland*, 18.
76. Wagner, *Kunstwerk der Zukunft*, 78–79.
77. Ibid., 89.
78. Ibid.
79. Wagner, *Oper und Drama*, 264.
80. Ibid., 266.
81. Ibid., 269.
82. Ibid., 267. We will return to this theme of the universality of nationality in the fourth chapter.
83. Wagner, "'Le Freischutz'—Bericht nach Deutschland," 220.
84. Wagner, *Oper und Drama*, 258.
85. Ibid., 260.
86. Ibid.
87. Wiora, *Europäische Volksmusik und abendländische Tonkunst*, 145, makes this point.
88. Wagner, *Kunstwerk der Zukunft*, 79.
89. Wagner, *Oper und Drama*, 266.
90. Ibid., 267.
91. Ibid.
92. Wagner, *Beethoven*, 98.
93. Wagner, *Tagebücher* 1878–1880, 479.

94. Ibid., 201.
95. Wagner, *Eine Mitteilung*, 324–325.
96. Ibid., 325.
97. Wagner, *Tagebücher* 1869–1872, 456.
98. Ibid., 115.
99. Marion Bless, *Richard Wagners Oper "Tannhäuser" im Spiegel seiner geistigen Entwicklung* (Eisenach: Verlag der Musikalienhandlung Karl Dieter Wagner, 1997), 121.
100. Wagner, *Eine Mitteilung*, 269.
101. Bless, *Richard Wagners Oper "Tannhäuser,"* 70.
102. Wagner, *Briefen*, Band II, 434.
103. Carl Dahlhaus, *Richard Wagners Musikdramen* (Hildesheim: Friedrich, 1971), 32.
104. Séquardtová, *Bedřich Smetana*, 18.
105. Ibid, 26.
106. Large, *Smetana*, 256.
107. Bartoš, *Bedřich Smetana*, 203.
108. Smetana, *Smetana-Procházka vzájemná korespondence*, 13.
109. Erben, *Próza a divadlo*, 146.
110. Jaroslav Jiránek "Regarding the Question of Smetana's Originality," in *Bedřich Smetana 1824–1884*. See esp. p. 16.
111. Séquardtová, *Bedřich Smetana*, 58.
112. Racek, *Idea vlasti, národa a slavy v díle Bedřicha Smetany*, 31.
113. Zdeňka Pilková, "Doba osvícenského absolutismu (1740–1810)," in *Hudba v českých dějinách*. See esp. p. 271.
114. Bartoš, *Bedřich Smetana*, 67–68.
115. Zdeněk Nejedlý, *O Bedřichu Smetanovi* (Praha: Academia, 1980), 109.
116. Bartoš, *Bedřich Smetana*, 81.
117. Deník, July 17, 1861, MČH#1098.
118. Racek, *Idea vlasti, národa a slavy v díle Bedřicha Smetany*, 74.
119. Bartoš, *Bedřich Smetana*, 174.
120. Smetana, *Kritické dílo*, 77.
121. Sidney Finkelstein, *Composer and Nation: The Folk Heritage in Music* (New York: International Publishers, 1989), 163.
122. Bartoš, *Bedřich Smetana*, 203. (italics mine).
123. Large, *Smetana*, 31.
124. Séquardtová, *Bedřich Smetana*, 252.
125. Large *Smetana*, 345.
126. Vladimír Tichý, "The Structural Role of Kinetics in Bedřich Smetana's České Tance" in *Report of the International Musicological Conference on*

*Bedřich Smetana, 24 to 26 May 1994* (Praha: Muzeum Bedřicha Smetany, 1995), 141.
127. Cited in Séquardtová, *Bedřich Smetana*, 254.
128. Large, *Smetana*, 186.
129. Ibid., 177.
130. Jiránek, *Dílo a život Bedřicha Smetany*, 202.
131. Gaukstad, *Edvard Grieg*, 49.
132. Grieg, *Dagbøker*, 21.
133. Gaukstad, *Edvard Grieg*, 49.
134. Benestad and Schjelderup-Ebbe, *Edvard Grieg: mennesket og kunstneren* (1990), 320.
135. Grieg, *Brev* Bind I, 371.
136. Grieg, *Briefwechsel mit dem Musikverlag C.F. Peters*, 495 and 513. See also Benestad and Schjelderup-Ebbe, *Edvard Grieg: mennesket og kunstneren* (1990), 369, for the Dahle story more generally.
137. Grieg, *Brev* Bind II, 324.
138. Gaukstad, *Edvard Grieg*, 54.
139. Ibid., 183.
140. Gerhard Schjelderup, "Edvard Grieg," *Allgemeine Musik-Zeitung*, 30, no. 26 (June 26, 1903): 434.
141. Ibid.
142. Grieg, *Brev* Bind I, 76.
143. Benestad and Schjelderup-Ebbe, *Edvard Grieg: mennesket og kunstneren* (1990), 339.
144. Grieg *Brev* Bind II, 33.
145. Benestad and Schjelderup-Ebbe, *Edvard Grieg*, 14; Herresthal, *Med spark i gulvet og quinter i bassen*, 100; Gaukstad, *Edvard Grieg*, 98.
146. Ibid. (1990), 338.
147. Ibid.
148. Gaukstad, *Edvard Grieg*, 73.
149. Ibid., 195.
150. Ferdinand Rojahn, "Edvard Grieg som national tonedigter," *Norsk Musik-Revue*, 3, no. 12 (June 15, 1903): 90. Though these words are not Grieg's own, he said explicitly that he was in complete agreement with everything that Rojahn had written about him in this article; see the letter to Olav Anton Thommessen of June 21, 1901, in *Brev* Bind I.
151. Gaukstad, *Edvard Grieg*, 50.
152. Ibid., 51.
153. Benestad and Schjelderup-Ebbe, *Edvard Grieg*, 102.
154. Gaukstad, *Edvard Grieg*, 51.

155. Grieg, *Brev* Bind I, 626.
156. Gaukstad, *Edvard Grieg*, 50.
157. Grieg, *Brev* Bind I, 616.
158. Benestad and Schjelderup-Ebbe, *Edvard Grieg*, 185.
159. Grieg, *Brev* Bind I, 372.
160. Gaukstad, *Edvard Grieg*, 44.
161. Ibid., 195.
162. Benestad and Schjelderup-Ebbe, *Edvard Grieg: The Man and the Artist* (1988), 369.
163. Ibid., 368.
164. Ibid., 106.
165. Hella Brock, *Edvard Grieg* (Leipzig: Reclam-Verlag, 1990) 299.
166. See Hroch in Eley and Suny, *Becoming National*.

CHAPTER 4

# CONSTRUCTING "DIFFERENCE" IN THE NATIONAL CULTURE

When Wagner, Smetana, or Grieg present in one of their works some vision of their nation and its culture, they are presenting this national self-image to the envisioned national populace itself. The idea is that the nation will recognize itself in its "own" artwork. This is in its purest sense the creation of the national idea, the elaboration of a national culture that would constitute the nation. However, there is another ingredient in constituting the nation, and that is the creation of *boundaries* to the nation, of delimiting in some way the national membership—who belongs and who does not. This is an essential element of the effort to build a national high culture, as well. In order to define what the German, Czech, or Norwegian national culture was, nationalist intellectuals had to define it in relation to something else, most often in relation to another national culture. The goal, after all, was to create a national culture that was distinct from that of other nations.

In the attempt to create boundaries between their envisioned national art and the art and cultural traditions of other nations, nationalist intellectuals rely above all on a discursive production of difference. A twofold dynamic is at work here: first, nationalist intellectuals strive specifically to create these boundaries, that is, to define the characteristics of the envisioned national art in relation to the arts of other nations with the goal of producing something distinct, unique, and of course "truly" national. Second, some nationalists also engage in an "Othering" of different national cultural traditions. In these latter instances, nationalist intellectuals regard a different national culture as the antithesis of their own nation's culture. They espouse not just an argument for distinctiveness but also a normative judgment on the inherent qualities of the "Othered" culture—and that judgment is always negative.

Wagner, as we will see, thoroughly and vituperatively "Others" both the French and the Jews. Smetana is different, in that he actually accepts outside cultural traditions (principally German) to a significant degree. However, some figures within Czech society, in a sense, "Other" Smetana by attacking his perceived Germanic tendencies: they accuse him of "Wagnerianism," which these critics reject as an imposition on a "pure" Czech musical culture. Not unlike Smetana, Grieg largely accepts the inheritance of German traditions in music, though he does also espouse a need for Norwegian independence from these traditions. With the case of Grieg, however, we will see how, as his career progresses, he is subsequently "Othered" by German critics, who accuse him of willfully rejecting "universal" norms of art music in favor of a particularistic obsession with nationalist expression. Yet these claims of universality are in themselves actually grounded on German, nationally biased assumptions.

Wagner's, Smetana's, Grieg's, and others' production of difference in national art is motivated by what I call a fetishization of difference. This fetish demanded a uniquely identifiable cultural expression for every nation. By fetishizing difference, nationalist artists were invoking one of the bedrock assumptions about nationality, that it is a unique quality, with every nationality somehow distinct. Thanks to this assumption, nations are almost inevitably conceived by their members as inherently exclusionary—after all, not everyone is a member of the same nation. It is, in fact, through such exclusion that the qualities of the nation come to be defined. Often, this exclusion takes the form of what Eley and Suny call "systems of negative distinction."[1] This formulation we can equate with the basic idea of the Other—the "Othered" nation embodies the opposite of "our" nation. As the term "negative" implies, this kind of conceptualization of group identity typically involves a judgment that the "Othered" group is in some way inferior to "our" group.

Yet such a claim of inferiority is not a necessary or a constant element in conceiving group distinctiveness. Indeed, as Frederik Barth has proposed, groups also rely upon a notion of "boundaries" for their self-definition.[2] Boundaries do not automatically imply inferiority. Rather, they simply involve an idea of distinction. Some conception of boundaries enables a group to distinguish itself from another group, without implying a normative hierarchization of group status or worth in relation to each other. Boundaries can also be "hard" or "soft." Soft boundaries, Prasenjit Duara writes, help identify a group but "do not prevent the group from sharing and even adopting, self-consciously or not, the practices of another."[3] Boundaries are or become hard, on the other hand, when someone seeks to mobilize a community by privileging "a particular symbolic meaning (or set of cultural practices) as the constitutive principle of the community." The goal is to heighten the self-consciousness of this community in relation to those around it: boundaries are "hardened" as part of a concerted effort to distinguish group difference. "Not only do communities with hard boundaries privilege their differences," Duara adds, "they tend to develop an intolerance and suspicion toward the adoption of the Other's practices."[4]

The process of creating boundaries involves elaborating cultural differentiae between groups. Nationalist artists are concerned with the discursive production of cultural differentiae in the realm of high culture, in the effort to produce a distinct national art. For nationalist composers, such differentiae are a means of creating boundaries between their national musics. Difference can be emphasized and privileged, though, even while maintaining "soft" boundaries: Smetana's and Grieg's attitudes toward German culture prove excellent examples of this possibility. It is nonetheless clear that Wagner's insistence on "hard" boundaries does also carry with it an intolerant "Othering." Ultimately, these composers demonstrate that nationalist intellectuals can and do advocate both hard and soft boundaries between their and other nations. In fact, the relative "hardness" or "softness" can be applied with differing standards to different groups.

Difference, then, is both conceived and produced in different ways. The discourse on nationalist music illustrates the varying ways difference is conceived. The Other is actually more an opposite than merely an embodiment of difference. Implicit in the conception of the Other—as Wagner, Pivoda, and the German critics will conceive it, following—is indeed a notion of antithesis. For them, the cultures they criticize are not merely different but, in a sense, *wrong*. Hence they openly and fully reject these Others. And yet, some conception of an Other is not absolutely necessary for a sense of self. That is, "our" group does not inevitably need some idea of an "anti-us" in order to understand who we are. Smetana and Grieg are both able to formulate a national art without clinging to antitheses. They do discursively construct difference, but they do not portray that difference as somehow inherently wrong. Too often the terms "Other" and "difference" are conflated to mean essentially the same thing. Conflating them, however, fails to capture the different dynamic by which "Othering" and alternative means of the construction of difference can operate.

"Othering" and boundary making in the national art are best understood as being built upon relational processes. Boundaries tend to be created because of the interaction between groups.[5] It is not isolation that spurs attempts to create distinction, but rather a contact or fluidity between "ours" and "theirs." Indeed, the interplay between differing group conceptions can even be based on a common fundament over which distinctions are then constructed. So, the desire to construct difference may be motivated by the perception of commonality—a commonality that would seem to undercut the difference that nationalists wish to construct.

The construction of difference between national cultures provides a paradigmatic example here. National arts *do* interact—they are not isolated or cut off from one another. The geographical boundaries of high culture, quite simply, are not discrete: French operas were performed in Prague and Dresden, not to mention St. Petersburg and Christiania. Similarly, German symphonies were heard all over Europe. Part of the nature of the relationship between various national arts, though, is that these arts had to be truly national (i.e., unique) in order to take their place on the European stage, as I discuss in the next chapter. Thus, in a sense, the interaction of art on a Europe-wide level is a major motivation for the effort to create national distinction in music. Czech art can learn from German models, for instance, but it must also be different from those models in order to be authentically Czech. Given the diffusion of widely shared art music forms across the European continent, composers with a nationalist agenda felt the need to create music that was distinct, in order to differentiate their own, national production from that of other artists.

There is another way in which the various national traditions interact, however, and I suspect that this is particular to the realm of music. Particular, because music has famously been described as the "universal language," and in fact this idea was quite common in the nineteenth century. Though of course the genuine universality can be questioned, it is nonetheless certain that the musical language that composers as diverse as Auber, Wagner, Meyerbeer, Smetana, Balakirev, Verdi, and Grieg shared is generally the *same* language. Without ignoring the differences in their individual musical expression, they nonetheless do all speak the same basic language of European art music as it evolved over the course of several hundred years, with its particular structural forms, melodic and harmonic conventions, and instrumentation. Metaphorically speaking, if we equate this fundamental musical language with the "whole," then the various national musics are the groups within that whole that seek to distinguish themselves from one another. Hence even the distinctive musical language that Wagner claims for the Germans includes, in a sense, the Others of French and Italian musical expression—simply because they are all rooted in the same artistic form.

It is perhaps doubtful that Wagner himself would have accepted this notion of similarity. Nonetheless, he was certainly conscious of the mutual imbrication of his own envisioned national culture with the Others—whether French, Italian, or Jewish—that he sought to discharge from German culture. And indeed, I suggest that even lacking an explicit acknowledgement of the shared universal language, we can consider such an acknowledgement as a presupposition of the effort to create a distinct national music. That is because the very commonality of the musical language would play a major role in fostering the fetishization of difference that characterizes this discourse. Here, of course, I rely on the assumptions behind the construction of difference: a perception of similarity, together with a belief in group distinctiveness, generates the effort to produce markers of difference. Given, then, the broadly shared characteristics of the musical language, composers recur to a search for totems of difference that will distinguish their artistic production as national and hence distinctive. These totems can amount to boundary creation or to a more thoroughgoing "Othering" with the normative assumptions that this implies.

## WAGNER'S VILLAINS

Wagner, as it turns out, is unquestionably normative. To him, the French and the Jews are the villains against whom a German culture must fight in order to realize itself and thereby to save art. They are villains because the tone with which Wagner "Others" the French and the Jews is so venomous that there can be no doubt of his antagonistic rejection of what he saw as their influences on Germany. Wagner's anti-Semitism has of course provoked much controversy and many reams of writing; not wishing to add too much to either, I will treat the topic here only as it relates to his Francophobia. Wagner's Francophobia relies on a slightly different principle than does his hatred of the Jews: the former posits a clear antinomy between two distinct national cultures, while in the latter case he presents the Jews as having no genuine culture of their own at all. Regardless, they are both powerful examples of "Othering" as a means of cultural boundary drawing. My discussion is directed primarily at a comparative purpose—and so draws the parallels between his treatment of the Jews and the French, and the role these bugbears play in his discourse on creating a national art, as material for examination in relation to Smetana and Grieg. I begin first with the French, and the background of the anti-French sentiment that informed Wagner's own opinions in this area.

Sparked largely by the Wars of Liberation during the struggle against Napoleon, the idea of the French as the corrupt antithesis of everything German is a well-established trope in German nationalist discourse, not just in Wagner. Early patriots such as Arndt, Fichte, Schleiermacher, Luden, and Jahn all pounded the drum to stir up resistance to the French. In fact, Arndt called for hatred of the French to be the "religion of the German people." This hate would be "a bright mirror...in which we will be able to see our glory as well as our ruin."[6] That statement is an obvious expression of the sort of ideas behind "Othering": the German people would realize its own self through the mirror image of its opposite, the French. Thus the French came to be presented as the "eternal enemy" (*Urfeind*) (as the motto of the Wartburgfest proclaimed)[7] of the German nation, against which many of the ostensible traits of German nationality would be projected by German nationalist intellectuals.[8] Dieter Düding summarizes this trend succinctly:

> To the implied national contrast between Germans and French was attributed a deep power, such that one saw the intrinsic qualities of the French people, their spiritual-intellectual disposition, as a diametric contradiction of the natural conceptualization of the German Volk. Thus this purported antipathy of the national characters was elevated to a dimension not merely of a historically-grounded difference, but also to the status of an ethical opposition.[9]

In art, the heritage of anti-French expressions can be traced back to the numerous patriotic songs written during the years of the Wars of Liberation. These were lyrics written by the likes of Ernst Mortiz Arndt,

Max von Schenkendorff, and Theodor Körner, set to music usually by various, generally minor composers. Members of the Burschenshaften and the Turnvereine, in particular, avidly sang these songs, and they kept both the songs and the sentiments therein alive in the decades following Napoleon's defeat.[10] These lyrics' attack on "welscher Tand" (very loosely translated, "foreign humbug") finds a direct echo in the speech Wagner gives Hans Sachs in *Die Meistersinger*, where the latter berates "falsche welsche Majestät"—*welsch* being a euphemism for the "Latin cultures" generally, and the French especially. Indeed, we know that Wagner viewed the French as "bloodthirsty" and the Wars of Liberation as a "holy cause."[11] Thus, where Arndt called for an "uprising" against the Napoleonic occupation at the beginning of the nineteenth century, later on Wagner takes up this call for an uprising against the hegemony of French culture.

All the components Düding mentions previously—the "spiritual-intellectual" opposition, the historical foundations, and the escalation of the antinomy into ethical claims—appear in Wagner's own discourse. Wagner even adds the idea that German art had to save the world from degenerate French culture. The problem, at least as Wagner framed it late in his life, was one of a conflict between a "pure race" versus a "mixed race."[12] The Germans, as a "pure race," enjoyed a "still unbroken racial natural power," whereas other races such as the French (or the English, for that matter) were merely degenerate. The entire French civilization developed "without the Volk."[13] Given the emphasis Wagner laid on the Volk's importance in giving birth to culture, this is a very serious charge indeed. It is one Wagner also uses against the Jews, as we will see later. The French, having no "Volk basis" to their civilization, could only develop a shallow, hollow culture.

From the fact of their own degeneracy stems the "murderous" damage that the French wreaked upon the world, particularly on the cultures of other lands.[14] More than once, Wagner accuses French composers of ruining opera. They made modern opera music not an art but a "manifestation of fashion."[15] Then, when the incorporation of folk elements into opera became the "fashion," the French composers went out and plundered folk sources, sucking the folk source dry.[16] This was a crime against humanity in general, but Wagner has a special bone to pick with what he regarded as the French destruction of German culture in particular. The Italians also played an accomplice role here. The forms of both the theater and opera came from outside Germany, Wagner says; Germany did not have its own forms.[17] France and Italy not only had "their own"—that is, uniquely national—forms, but they had their own conservatories as well. These conservatories allowed the French and the Italians to develop their own national styles. And in Wagner's day, since France ruled the world in terms of taste, French taste came to dominate that of "all nations." As a result, the Germans had no national style of their own—all they could do was imitate Italian and (especially) French styles.[18]

These "foreign" styles were founded on inherently "un-German" characteristics. For example, the entire melodic, virtuosic nature of Italian opera is based on the Italian's "preference for song."[19] The Germans do not have this gift, which means their art should take a different direction.[20] Regardless, the Germans just imitate. However, their imitations are never as good as the originals (though the originals are by no means "good" in terms of their aesthetic value). So, the Germans just end up producing bad copies of others' bad art.[21] Wagner detested the fact that these foreign styles dominated German society.[22] The prevalence of French (i.e., *bad*) taste in the theater meant that the German public was losing its own good taste. Wagner complained that German audiences more easily fall into ecstasy over an Italian soprano than they would over Bach's or Beethoven's music.[23]

The deeper, social effect of this French domination is that, historically, it caused the German princes to be estranged from the German Volk.[24] The ruling classes were "Frenchified" before the masses, so the masses at least retained a connection to the German Volksgeist. However, as the nineteenth century progressed and French hegemony remained unchallenged, Wagner seemed to fear that even the mass German public was losing touch with its Volksgeist. The French were ruining even that most precious element of "Germanness." A metaphorical example of this kind of ruination is the staging of *Der Freischütz* in Paris in 1841. Wagner complains that the text was translated from German to French by an Italian, that the spoken dialogue was turned into recitative, that the cast was made up entirely of second-rate singers, and that various dances were added to the score to satisfy the Parisian mania for ballet music. Far from doing justice to this treasure of the German Volk's culture, Wagner says, the French used the production to make fun of German taste and Germans in general.[25]

It might seem questionable what "German taste" would even be, since Wagner did not think that there was much German taste left. What he means in the case of *Freischütz* is that it was a pure expression of the German Volksgeist, and as such represented the true values (what German taste *should* be) of German art.[26] Also seemingly contradictory are Wagner's statements that Germans feel shame at their domination by the French. If French taste has infected the Germans so thoroughly, how would they feel shame in being so dominated? Nonetheless, that is how Wagner characterized German society: in 1870 he wrote that as the mighty German army marched victoriously on Paris, "suddenly inside us stirred our shame over our subordination to that civilization."[27]

Surprisingly, Wagner occasionally expressed admiration for some of the products of French and Italian cultures. He liked, for instance, Auber's opera *La muette de Portici* when it was given a production in Leipzig in 1829.[28] He also admired Cherubini, and at one point claimed that the "continuity of song" in *Lohengrin* comes more from Spontini than from Weber.[29] Despite what he called their "Pauvretät" (a particularly, possibly unintentionally ironic use of a Germanized French word in this instance), he enjoyed the "passion and feeling" of themes from operas such as *Romeo and Juliet*, *La straniera*, and *Norma*, even admitting that he learned from them melodically.[30] Wagner was not so hostile toward Italian culture, in part because it did not rule the world. There can be no doubt of his intense hatred for the French, however; statements such as "The French are the rot of the Renaissance" are too colorfully descriptive in that regard.[31]

Wagner's antipathy toward the Jews takes broadly similar forms to his Francophobia, in terms of his portrayal of the Jews' inherent degeneracy and their lamentable impact on artistic life. "Das Judentum in der Musik," written in 1850 but published several years later, is of course the most infamous document of Wagner's anti-Semitism. In it, he claims that everyone, as a matter of course, shares an aversion to Jews.[32] This may well be because people feel instinctively that Jews are "the bad conscience of our modern civilization."[33] In addition to this more metaphysical antipathy, however, Wagner is also outraged that Jews rule public taste.[34] They rule because money is power, and Jews control the flow of money. Money in turn has come to control art, with the result being the "Jewification of modern art." Wagner's purpose in this essay is to protest this "Jewification," exhorting his readers to emancipate themselves from the "oppression of Jewry."[35]

Besides the subjection of art to money—which in itself is an evil, according to Wagner—the Jews' control of art is also a disgrace because they are a people absolutely incapable of art. The root of the Jews' inability to produce true art is that the Jews completely lack a Volk commonality (*Volksgemeinsamkeit*). The Jews are the product of a "splintered, rootless tribe, to which is denied all development out of its own self."[36] In a search for belonging and a basis for his own art, the Jew looks to the Volk of whatever land he resides in. However, the Jew is always an outsider—he does not actually belong to this Volk or that Volk. The Jew is therefore incapable of appreciating or expressing any people's Volksgeist, because he is always foreign and lacks any Volksgeist of his own.

And since there is no Jewish Volksgeist, the Jew has no folk art to inspire him. Instead, the only source of inspiration for a Jewish composer is the musical material of the synagogue service; that is the closest the Jew can come to "folksy motives." However, this source is repugnant, Wagner claims: "Who has not been seized by the repellent feeling, mixed with horror and absurdity, when he hears that mind- and spirit-bewildering gurgling, yodeling, and babbling [in the synagogue service], that no intentional caricature could make more disgusting than it already is presented there with all its naive earnestness?"[37] This "gurgling, yodeling, and babbling," though, calamitously finds its way into the music of Jewish composers. This is an inevitable result, as Wagner frames it, since Jews must fall back on their own language when composing, due to their inability to compose in the language of any other Volk—again because the Jews lack a connection to the relevant Volksgeist.

However, Jews are of course unaware of their inability to produce great art, so they attempt it regardless. But what they create inevitably ends up being "cold, strange, unnatural," inevitably "foreign" *imitations* of other peoples' cultures.[38] Jewish music ultimately only evinces a striving after effect, a constant search for entertainment, and an impossible attempt to seem natural, which can never amount to art. In this search for effect, Wagner's denunciation of Jewish music echoes his similar charges against French style. The deficiencies of both stem from the missing connection between the Volk and the artist. Either the Volk is completely lacking, as in the case of the Jews, or the artist is so cosmopolitan that he no longer has any Volk to communicate with. This last charge applies to both the French and the Jews, since the latter are scattered all about the world, everywhere foreign, having no actual home. The embodiment of all these ills are men such as Mendelssohn and Meyerbeer and their "trivial" music. In fact, Meyerbeer unites both the deficiencies of the Jews and the French in one, since besides suffering from all the Jew's incapacity for art, he also conquered the French operatic scene, the ultimate cosmopolitan who destroys good taste everywhere from his throne in Paris. In this way, Wagner suggests, Jews are capable of wrecking high culture itself, by substituting their own, uniquely corrupt expression for true art.[39]

Against the worthlessness of French and Jewish culture, then, Wagner posits German art. To a significant degree, Wagner's attempt to outline the definition of "Germanness" in the arts depends precisely on what these "Othered" cultures *are not*. Indeed, Wagner posits the resistance to the infection of French culture as one of the defining features of the German nationalist movement: the "German movement could almost only take the character of a reaction against the foreign, deformed and thus also deforming, Latin model."[40] The goal of this "reaction," of course, would be to produce an art of real value, not just for Germany but for the world. Wagner enunciated this goal succinctly in 1842: "The limp characterlessness of today's Italians, as well as the frivolous stupidity of recent Frenchmen, seem to me to encourage the earnest, conscientious German to take control of the more fortuitously elegant and cultivated resources of these rivals, thereby resolutely to bring forth true works of art."[41]

According to this conception, the Germans will bring forth "true works of art" because the German Volk is still natural, not just a parasitic creature of "fashion" like the French. For Wagner's own envisioned artworks, likewise, German was the only language that could bring about the necessary reform of opera—precisely because German, unlike French or Italian, was still natural, tied to its roots.[42] Moreover, only the Germans know "'music' as music"—that is, as something other than mere accompaniment to "song or dance virtuosity."[43] The German, he says, "loves music for its own sake, and not as a means to delight or of attaining money and admiration, but rather, because music is a beautiful, divine art."[44] As with music, in the theater only Germans (namely Goethe and Schiller) have shown the world the sole possible path for the further development of the art form.

In a half-delirious description of a portrait he saw of one Pastor Niemann, a founder of the Burschenschaft, Wagner overflows with praise for what he calls "German ideality": "Little movement, no Hungarian, Polish, or French suppleness, somewhat heavy, not dainty: but this piercing mind! The naive look, the marvelous faith therein, the rapture!...But what is this *Germanness*? It must be something wonderful, for it is more humanly beautiful than everything else?"[45] Wagner directly juxtaposes here the German and the "Othered" cultures, revealing the latter as antitheses that pale in comparison to the power of Germanness. Thanks to the love of art for art's sake, as well as the inherent German qualities of naturalness, "nobility and perceptiveness," and the direct contact to the Volk, the salvation of art can only be brought about by *German* art. This salvation, of course, he locates in his own art, which not surprisingly he also identifies as the epitome of Germanness. Wagner's take on foreign artistic traditions is so thoroughly critical—portraying those traditions as the antithesis of German culture—that his discourse is the best example of a true "Othering," of our three composers. The boundaries between national cultures that Wagner seeks to create are not just boundaries, but more accurately fortifications: French and Jewish influences are so deleterious that only completely sealed off from them can a German national culture thrive.

## SMETANA AND THE BATTLES OF "WAGNERIANISM"

Historically speaking, what the French are for German nationalism, the Germans are for Czech nationalism. Czech patriots' nationalism was predicated not just on a struggle for greater sovereignty within the Habsburg Empire. Rather, it was resistance to a broader process of what they perceived as the "Germanization" of the Czech lands. Germans dominated economic, political, and social life in Prague. Concomitantly, the supremacy of the German language was viewed as driving the Czech language to near extinction. Of the major figures in the Czech movement, Karel Havlíček was one of the most ardent anti-German nationalists, portraying "all of Czech history" as a "permanent fight" of "a weak Slavic tribe against the entire German nation always pressing toward the east."[46] František Palacký represents a more moderate approach; in the first edition of his history of the Czech lands (1836, written in German) he emphasized that the civilization there was a synthesis of Czech and German elements. Later, though, while still relatively tolerant of the German presence in Bohemia, he instead viewed the Czechs as a "bridge" between West and East, thus emphasizing their distinctiveness vis-à-vis the Germans and downplaying the "synthesis" idea.[47]

Both the antagonistic and moderate positions are represented in the efforts to build a Czech national culture. On the one hand, documents like the forged "historical chronicles" of the Kralovedvorský and Zelenohorský manuscripts are decidedly anti-German. We can view these documents (newly "rediscovered" in 1817–1818 after being "lost" for centuries) as in a sense the counterpart to Havlíček's efforts to portray Czech history as a battle against Germans, since they purported to actually be *records* of that history. Their author, Václav Hanka, sought thereby to ground Czech national resistance to Germanization all the way back in the early medieval period. In trying to create a Czech verse style, men such as Pavel Josef Šafařík explicitly rejected what they viewed as "German forms" of poetry, insisting on the need to create something "purely" Czech.[48] Similarly, Havlíček rejected what he perceived as the "philosophizing" tendencies of German culture—he called for the Czechs in contrast to be a nation "without philosophy," founding their culture on "common sense" instead of on (implicitly) unhealthy philosophical noodling. In general, the Czech nationalist intellectuals who took this antagonistic attitude toward German culture insisted that, in order to "liberate" Czech culture from the Germans, Czech culture had to be built not only from its "own" foundations, but that these foundations must be "opposite" from those of German culture. The demands of Havlíček and the like for a Czech culture that is a "mirror image" of German culture are an obvious instantiation of the "Othering" idea.

Never as rabidly anti-German as Havlíček, Smetana was one of the major figures in the more moderate camp that accepted German influence on Czech culture. Nonetheless, he was a Czech patriot and he did occasionally voice anti-German sentiments, both politically and artistically. For instance, in 1869 he protested against the Imperial government's policies, "which would so dearly like to throw *all* the nations of Austria into one pot—that of Germanization—in order to rule over all of them with *beaucoup de plaisir*. Praise be to God, our nation fights back uncowed and as *one* man."[49] This theme of the German-biased rule of the Habsburgs appears at various times over the years in Smetana's correspondence.[50] Artistically, Smetana and his circle sometimes claimed to reject "foreign" forms in general, and not just German. Smetana criticized the "fad-ish jangling" of modern Italian opera music and did not want that style to dominate in Prague. Similarly, his student and supporter

Ludevít Procházka resented the popularity of Italian "trends" in music, and called for the Czechs "to completely abandon foreign courses little by little and to move toward artistic independence and originality."[51]

Smetana's relationship specifically to German music is quite complicated. On the one hand, he sometimes denied his inheritance from German culture. For example, he said that he could not allow himself to compose to a German text, since apparently it would be an affront to his Czech patriotism to do so.[52] This is despite the fact that throughout his life, Smetana actually spoke German better than Czech. On one occasion, he also explicitly rejected Wagner's influence, according to an acquaintance: "Speaking of Wagner's declamatory style of composition and his endless melody in orchestration, Smetana once said in the circle of his friends: 'We Czechs are a singing people and can't accept those methods.'"[53] He claimed that there is "no Wagner" in his opera *Dalibor*.[54] On the other hand, Smetana also acknowledged what he had learned from German examples. The last two quotations in particular seem contradictory, given his avowed reverence for Wagner's achievements. For example, a diary entry of 1862 reads, "Insofar as the neo-German school means *progress* I belong to it."[55] The "neo-German school" was commonly identified with Wagner and Liszt. In a letter to a Swedish friend, Smetana describes the personal attacks he suffered because of his artistic allegiances: "The Old Czechs made me out as dangerous for the national independence of art because I recognize the German direction in music—Wagner—too much."[56]

One likely reason for the seeming self-contradiction is precisely the attacks on Smetana that took place within the context of the debates on "Wagnerianism." The smear campaign to label him a kind of "German spy" within Czech culture probably provoked these denials of German influence as Smetana sought to emphasize his own Czechness. The controversy surrounding this debate is well illustrated by an anecdote from Eliška Krásnohorská, one of Smetana's librettists, that is worth quoting in full for the way it captures the spiteful tone and some of the issues of the time. Krásnohorská tells of an encounter with an acquaintance who warned her against working with Smetana.

> First of all [Krásnohorská's acquaintance warned her] everybody
> knows that Smetana is trying to Wagnerize Czech music, that is
> to say to germanize it, a thing which is not a merit but a crime for
> which he ought to be generally condemned and not honored! And
> then that fraud with his pretended deafness! Uncle has asked me
> to tell you—and any sane person would agree with him—that a
> deaf person cannot compose music any more than a blind one can
> paint pictures.[57]

As this anecdote suggests, Smetana stood at the center of the fights about Wagnerianism. It is largely coincidental that the pinnacle of Wagner's career came in the later 1860s and early 1870s, which also happens to be the time of the highest interest in producing Czech national opera. This period is also the peak of Smetana's own public career, before deafness forced him to retire from the directorship of the Czech opera house. (Krásnohorská's anecdote evidently dates from after his retirement, but that does not lessen its applicability.) The Wagner debate really exploded with the premiere of *Dalibor* in 1868. On one side were those such as F. L. Rieger and especially František Pivoda, who lambasted *Dalibor* as a Wagnerian affront to Czech art, and on the other were Smetana and his supporters, who advocated musical "progress" on the basis of Wagner's "reform" of opera.

The epithet "Wagnerian" in this context is of course polemical and needs to be explained. In general, as Ottlová and Pospíšil make clear, music that was described as "Wagnerian" could consist of a "richer web of orchestral voices or more developed interludes and gradations."[58] Features such as complex instrumentation and "unusual" harmonies thus sufficed for commentators to label a piece Wagnerian. This view of Wagner led supporters such as Smetana to accuse Wagner's critics of misrepresenting what Wagner had accomplished—Smetana in fact even offered to teach Pivoda what Wagnerism "really is."[59] In the Czech lands, when a work was accused of being "Wagnerian," the accusation was indeed based on the stylistic features that Ottlová and Pospíšil outline—and this accusation (for the anti-Wagnerites) also presumes a negative aesthetic judgment about those very features. However, another crucial element in the debate was the perception of Wagner and "Wagnerian style" as something inherently German, which thus was regarded by anti-Wagnerites as inappropriate for Czech music. In the following discussion of the Wagner debate, I will first present the anti-Wagnerian side, in the form of František Pivoda's attack on Smetana. Then I will turn to Otakar Hostinský's defense of why Wagnerian style *is* an acceptable basis for Czech national music. In a letter to Pivoda of June 16, 1870, Smetana mentioned that he was entirely in agreement with Hostinský's article "Wagnerianism and Czech national opera," on which I base my analysis.[60] Thus in this particular area, we can safely equate Smetana's ideas with Hostinský's.

Pivoda was a musician known mostly for running a prominent singing school in Prague. He was actively interested in the question of a Czech national music, and in fact quite liked *The Bartered Bride* since it corresponded to his ideal of a *prostonárodní* folk opera.[61] The musical direction Smetana took after *The Bartered Bride*, however, provoked Pivoda's ire. Hostinský, though by no means an impartial commentator, suggests that Pivoda's resentment against Smetana may also have been motivated by the incident when the latter, together with the directors of the opera, turned down Pivoda's proposal to affiliate his singing school with the theater.[62] In any case, Pivoda did take over as the director of one of Prague's musical journals, the *Hudební listy*, which he turned into the main mouthpiece for attacking Smetana and the threatening "German direction" in Czech music. Smetana's supporters, in turn, defended him in the journal not coincidentally named *Dalibor*, and the pages of these two publications became the battleground of the Wagnerianism debates.

Pivoda's attack on Wagnerianism in Czech music is two pronged: first he rejects the music because it is inherently "foreign," and then he criticizes it on aesthetic grounds, arguing that Wagner's music and that beholden to it is simply bad art. In this way, his critiques take the same basic form as Wagner's own harangues against the French and the Jews. For Pivoda, Wagner represents the "peak of unacceptable foreignness," as Ottlová and Pospíšil term it, and that foreignness was of course Germanness.[63] He was not alone, though, in regarding Wagner as indelibly German—Wagner was widely conceived as the "summation of German music" in the Czech lands, and even Hostinský agreed that Wagner's music was German "through and through."[64] Pivoda, however, thought that the only way to create a truly Czech music was if it was *exclusively* Czech through and through.[65] Czech music could not be Czech if it was based in some way on foreign models—though Pivoda's objection always seems to have been aimed just at German models, since he in fact taught the Italian style of *bel canto* at his singing academy and encouraged this as the proper vocal style for Czech opera. He thought that Smetana's *Dalibor* was so full of "indigestible foreignness" that it should more properly be named *Dalibor Wagner*.[66] Smetana also reports that with *Dalibor* he was accused of trying "to outdo *Tristan*, that [he] was only just beginning where Wagner had left off."[67]

Besides his Germanophobic sentiments, Pivoda simply found Wagner's music incomprehensible. He evidently had read *Das Kunstwerk der Zukunft* and did not necessarily disagree with it. However, subsequently when he actually encountered Wagner's music, Pivoda found he could not accept the aesthetic principles Wagner had laid out in his writings if such principles produced this kind of music that Pivoda thought was awful. Thus the acceptance of such principles—which Hostinský also advocated—would lead, in Pivoda's opinion, to the same incomprehensible standard for a Czech national music. Against this "incomprehensibility," Pivoda juxtaposed his own vision of the inherent qualities of the Czech spirit and musical expression. He emphasized the "natural" qualities of Czech music, that it was gifted "naturally" with simplicity and melodicness.[68] German art, and particularly Wagner, thus became "unnatural."

As Ottlová and Pospíšil explain, Pivoda's emphasis on simplicity, while grounded on the *prostonárodní* idea that folk songs should be the basis for national opera, involves more than just that. In fact he was insisting on opera that would continue to be based on organized forms—traditional structures such as arias, duets, and choruses as they were found in French and Italian opera and which Pivoda perceived to be missing in Wagner. It was the perceived lack of these familiar forms of "orientation" (including more traditional melodic and harmonic musical language) that provoked Pivoda's complaint of Wagner's incomprehensibility.[69] In fact, Smetana was not the only composer to be criticized for a "Wagnerian" abandonment of traditional forms: Pivoda also derided Karel Šebor's (a contemporary of Smetana's) use of the orchestra to express emotional content, and the consequent "neglect" of the solo singing parts.[70] The importance of the orchestra was one thing about Wagner that particularly frightened Pivoda. He held to the idea of opera as a vehicle for discrete numbers that showcased singers, and in this sense he opposed Wagner's claims for the *Musikdrama*, which put the principle of drama before that of virtuosic display. So, for Pivoda, not only did German influences scupper the possibility of a truly national opera, but in fact the entire aesthetic direction Wagner proposed could only lead Czech music down the wrong path.

Hostinský (and by extension Smetana), on the other hand, praise Wagner precisely for indicating the direction in which music, as an art form, must progress. In order to found a Czech music, they argued, Czech artists should look to the best examples of modern art they can find. This model happened to be German. With a conspicuously Wagnerian line of argument, Hostinský says that Italian and French models brought about the decline of opera that he saw as readily apparent in the contemporary period.[71] He characterizes these models, disapprovingly, as based on "vocal virtuosity" and "insignificant, entirely perfunctory music."[72] Again like Wagner, Hostinský criticizes the number-opera form as being a product of the cult of virtuosic, empty singing. Hence this particular artistic style, which Pivoda argued for, is illegitimate. Hostinský also rejects following what he terms a "cosmopolitan" path, that is, picking and choosing trends from various artistic traditions. Such an approach would only result in a "colorless" music, not Czech, not of any unified style, and not based on worthy aesthetic principles.[73] Hostinský specifically denounced "eclecticism," which he (following Wagner) identified with Meyerbeer, calling it the "negation of all principle."[74] Instead, opera should have a "rounded form," with sections almost like the movements of a symphony. Not surprisingly, he also advocated the full use of the modern orchestra to exploit its potential for polyphony and color—and this proposal again ties in to the idea of not letting opera be solely a vehicle for virtuosic vocal display.

Given the deficiencies of other possible models for Czech music, German music and specifically Wagner's example were the highest quality musical expression in the contemporary period, and so the only viable model. One reason why German music had attained its exalted position was because Wagner also rejected the debasing Italian and French influences, looking back to the example of the Greeks to restore dramatic truth to opera. However, there was another, critical reason why Czechs should follow Wagner's example: he showed the world how to express the national in music. As Hostinský explains,

> Wagner's operas are authentically of a German character through and through, but just for that reason I remain a convinced Wagnerian, even with regard to our opera, to our Czech national opera…Richard Wagner showed us, with his excellent example, where to proceed from, which direction to take and what means we must use if we want our own uniquely Czech national opera, just as a uniquely German national opera is his accomplishment. It goes without saying that the departure point must be different for every individual nationality, natural and appropriate to it, its own and particular. And this specific departure point, to which Wagner pointed us, is—our national language.[75]

In this way, despite the undeniable Germanness of Wagner's art, it is valuable to Czechs as a kind of recipe for the national opera. And when Czech composers rely on Wagner's example, their art is nonetheless thoroughly and exclusively Czech because it is based on the Czech language. The Czech language would automatically determine the music, in Smetana's and Hostinský's formulation, and thereby produce both an original and national music. The emphasis on speech is also associated with the subjugation of absolute melody. In contrast to Pivoda, who emphasized that melody must be primary, Hostinský and Smetana believed that the dramatic composer must create his sung melodies on the basis of human speech patterns.[76]

This linguistic basis was the ultimate defense of the Czechness of a piece, despite a Wagner-influenced style. It was also the argument that Smetana's supporters used to defend him against the charges of Wagnerianism. As Jan Neruda wrote:

> They say that Smetana is a Wagnerian. Where they are right in principle, is that Smetana watches severely to see that the music should correspond to the words. If you meet Smetana walking along the embankment, you will hear in passing how he declaims under his breath. Preoccupied with a new operatic composition, he declaims the text, repeating it a hundred times until melody flowers from the words in the most natural of chords. That is why his music, in spite of all "Wagnerianism," is so Czech. And because it is so Czech it is so elegiac.[77]

Interestingly, Neruda here also urges that the character of the language naturally comes out in the music, insisting that elegiacness is an inherent Czech quality, distinct from any German character. Thus the elegiac Czechness in a piece of music also serves to emphasize its nationality, regardless of German influence. Additionally, however, a national color could be granted to a piece through the use of Leitmotivs, according to Hostinský. For example, when Smetana gave the character of Zdeněk in *Dalibor* a Leitmotiv with a clear "national character," as that motive appears throughout the opera, the national character of the work is reaffirmed.[78] Moreover, by treating those motives in a truly Wagnerian fashion (i.e., developing them so that they can express particular dramatic facets of the work), the composer unites the most "progressive" musical techniques with the national melodic elements.

Actually, Pivoda would not have disagreed completely with this last claim of Hostinský's. He, too, was in favor of incorporating national tunes into Czech opera. He would have rejected, however, treating those tunes along the principles of Wagner's musicdrama. This case, then, is a good demonstration of the distinction to be drawn between "Othering" and boundary creation as processes of the social construction of difference. The Germans really are the Other for Pivoda, the enemy that Czech art must resist, the image of which Czech art must be the opposite. For Hostinský and Smetana, the boundaries between German art and Czech art are not so hard. Hostinský and Smetana are not interested in a complete exclusion of German influences from Czech art. They wish to create a distinctive Czech music, but in order to create a quality art, Czech composers must be open to allegedly "foreign" impulses. In a sense, Hostinský and Smetana are convinced that the boundaries of their community are secure—that the uniquely Czech character of music can be maintained—even with communication across those boundaries.

## GRIEG, GERMAN MUSIC, AND GERMAN CRITICS

In contrast to the Czechs and Germans, there really is no "eternal enemy" for the Norwegian nationalist movement. Sometimes nationalists would complain about the Danish influence in Norwegian culture, or about the Norwegian-Swedish Union, portraying the Swedes as aristocratic and autocratic in comparison to the earthy, homey Norwegians. But, in general, "Othering" discourse has a low profile in the Norwegian movement. This does not mean that criticisms of other peoples were entirely absent in the drive to create a Norwegian national culture. In fact, as members of a small, peasanty country on the periphery of Europe, Norwegian patriots often seem to have felt that their culture was in danger of being squashed by the bigger nations. As good patriots, though, these nationalists believed that Norwegian culture was inherently worthy and deserved to be freed from the domination of external, less worthy national cultures.

An early outburst of this kind came from Lars Roverud, who, along with various Christiania critics of the early 1800s, complained about the popularity of empty and virtuosic Italian music.[79] Roverud doubted that Norwegians' ears were made to hear such "southern," "luxurious" music; instead, he advocated a more "simple, natural" music that would be in line with Norwegian character.[80] In 1830 Henrik Wergeland even wrote a little play called *Harlequin Virtuos* as a critique of Italian and French music. Such perceived foreign influence also annoyed Ole Bull in the late 1850s, when he complained that Norwegian theaters, and Bergen's in particular, were filled with Danish actors doing French plays, instead of, properly, Norwegian actors in Norwegian plays set to Norwegian music.[81]

Nonetheless, the principal adversary in the drive for a Norwegian art came to be the Germans. Herresthal covers in detail anti-German resentment in early nineteenth-century Norwegian cultural life, and I am indebted to his work in this area. In general, it seems that this resentment, though it produced some invective, rarely reached the bitterly divisive levels that it did in the Czech lands. The reason for the more moderate character of Norwegian resentment is assuredly because Germans did not occupy the same positions of dominance in Norway as they often did in the Czech lands. Still, though, Ole Bull, Bjørnstjerne Bjørnson, and A. O. Vinje, among others, decried especially Germans' influence on Norwegian music. Many of Norway's orchestras were made up of a size-able number of Germans, which irritated Bull and provoked Bjørnson to declare that these Germans would hinder a "national art" because they do not understand the "Norwegian spirit."[82] In an article of January 1860, Bjørnson pinpointed the danger here:

> One must remember that effectively all of our music is still in for-eigners' hands, and that music's wondrous power is not being used towards the awakening of the national spirit, as it does over the entire civilized world. Thanks to its immediacy, music more than any other art can conquer the great masses by speaking to their fantasy and feeling, and if this happens continually and repeat-edly in a particular direction, then there is finally established also something in the listener's mind, upon which he can later, without knowing it, build further.[83]

This quotation also shows the importance Bjørnson assigned to music's role in the nation-building project; clearly, that role was too critical to let music remain in "foreigners' hands."

Once Edvard Grieg arrived on the scene, he, too, voiced many similar opinions on the potentially pernicious German influence. However, Grieg's statements actually reveal a move away from accusations of the influence only of German musicians in Norway and toward an indictment of the broader dangers of "foreign," and particularly German, artistic traditions. By exposing the risks behind foreign influences, he of course espoused a particular idea of what "German art" was. We see him characterizing (one might even say "caricaturing") German music in order to contrast it to his own view on Norwegian music.

One of the biggest problems, he claimed, was the extent to which German music could adversely affect Norwegian composers' art— particularly since most Norwegian musicians, perhaps up until the end of the nineteenth century, were trained, like Grieg, in Germany. He wrote in his diary in 1907,

> The Norwegian artistic nature still has the ability in itself to pro- duce naive, healthy, straightforward art, only so long as it is formed from out of the national temperament and not out of the foreign. And just now the Germans' music has gotten so far away from a healthy nature that their modern interpreters produce a pure cari- cature of their own masters. So badly has the Wagnerians' music… affected today's musicians, that they feel *all* music Wagnerian (I intentionally don't mean Wagner's music) in the sense that they can't create or reproduce four measures in the same tempo.[84]

Grieg takes a position here not unlike Pivoda's, in the claim that German music has gotten away from "healthy nature"—which in turn contradicts Wagner's own insistence that German music was a paragon of naturalness in relation to French music. However, Grieg does not apply his criticism to Wagner, which is why he specifies that he is not referring to Wagner's music but rather to *Wagnerians'* music, that is, to those German composers who took Wagner's innovations but (Grieg thought) used them to excess.

Interestingly, Grieg admitted that Norwegians, as "Northern Germans," had much in common with Germans and with their music, such as a certain "propensity toward melancholy and brooding."[85] However, for that very reason, Norwegian musicians must be careful with German music, in order to "clear and rinse their ideas from the one-sidedness that only loses itself in Germanness."[86] He wrote that "a Scandinavian is in his national character so gloomy and reflective that in truth he can find no counterweight in the exclusive study of German art."[87] To "rinse" oneself from German music—which had become merely a "school-art" that "smells like it does in a schoolroom or an anatomy chamber"—a Norwegian artist should look home, to "Nature," as an antidote.[88]

As with his accusation of German music becoming unnatural, Grieg turned Wagner's arguments on their head in another way as well. Grieg accused German musicians of being "one-sided" because they knew only the history of German music: they were so steeped in their own musical traditions that they never looked beyond them. Composers of other nationalities, Grieg argued, and particularly those from small countries, must have a "wider horizon" to appreciate the fruits of a variety of musical styles and traditions.[89] So, an excellent way to broaden one's horizons was to study the great musical traditions of France and Italy. In fact, one of Grieg's stated justifications for his government travel stipend in 1869 was to go to Italy to take the necessary remedy to an exclusive education of German music.

In an article on "French and German Music" published in *Le Figaro* in October 1900, Grieg elaborates on a definition of Norwegian music in relation to these two other traditions. As he did with his study of Italian music, Grieg here juxtaposes French music against the German. However, whereas Wagner used this juxtaposition to proclaim the worthlessness of French and Italian art, Grieg advocates it as a beneficial element of musical education. In the process, of course, he essentializes German, French, and Italian music, underlining the ways in which they are different from one another. In trying to establish boundaries among these national musics, he also advances an idea of what Norwegian music must be. French art, with "its light, free form, its transparent clarity, its euphony," will be the Norwegian musician's "salvation." This would be the necessary foil to the Norwegian's German inheritance, since Norwegians do not have "[the German] race's need to express itself in an expansive and exalted manner." Quite the contrary, he claims:

> We have always loved the short and brief, the clear and concise in expression, as is found in our sagas and which any traveler today can find amongst us. These characteristics are also the goal of our

artistic efforts. But with all our boundless admiration for German art's profundity, we cannot enthuse in the same degree over its modern manner of expression, which we often find ponderous and overloaded. The Nordic musician has, generally speaking, studied in Germany. One would thus believe that that land's immortal masterworks from its great classical period, with their pure lines and noble architecture, would serve as a lesson for him for his entire life. But alas! That period belongs to the past and youth seeks today's ideals with their merits—and mistakes. It is therefore painfully human that he gets intoxicated with German neo-romanticism's color orgies, and acquires its technical weight and vague lines, a ballast which later, when he must find expression for his individual and national particularity, is extremely difficult to cast overboard.[90]

As this citation shows, one of Grieg's reservations about German music was its present stylistic direction (again, identified with the "Wagnerians'" excesses), which earlier in his life he said "possesses no ability for a vigorous progress."[91] It is necessary to emphasize that Grieg did not reject German music completely, though. He fully acknowledged how much he had learned from it, writing, for example, that "No music and no musicians has [*sic*] gone to my heart like the German."[92]

However, as the long passage just cited makes clear, Grieg did think that "progress" in modern music could be attained by composers giving voice to "national particularity" in music. Yet this drive toward creating national styles in music seems to have antagonized German music critics, according to Grieg. A number of times in his correspondence, he complained about Germans' attitudes on national music, saying that according to Germans, "other nations are not allowed to write out of their national feeling."[93] Thus non-German nationalist composers often had to deal with resentment of their national music in Germany. That is how Grieg described Dvořák's reception in Germany, where he said that Germans could not digest Dvořák's nationality.[94] Looking back on his career, Grieg also complained of bad treatment: "In Germany critics treated me poorly because I didn't fit into the boxes they liked to put composers in. In Germany people like to say: 'Er norwegert!'"[95] This slur of "Norwegerei"—which must have been used against Grieg on more than one occasion—also provoked the following complaint:

> No one would permit himself to use as an insult descriptions like "Germanness" or "Germanism" [*Deutscherei*] of a German composer. But it is nonetheless a fact that German music critics take a distrustful and unsympathetic position not just towards Norwegian but indeed toward all national expressions in music *outside of Germany*. How narrow-minded and biased that is![96]

Grieg implies that Germans think that *all* music is really German music because so many of the greatest composers and masterpieces have come from German Europe. He said as much in a letter of 1889, originally written in English: "the great traditions of German music often make the German musicians and critic unjust in their judge of the works of foreign composers."[97] He suggests that the typical, intransigent German position is that any music that departs from "German" traditions thus is not really music, or at least is not really good music. Germans are so wrapped up in their own lofty tradition that they cannot—or will not—acknowledge other possible directions for art music.[98] This accusation echoes his statement, cited previously, about German "one-sidedness," and German composers' tendency not to look beyond their own musical traditions.

Grieg's reaction here becomes comprehensible in light of the severity of German critics' attacks on him, which target not just his art but also the idea of national music in general. These attacks are a kind of second-phase "Othering," since they come not from nationalist artists constructing difference in the national art, but rather from critics *reacting to* that art. These critics themselves, in their responses to the ideas of constructing difference, "Other" the nationalist composers who first advanced those ideas. The attacks have three different critical motivations. First, German critiques of national music are based on a perception that national music cannot be universal—indeed, that national musics are the rejection of universality in art. However, as we shall see, the criteria of universality in music are in fact *German* in origin. So, secondly, critiques of national music are often based on a perceived rejection of German musical forms. The third element in Germans' critiques is that national music is simply bad art, for the combination of reasons that it is particular rather than universal, and based on unworthy musical forms. In this way, German critics "Othered" non-German national musics, positing them as antithetical to the standards of high art—standards that had been elaborated by Germans but that were nonetheless portrayed as being universal rather than national. These critiques affected not just Grieg but a wide variety of nationalist composers; I focus specifically on German treatments of Norwegian and Czech music, however.

The fact is, as Grieg suggests previously, that German composers are almost never considered composers of national music. Somehow, by definition, German music is not national music. This attitude, Leon Plantinga says, is akin to the way nationalism from "the center" is typically ignored within the history of the Austrian Empire. The Germanic center of the Western Habsburg Empire occupied the position of power throughout the nineteenth century. The fact of this power has affected musicological and historiographical understandings, producing different conceptions of the music that is "in" (the music of the powerful center) versus music that is "out" (the music of the subordinated parts of the Empire). Thus "in our consideration of 'nationalism' as a force in the history of music and art we tend to limit our focus…to cultures of the powerless and the oppressed, to those where there is a longing to throw off rule from elsewhere and establish indigenous nations."[99] So, the artistic expressions of the "periphery" (Poles, Czechs, Hungarians, or, farther afield, Norwegians) are "national," while the art of the center (Germans, whether inside or outside the Habsburg lands) is not.[100]

In recent years, scholars have increasingly recognized the latent German bias of much previous musicological scholarship.[101] The roots of modern musicology, and hence of the scholarly understanding of national music, are firmly grounded in the evolution of music as an art form in the nineteenth century. The aesthetics of music in that century were largely a German concern: it was primarily Germans who advanced the major theoretical and philosophical conceptualizations of music that would come to dominate later understandings. Hence, German writers established the paradigms by which music was often measured. A major one of these paradigms was the idea of universality—and musicological practice, as its methodological underpinnings took shape in nineteenth-century Germany—encouraged the precise equation of *German* music with this universal ideal. While aspirations to universality in art are not restricted just to German artists (as we see in the next chapter), the obsessive privileging of this claim seems largely a product of German thinking.

Closely linked to the obsession with universality was the ostensible primacy of absolute music. This latter idea holds that music must not (and cannot) express anything "extramusical" like emotions, a story, or nationality. Absolute music was regarded by Germans not only as an achievement of German culture but in fact as the ultimate status that all music should aspire to. As Sanna Pederson has shown, though, "the idea of absolute music [did not become] the esthetic paradigm of German musical culture" but rather "the idea of German musical culture…became the paradigm of absolute music."[102] Despite its obviously localized and particular origin, German music became identified with absolute music—for which were made normative claims to universal applicability. Later commentators who were educated in this belief continued to propagate it. For example, Celia Applegate points to American musicologists writing in the 1940s who claimed that even when German musicians express "German traits" in music, these traits come across more as universal than as nationalistic. In fact, this trend is by no means dead: even a 1990 entry in the *New Oxford History of Music* treats nationalist music mostly in non-German terms.[103]

The identification of German music with universality is a surprisingly evident trend in nineteenth-century writing. This privileging consequently leads to criticism of music that is perceived as not attaining that standard. Nationality is viewed as incommensurate with universality (unless of course it is German nationality, which is inherently universal), and since universality is the requirement for art, nationality in art is wholly inappropriate. "Absoluteness" (identical in this sense with universality) is again the measuring stick, since "nonmusical" features such as nationality only detract from absoluteness. In this vein Philip Hale, an American critic, criticized Grieg's music:

> It is doubtful whether that which is first of all of national inter-est can ever appeal to the world as a musical masterpiece. We do not first think when listening to the great acknowledged masters of the nationality of these composers; if this thought occurs it is by way of digression, completely secondary...The nationality of Grieg is forced upon the attention by the man, his music and his friends.[104]

Critics of Grieg often perceived him as rejecting these absolute/univer-sal standards and hence pursuing only the "particular"—which takes the form of the national—in his art. In Hale's formulation, since national music is not universal, it cannot speak to a wider human audience; as a result, it fails to meet the aspirations of true art.

Similarly, the German critic Riemann said of Grieg that he "imposed on himself the limitation of national characteristics, and instead of speak-ing the musical world language preferred more or less a local dialect."[105] What Riemann means by "the musical world language" is, of course, really the Germanic tradition of music. Grieg, though, was not the only composer to be "demerited" for not speaking this musical world language. His colleague and friend Johan Svendsen also provoked a German critic's dislike of his *Second Symphony* on the same measure. Eduard Bernsdorf, who seems to have been a particularly cantankerous individual, objected to the national features in the symphony, writing that "[i]t interests us not in the slightest to be constantly reminded that a composer has been born and raised in some land that he is now attempting to reflect in music."[106] Besides his complaint that music should not express something "extra-neous" like nationality, Bernsdorf also particularly objected to national expression in forms such as the symphony and the sonata—forms which were exalted, above all, in the German musical tradition.

With these forms held out as ideals, as, in a sense, the "highest" musical structures, German critics established another standard by which nationalist composers who dared to work in these forms could be condemned. Bernsdorf, writing of Grieg's sonata for violin and piano (Opus 13) and his string quartet in G minor, spewed venom on the composer and his works:

> We have felt only displeasure and repugnance toward all the boorish and absurd stuff that is gathered together under the guise of a Norwegian national stamp, toward the mediocrity of the compositional inventiveness that lurks behind the rough-hewn and exaggerated Norwegian exterior (something non-Norwegians must accept in good faith), and toward the lack of any talent for structure and development—indeed, the lack of any ability whatsoever to create—adequately, without patchwork—a continuous whole in a movement (as here in the sonata and the quartet).[107]

As we will see later, composers such as Grieg, who seemed largely to eschew the classical forms, were especially liable to criticism. Alternatively, however, composers who were perceived as adhering to these forms *could* be praised, even "in spite of" their nationality. In her book on music criticism in Vienna in the years 1896–1897, Sandra McColl provides a number of illuminating quotes from critics who were judging music on the basis of German norms. These norms, she says, were the musical "yardstick by which all other music ought to be measured."[108] Behind this idea is the belief, apparently widely shared by the Viennese critics she examines, that "the successful construction of large-scale musical works" was a feature of "Austro-Germanic classical heritage."[109] That the perfection of these formal structures was an achievement particularly of German civilization is a claim also advanced by Wagner.[110] With this as the "yardstick" for achievement, then, national musics were acceptable in large part to the extent that they "measured up" according to these formal standards.

Thus one critic, Heinrich Schenker, regarded Smetana's and Dvořák's works as "successful" because of their reliance on German form:

> Smetana and Dvořák...succeeded more happily in bringing their national music into a system than did the Russian artist

[Tchaikovsky]. The system is naturally that of German art, for this is best able to solve the principal problem of the logical development of a piece of music. So it was first of all Smetana, who with his brilliant predisposition towards the classical simply applied the German system to Bohemian music, and because he understood the German logic of music as it were in its necessity and sensibleness as no other, it was granted to him to present Bohemian music in a perfection which will not be surpassed. Since then Dvořák has also succeeded, always with the German system as a basis, in nearly every field of composition, in the naturalization of his national tone. His chamber music in particular, with all its Bohemian roots, is blessed with such outstanding German virtues that it justly seems to us most highly attractive.[111]

This sort of German "aesthetic chauvinism," McColl suggests, corresponded to similar views held by other prominent writers, Eduard Hanslick among them. It is interesting, though, that whereas Smetana's *Dalibor* was perceived by some in the Czech lands (such as Pivoda) as formless in a Wagnerian way, later Viennese critics praised *Dalibor* precisely for its form. One commended the opera's "German classical form," indicating that the form is what lent the piece its greatness.[112] Making the link between *Dalibor* and its ostensible German influences explicit, the critic Helm held both Smetana and his opera in high regard precisely because they were indebted to Wagner.[113] When nationalist, non-German composers were not perceived as rejecting the "universal" German forms, then, their music was more acceptable, even potentially attaining greatness, albeit thanks in large part to that form.

Ironically for these praiseworthy comments about Smetana, however, "German classical form" seems to have meant relatively little to him. Apart from his two string quartets, his one completed symphony, and a handful of piano pieces, there are few works in his output that are easily identifiable as corresponding to German classical form. Even in his operas, while the influence of Wagner is indisputable, other models can be detected, such as that of French grand opera in *The Brandenburgers in Bohemia*. Erismann suggests, in fact, that after Smetana's first, early symphony, he refused to work any more in that form, precisely because he considered it German.[114] While direct evidence for such a claim is lacking, it is nonetheless clear that many Czech composers (Dvořák not among them) in the last decades of the nineteenth century saw the symphony form as "outmoded" and inappropriate for a Czech national music. Though Grieg also never directly voiced any rejection of German forms, his output, too, is fairly sparse in this area. His one symphony, the piano concerto, the three violin sonatas, and the one completed string quartet are his principle compositions in classical form.

Often, the critiques of national composers unite these aforementioned strands—the perceived rejection of "universality" and the supremacy of German form—into a more wide-ranging attack on the products of non-German national musical traditions in general. These sorts of critiques do not necessarily appeal to any higher standard of universality or the like—they often just judge national music as bad music in itself. Few critics could top the bile of Martin Röder in this regard, who in an 1884 biographical sketch of Grieg in the *Neue Musik-Zeitung* took the opportunity to lambaste the entire idea of national music:

> Those lands in particular that don't have the prophets [of universal music, apparently] in their midst wipe off as much as possible the accepted universal artistic expression, and they seek with all violence to present us with a kind of degenerated art [*Afterkunst*], in which the respective national element steps strongly into the foreground. This moment is usually the mask for their own natural poverty of invention—though thereby for a certain time-span they never fail in their goal of flinging sand in the eyes of the honorable public.
>
> In music this phenomenon, more than all the other arts…has become most especially prominent.
>
> We find almost regularly that in other lands (and since for longer than a century the belief in German music as the standard-bearer holds, we can refer strictly to our neighboring lands), which as a result of a certain music-chauvinism will not lend the respective ruling prophets their ears, [artists] declare the national side of art in the most purely outward musical work. One endeavors thereby to give artistic practice something new, unusual, in a

certain sense also ethical, in that one creates an art form on the basis of folk songs and the characteristic melodic, harmonic, and especially rhythmically colored national tunes, so that they will astonish in the first moment. Their right to existence however is highly doubtful, when one judges artistic practice from an ideal standpoint.

Namely the so-called Nordic and Slavic art has in this area a lot on its conscience...And from there stems the rather rancid after-taste that the word "Nordic school" has in our ideal artistic life.[115]

Röder here clearly identifies German music as the universal "artistic expression" to which all music must thus aspire. However, the fact that he perceives national music as rejecting this universal aspiration means that national music has no real right to existence. This is especially so given that such national music is usually poor in its "artistic practice," when judged from an "ideal" perspective. However, this "ideal" is, of course, the product of German musical traditions. What makes this attack so unintentionally laughable is that while Röder derides the "chauvinism" of national music, his own tirade is just as chauvinistic, based as it is on the privileging of German aesthetic standards.

## Conclusion

Two particular trends in "Othering" and boundary drawing become clear in the discourse on constructing difference in national music. First, nationalist artists seek to create distinctions on the basis of certain aesthetic criteria. This is the elaboration of cultural differentiae that will permit observers (whether in the "in group" or the "out group") to recognize a particular culture as belonging to a specific group. Second, it is apparent that sometimes there is a normative component to the aesthetic differentiation, and this normative component is the negative distinction inherent in the concept of "Othering." In these two types of claims, we see a difference between those who insist on a "pure" national music without foreign influences (such as Wagner and Pivoda), and those who are willing to acknowledge or learn from "foreign" models (Smetana,

Hostinský, Grieg). The former seek to draw harder boundaries, while the latter are comfortable with softer boundaries between the relevant national artistic traditions.

To a certain extent, then, this discourse evinces a very familiar language seen in many nationalist movements about subjugation and resistance. Nationalist intellectuals typically claim that their nation is being threatened in some way, often directly repressed by another nation. A classic example is Wagner's complaints about the hegemony of French music. Yet the discourse on national music actually represents an unusual and quite ironic instantiation of the subjugation and resistance theme. That is because German nationalists' protests against the French eventually ricochet when later nationalists from other movements turn these very same protests *against* German culture. The Czech and Norwegian cases are only two of many where later nationalist composers attack German music's hegemony; this theme in fact becomes a nearly indispensable weapon for most non-German nationalists.[116] Having "conquered" French music by the second half of the nineteenth century, and arrogating to itself status as the one true universal music, German music then becomes viewed as the oppressor of other national musics. So, this is a striking example of non-German nationalists taking up German nationalists' discursive strategies but inverting the target of the attacks.

Finally, I want to offer a few ideas locating the practice of "Othering" and boundary making within the history of nineteenth-century nation-building movements more broadly. These practices in the realm of high culture are closely associated with the rise of the nation form, specifically with the production of a vertically integrated versus a horizontally integrated culture, which is one of the goals of the nationalist movement. In relation to "Othering" and boundary creation, we see in the nineteenth century a move away from horizontal cultures that are shared transnationally among elites to a vertical culture that is shared *intra*nationally among the national populace. This is the production of distinct national cultures.

The "Othering"/boundary construction dynamic enters here as a means of establishing the boundaries of this vertical culture—that is, as a means to establish boundaries *between* national cultures. Admittedly, the move away from transnational cultures is not a perfect one, since it could well be argued that cosmopolitan elites such as Wagner, Smetana, and Grieg may have more truly "shared" a culture with one another than they did with the respective peasant populations of their countries. National integration across social divides, and across high and low cultures, was of course not complete—but it was the ideal of the nationalist movement. This is the ideal of the unified, vertically integrated culture that is differentiated from other national cultures. "Othering"/boundary construction is part of the process of creating this differentiation.

In turn, the process of creating differentiation refers back to the idea of the fetishization of difference that I mentioned earlier. The fetishization of specifically *national* difference is, naturally, also a product of a particular historical moment. For instance, did J. S. Bach espouse the same kinds of ideas on the distinctions between national arts that Wagner would, one hundred years later? Of course he did not. Bach's life preceded the rise of the nation form. He did perceive differences in communal cultural expression—for instance, he wrote pieces in what he called "French" or "English" style. He assuredly thought that different groups expressed themselves differently. Some idea of communal stereotypes and distinctive communal cultures ("the Italians are loud and create happy music," for instance) have been around for ages. However, the *nation* idea is absent in these earlier conceptions. That means that Bach did not share the same conception of a culture, vertically integrated across social boundaries, that identifiably belonged to a unified nation. Wagner, in contrast, not only perceives differences in communal cultural expression but also elevates that difference to the status of a norm. Whereas for Bach, communal cultural expressions simply *are* different, for Wagner, they *must* and *should* be different. Cultural expressions become indispensable in defining the nation and its characteristics. In this way, difference itself becomes positively valued, as both the condition and vehicle for a distinctive national art.

## Endnotes

1. Eley and Suny, *Becoming National*, 25.
2. See Frederik Barth, "Introduction," *Ethnic Groups and Boundaries*, ed. Frederik Barth (Boston: Little, Brown and Company, 1969), 1–31.
3. Prasenjit Duara, "Historicizing National Identity, or Who Imagines What and When," in Eley and Suny, *Becoming National*, 151–178. *See esp.* pp. 168–169.
4. Ibid., 169.
5. See Barth, *Ethnic Groups and Boundaries*, 9.
6. Michael Jeismann, " 'Feind' und 'Vaterland' in der frühen deutschen Nationalbewegung 1806–1815" in Ulrich Herrmann, ed. *Volk—Nation—Vaterland* (Hamburg: Felix Meiner Verlag, 1996), 279–290.
7. Johannes Willms, *Nationalismus ohne Nation* (Düsseldorf: Claassen, 1983), 115.
8. Jeismann, " 'Feind' und 'Vaterland' in der frühen deutschen Nationalbewegung 1806–1815," 285.
9. Dieter Düding, *Organisierter gesellschaftlicher Nationalismus in Deutschland (1808–1847)* (München: R. Oldenbourg Verlag, 1984).
10. Dieter Düding, "The Nineteenth-Century German Nationalist Movement as a Movement of Societies" in *Nation-Building in Central Europe*, ed. Hagen Schulze (Leamington Spa: Berg Publishers, 1987), 19–49. *See esp.* p. 29.
11. Wagner, *Das Braune Buch*, 85.
12. Wagner, "Ausführungen zu 'Religion und Kunst,' 1; 'Erkenne dich selbst'." *See esp.* p. 269.
13. Wagner, *Deutsche Kunst und deutsche Politik*, 34.
14. Ibid., 32.
15. Wagner, *Oper und Drama*, 308.
16. Ibid., 264.
17. Wagner, *Oper und Drama*, Parts II and III, 18; *Zukunftsmusik*, 91.
18. Wagner, *Bericht an Ludwig II*, 5.
19. Wagner, *Beethoven*, 62.
20. Wagner, *Über deutsches Musikwesen*, 85.
21. Wagner, *Deutsche Kunst und deutsche Politik*, 94.
22. See his letter to Robert Schumann, in Wagner, *Briefen* Band I, 577.
23. Wagner, *Deutsche Kunst und deutsche Politik*, 94.
24. Ibid., 34.

25. Wagner, " 'Le Freischutz'—Bericht nach Deutschland," *passim.*
26. See Wagner, "Der Freischütz—an das Pariser Publikum."
27. Wagner, *Beethoven,* 113.
28. Gregor-Dellin, *Richard Wagner,* 69.
29. Cosima Wagner, *Tagebücher* 1878–1880, 289.
30. Ibid., 54.
31. Ibid., *Tagebücher* 1869–1872, 258.
32. Wagner, *Das Judentum in der Musik,* 66.
33. Ibid., 85.
34. Ibid., 73.
35. Ibid., 68.
36. Ibid., 71.
37. Ibid., 76.
38. Ibid., 78.
39. Ibid., 71.
40. Wagner, *Zukunftsmusik,* 93.
41. Wagner, "Autobiographische Skizze," 10.
42. Wagner, *Oper und Drama,* Parts II and III, 211.
43. Wagner, "Zur Einführung in das Jahr 1880," 30.
44. Wagner, *Über deutsches Musikwesen,* 83.
45. Wagner, *Das Braune Buch,* 85–86.
46. Karel Havlíček Borovský, *Lid a národ* (Praha: Melantrich, 1981).
47. Jan Křen, *Konfliktní společnosti: Češi a Němci 1780–1918* (Praha: Academia, 1990).
48. Vladimír Macura, "Paradox obrozenského divadla" in *Divadlo v české kultuře 19. století* (Praha: Národní galerie, 1985), 36–43.
49. Bartoš, *Bedřich Smetana: Letters and Reminiscences,* 114.
50. See, for example, BS: J. Valentin, January 24, 1864. MČH #2117.
51. Marta Ottlová and Milan Pospíšil, *Bedřich Smetana a jeho doba* (Praha: Nakladatelství Lidové noviny, 1997), 30–31.
52. Bartoš, *Bedřich Smetana: Letters and Reminiscences,*250.
53. Ibid., 127.
54. Ibid., 130.
55. Ibid., 65. Italics in the original.
56. BS: Charlotta Valentin, approx. November 4, 1874. MČH #2122.
57. Bartoš, *Bedřich Smetana: Letters and Reminiscences,* 278.
58. Ottlová and Pospíšil, *Bedřich Smetana a jeho doba,* 33.
59. Otakar Hostinský, *Bedřich Smetana a jeho boj o moderní českou hudbu* (Praha: Jan Laichter, 1941).

60. BS: František Pivoda, June 16, 1870. MČH #273.
61. I explain the *prostonárodní* idea in the chapter on folk sources in the national music.
62. Hostinský, *Bedřich Smetana a jeho boj o moderní českou hudbu*, 196. We have to beware of Hostinský's impartiality because of his recognized status as a champion of Smetana. Hostinský was also the founder of Czech musicological scholarship, and his biases in favor of Smetana tended to inform the subsequent direction of Czech musicology. Nonetheless, Hostinský was a serious, intelligent writer, and no crackpot, so his work still represents a valuable historical document of the intellectual/aesthetic concerns of his time.
63. Ottlová and Pospíšil, *Bedřich Smetana a jeho doba*, 105.
64. Lebl and Ludvová, "Nová doba (1860–1938)," 419; Hostinský, *Bedřich Smetana a jeho boj o moderní českou hudbu*, 150.
65. This is the gist of a Pivoda article of 1870 cited in Hostinský, *Bedřich Smetana a jeho boj o moderní českou hudbu*, 180.
66. From the article of 1870, cited in Hostinský, *Bedřich Smetana a jeho boj o moderní českou hudbu*, 186–187.
67. Bartoš, *Smetana ve vzpomínkách a dopisech*, 112.
68. Ottlová and Pospíšil, *Bedřich Smetana a jeho doba*, 102.
69. Ibid., 103.
70. Ibid., 100.
71. Hostinský, *Bedřich Smetana a jeho boj o moderní českou hudbu*, 153.
72. Ibid., 159.
73. Ibid., 152.
74. Ibid., 159.
75. Ibid., 150–151.
76. Ibid., 157.
77. Bartoš, *Smetana ve vzpomínkách a dopisech*, 128.
78. Ottlová and Pospíšil make this point, *Bedřich Smetana a jeho doba*, 107.
79. Herresthal, *Med spark i gulvet og quinter i bassen*, 36.
80. Roverud, *Et Blik paa Musikens Tilstand i Norge*, 3.
81. Herresthal, *Med spark i gulvet og quinter i bassen*, 140.
82. Ibid., 144.
83. Ibid., 146.
84. Grieg, *Dagbøker*, 176.
85. Gaukstad, *Edvard Grieg*, 184.
86. Grieg, *Brev* Bind I, 479.
87. Ibid.

88. Ibid., 357.
89. Grieg, *Dagbøker*, 115.
90. All aforementioned citations in this paragraph are from Gaukstad, *Edvard Grieg*, 184.
91. Grieg, *Brev* Bind I, 246.
92. Ibid., 111. Originally written in English.
93. Ibid., 623.
94. Gaukstad, *Edvard Grieg*, 208.
95. Benestad and Schjelderup-Ebbe, *Edvard Grieg: mennesket og kunstneren* (1990), 338. "Er norwegert!" is basically untranslatable, but the sense of it is, "He's doing that Norwegian thing again!" This insult seems to be predicated on the idea that if Grieg is making music strongly Norwegian in character, then he is just playing around, indulging in flashy national colors, and not being "serious." If he is "doing that Norwegian thing," he is not making true art.
96. Grieg, *Brev* Bind II, 529.
97. Grieg, *Brev* Bind I, 111.
98. This is the gist of his comment in the letter to Finck, Gaukstad, *Edvard Grieg*, 50.
99. Leon Plantinga, "Dvořák and the Meaning of Nationalism in Music" in *Rethinking Dvořák: Views from Five Countries*, ed. David Beveridge (Oxford: Clarendon Press, 1996), 117–124. *See esp.* p. 117.
100. Dahlhaus, *Between Romanticism and Modernism*, also makes this point.
101. See Celia Applegate, "What Is German Music? Reflections on the Role of Art in the Creation of the Nation," *German Studies Review* vol. XV (winter 1992): 21–32.
102. Cited in Celia Applegate, "How German Is It? Nationalism and the Idea of Serious Music in the Early Nineteenth Century," *19th-Century Music* XXI/3 (spring 1998): 278–279.
103. See Applegate, "What Is German Music? Reflections on the Role of Art in the Creation of the Nation," 275–276. She refers to Robert Pascall's entry "Romanticism, 1830–1890" in volume IX of the *New Oxford History*.
104. Philip Hale, "Edvard Grieg," in *Famous Composers and Their Works*, ed. John Knowles Paine, Theodore Thomas, Karl Klavser (Boston: J. B. Millet Company, 1892). *See esp.* pp. 835–836.
105. Cited in Henry T. Finck, "Grieg's Influence on the Musical World," *The Musician* vol. III, no. 7 (July 1898): 191.
106. Finn Benestad and Dag Schjelderup-Ebbe, *Johan Svendsen: mennesket og kunstneren* (Oslo: Aschehoug, 1990).

107. From an 1878 review in the journal *Signale*; cited in Benestad and Schjelderup-Ebbe, *Edvard Grieg: The Man and the Artist* (1988), 221.
108. Sandra McColl, *Music Criticism in Vienna 1896–1897* (Oxford: Clarendon Press, 1996), 107.
109. Ibid., 171.
110. See Wagner, *Die deutsche Oper*, 9.
111. Cited in McColl, 176.
112. Cited in ibid., 171.
113. Ibid., 95.
114. Guy Erismann, *Smetana l'éveilleur* (Arles: Actes Sud, 1993).
115. Martin Röder, "Edvard Grieg. Biographische Skizze," *Neue Musik-Zeitung*, no. 11 (June 1, 1884) fünfter Jahrgang.
116. See Robert Stradling and Meirion Hughes, *The English Musical Renaissance 1860–1940* (London: Routledge, 1993) for an excellent account of this theme in the English discourse; and Victor I. Seroff, *The Mighty Five: The Cradle of Russian National Music* (New York: Allen, Towne & Heath, 1948) for a less in-depth consideration of the Russian case.

## CHAPTER 5

# UNIVERSALITY AND THE NATIONAL MUSIC'S PLACE IN THE WORLD

Nationalists invariably insist that their nation's culture must be "its own," that each culture must be unique to each nation. Yet this claim does not automatically presuppose the rejection of outside influences on that culture or national identity. Indeed, the particularistic, narcissistic gaze of nationalism does not preclude aspirations to *transcending* the nation, of attaining something that is conceived as universal. So, where the previous chapter investigated how nationalist artists seek to create boundaries, this chapter will show how nationalists are also concerned with transcending them, to be both national and *inter*national at the same time. How do nationalists try to have it both ways? How do nationalism and cosmopolitaneity both conflict and coincide? How and why does nationalism reject universal transcending authority but itself claim universality? These are the questions that we will examine through the discourse of Wagner, Smetana, and Grieg.

These three composers do have an aspiration and in a sense an audience beyond that of their own nations—they are aiming at the world. They demonstrate that there are international claims to nationalism, that nation building is not entirely an inward-looking process. These nationalist artists' method of navigating the tensions between nationalism and cosmopolitaneity is through the principles of the universality of art, of art that springs from a national source but that goes out to enrich the whole world. Through their ambitions to create great, universal art, Grieg, Smetana, and Wagner did hold to a value that they thought transcended nationality. By adhering to cosmopolitan standards of what makes art "great," an artwork could be both national and universal.

Before we turn to the analysis of their discourse, however, I need first to explain what I mean by universality and cosmopolitaneity. Universality, obviously enough, is some value that surpasses the national, that is conceived as applying equally and eternally to all of humanity. A universal is a truth that is absolute, valid regardless of the particularistic truths or values that individual nations may claim for themselves. As for cosmopolitaneity, it is associated with universality in part through nationalists' discourse and also in part because these ideas do have deep conceptual affinities. They both imply a transcending of particularity. Amanda Anderson has provided a useful definition of what it means to be cosmopolitan: "In general, cosmopolitanism endorses reflective distance from one's cultural affiliations, a broad understanding of other cultures and customs, and a belief in universal humanity. The relative weight assigned to these three constitutive elements can vary, as can the cultural identities against which 'reflective distance' is defined."[1] Cosmopolitanism is sometimes accused of entailing the complete absence of nationality, of any belonging or "roots." However, being cosmopolitan does not necessarily mean a detachment from one's roots. Kwame Anthony Appiah and others have argued for a "rooted cosmopolitanism," by which an individual will belong to the wide world but still remain "attached to a home of her own, with its own cultural particularities...taking pleasure from the presence of other, different, places that are home to other, different, people."[2] In fact, this is the very view that Grieg and other "cosmopolitan patriots" (Appiah's term) espoused already in the nine- teenth century, as we shall see.

Nationalism has often been regarded as the antithesis of universality and cosmopolitaneity. When equated with chauvinism, nationalism is typically assumed to demand a blind favoring of one's own commu- nal group at the expense of other, broader, concerns. Many writers, in fact, argue that as an ideology, nationalism arose historically in oppo- sition to supranational creeds and cultures. Isaiah Berlin, for instance, describes the growth of nationalism as a resistance to various forms of what he calls universalism, such as Roman law, papal authority, natural law, "and other claims of supranational authority."[3] Historically speak- ing, the rise of nations does indeed put an end to what one might call the "universalism" of earlier eras such as the Middle Ages, when there truly was "one" religion and one elite language. As an opposition to universal truth, the idea of the nation engenders the claim that no authority other than that of the nation itself should be recognized, Berlin says:

> There is no over-arching criterion or standard, in terms of which the various values of the lives, attributes, aspirations, of differ- ent national groups can be ordered, for such a standard would be super-national, not itself immanent in, part and parcel of, a given social organism, but deriving its validity from some source outside the life of a particular society—a universal stan- dard, as natural law or natural justice are conceived by those who believe in them.[4]

This is a view that posits nationalism as a historical reaction against the ostensibly universal values of the Enlightenment. Where the En- lightenment (particularly in France and England) trumpeted the equal- ity of all men, with unity as the ideal of humanity, nationalism instead exalts diversity and the organic, metaphysical bond to a sort of national/ tribal community. Elie Kedourie is most famous for advancing this char- acterization of nationalism as based on irrationality and emotion versus the Enlightenment's reason and intellect.[5] Many scholars, though, have also pointed to Herder as fathering the cult of diversity, rejecting the "unnatural" cosmopolitanism of the so-called "Age of Reason."[6] It is often alleged that the spread of nationalism in the nineteenth century historically negates an earlier cosmopolitan ethos, as the world becomes divided into vertically integrated national societies.[7]

This account of nationalism is not purely the creation of scholars, of course. Nationalists themselves also sometimes have seen nationalism and cosmopolitanism as incommensurable. Certainly a critical component of nationalist discourse has always been the need to build up a particularistic, unique identity for "the nation's" people—an identity, usually, that is free from foreign influence. In the realm of the national art, Wagner lambasted the cosmopolitanism of the French and the Jews, and Smetana and like-minded Czech nationalists also criticized "cosmopolitan" national styles, as we have seen. Their complaint was against music (and composers) who were not rooted somewhere, in some particular, "natural" Volk style. So, we do see in the discourse on creating a national culture some kind of resistance to "supranational" authority of the sort that Berlin refers to. Nationalist artists rebelled against the idea of a homogeneous, monolithic, one-size-fits-all aesthetic or artistic style. They obviously desired to create individual "national" styles that would be grounded in some unique and uniquely identifiable brand of cultural expression. Such national styles were seen as an antidote to any sort of cosmopolitan, and thereby "non-national," artistic style.

However, this antinomious view of nationalism and universality/cosmopolitaneity is much too blunt, failing to capture the intricate relationship between these ideas. Bruce Robbins does well to caution against the "overly simple binary of universal and particular."[8] Nationalist artists' aspiration to be both national and universal is one prime example that disproves this supposed incommensurability. In fact, for many nationalists, not only were nationalism and cosmopolitaneity not mutually exclusive, but particularism was *the vehicle* for achieving universality. Nations are part of a greater whole, "the body parts of humanity" as one nineteenth-century German writer phrased it.[9] In a passage from his *The Duties of Man*, Mazzini passionately formulated how national particularity is a step toward a more universal goal:

> God gave [the means of working for the moral improvement, the progress, of humanity] when he gave you a country, when, like a wise overseer of labor, who distributes the different parts of work according to the capacity of workmen, he divided Humanity into distinct groups upon the face of our globe, and thus planted the seeds of nations…Without Country you have neither name, token, voice, nor rights, no admission as brothers into the fellowship of Peoples…In labouring according to the true principles for our Country we are labouring for Humanity; our Country is the fulcrum of the lever which we have to wield for the common good…Before *associating* ourselves with the Nations which compose Humanity we must exist as a Nation.[10]

The appeal to particularity in creating a distinct national community or culture is not an appeal purely to difference for its own sake—there is also an appeal to a "higher" standard, one that transcends nationality and applies to all of humanity. Nationalism, as Mazzini suggests, is not just about group distinction. Rather, it is a condition for membership in human society at large.

In much the same way, nationality could be the criterion for art's place in the world. Three broad themes appear in this discourse, which I have termed prestige, dissemination, and universality. I explain these themes in more detail at the beginning of each relevant section. Briefly, however, prestige refers to the quest for status for the national culture, to assure it an acknowledged, respected place on the world stage with the cultures of other nations. Dissemination deals with how nationalist composers sought to gain for their works an audience beyond their nation's boundaries. This was a means of spreading the national culture abroad precisely so it would achieve the prestige that these artists thought it was due. The idea of universality I have already explained; it comes last because, in an important way, it is the ultimate goal of the drives for prestige and dissemination. All three themes show nationalists wanting to transcend the nation, and each theme assumes a varying importance for each of my three composers. However, for all of them, the universality of art is what finally grants nationalist music its transcendence.

## PRESTIGE

The implicit, and sometimes explicit assumption behind the call for a prestigious national art was that there existed a kind of "race" between nations to produce great but distinctively national cultures. The process of national particularization in nineteenth-century Europe was viewed by many nationalists as a kind of "competition among nations."[11] No nationalist wanted his people's culture not to be represented on the world stage. The goal was to develop a national culture that would be the equal of the great *Kulturnationen* (usually conceived as France, England, and Italy, and later, Germany). As one Czech writer urged his fellow poets and playwrights, every nation had to assure itself of a "place on Parnassus."[12] Successive waves of nationalist movements looked to what were considered to be previously established, prestigious national cultures; the Germans compared themselves to the French, the Czechs to the Germans, and so on.

In music, this "competition" took a somewhat special form, since over the course of the century a distinctive national style became an important vehicle for international recognition. As I discussed in the Introduction, folk traditions in music carried a hint of the "exotic" with them. They constituted an extremely useful part of the palette for the artist striving for originality, and so nationality was regarded as a major contributor to artistic value. Nationalistic artworks, then, were very often created with an eye to how they would compare to the products of other national cultures. There was an audience beyond the artist's home nation, and the artwork was to be measured by international standards. In this way, the products of the national culture, though created for the artist's nation, were also meant to be, in a sense, cosmopolitan by contributing to an international high culture.

These composers' quests for prestige also involved transcending their nations because they looked outside of their nations' borders for models. The idea of an international standard by which the national culture must be judged encouraged nationalists to create something that would be measured not exclusively on its value to the home nation. Thus their cultural products had to have a value even to "foreigners," since others besides the national citizens would be appreciating or consuming what the nationalist artists created. Moreover, the very fact that widespread international models—such as music festivals or national theaters—were employed in the effort to create a prestigious national art means that the national culture was unavoidably impregnated with a certain cosmopolitanism. These models were imported from "outside," after all. By aspiring to have their "own" theater, though, nationalists did recognize an authority outside of their nation, since it was the example of how these theaters or festivals promoted national cultures in other lands that motivated the nationalists' desire for their own versions in the first place.

Surprising though it may seem—given the fame that many German writers, composers, and painters enjoy today—in the earlier nineteenth century, German patriots worried about the place of German art in the world. Certainly the likes of Goethe, Schiller, Bach, and Beethoven were often seen as having already achieved renown for German culture. Yet nonetheless, many people, inside and outside of Germany, regarded it as a "delayed nation" that needed to catch up with others both politically and culturally. German nation builders were predictably concerned that a German national high culture had to be "competitive" with the established national cultures, of equal value and quality. For Wagner, France and Italy were the chief competitors, as these were the two lands whose musical styles largely determined the tastes of the opera-going public in his day. Throughout his writings, he laments repeatedly the fact that the French and Italians have their "own" opera, and hence they and their music are "already" national.[13] To compete, then, Wagner called for the Germans to develop their own "cultural institution" such as the French and Italians have.[14] Their own institution would free the Germans from the hegemony of French and Italian opera music.

Wagner's complaint is neatly summed up by a quotation from his report to King Ludwig II, in which he proposed the creation of a German national theater:

> The peculiarities of French taste, together with the collaboration of the greatest artistic powers of all nations, founded the style of the Parisian institution [meaning the Opéra de Paris] towards the end of the last and the beginning of this century. From there the taste of almost all European nations has been ruled up until today. The Germans also have not escaped the mere copying and imitation of the stylistic characteristics of the Italians and French, namely in regard to the current performance style in the theater.[15]

Rather than merely imitating French and Italians, as the Germans presently do, Wagner argues for the establishment of a style that would be uniquely German. With a truly German national art, the Germans would finally deserve the place they claim for themselves "at the peak" of European peoples.[16] Wagner's argumentation here follows a pattern established by earlier figures such as Schiller, Lessing, and Klopstock, who had all, with much the same motives, called for the establishment of a German national theater.

As the report to Ludwig II demonstrates, Wagner had assigned *himself* this task of creating a national theater. The specific plan that he outlined in this document to the king was not realized, but Wagner's goal did come to fruition in the form of his Bayreuth theater. As I have shown in the second chapter, Bayreuth embodies virtually all of Wagner's ambitions for a German national art. Bayreuth, then, was the ultimate stepping stone to the realm of prestige that the French and Italians enjoyed with their own national arts. Bayreuth would be the vanguard of a German art that could compete with the more established national traditions. However, Wagner was not interested simply in attaining equality with the French and Italians. In fact, his idea of prestige for the Germans explicitly poses the Germans *above* the French and Italians. The Germans, as a Volk, are not merely equally endowed artistically as the French, but are actually superior to them. Hence, although French was the hegemonic culture of educated European society, that culture was in fact degenerate.

However, given this French hegemony, Wagner aspired for the Germans to become the "equally powerfully armed rival" to the cultural might of Paris.[17] Germany's mission was to save the world from French culture. Wagner's goal was thus not only to win recognition and prestige for German art, and a place for it at the highest levels of European culture, but actually for German culture to stand supreme among the other "culture lands." This superiority complex is an integral element of the messianic impulses within German nationalism and Wagner's own thought, which we will investigate in more detail later.

For the Czechs—self-consciously one of the "small nations" of Europe—the theme of prestige took a very prominent place within nationalist discourse. Whereas even early German patriots could exalt the achievements of Goethe and Beethoven, up into the 1850s, Czechs had virtually no works of high art to point to as unique products of their nation. Czech nationalist intellectuals may have been particularly sensitive about prestige because they, like all educated Czechs, were very often steeped in the "colossus" of German culture. They seem to have felt an especially strong desire to demonstrate that a Czech art could stack up in every way to the German or that of the other large countries. It was not just the Germans with whom the Czechs were in competition, however. In 1826 Palacký wrote about the Czech language:

> At a time when nearly all second-class peoples in Europe are, so to speak, vying for their so recently neglected national languages as if to the most holy palladium of their existence, endeavoring to protect them through impressive, expensively-founded institutions (one need only think of the Poles, Magyars, Netherlanders, Danes, and Finns among others), it would not be proper for the Czechs to be left behind in their own cause.[18]

Palacký is obviously urging the Czechs to attain the same goals (the establishment of language institutes) that other "second-class" nations had. He did not want the Czechs to remain "second class" in the sense of falling behind their neighbors in national development.

As in the case of Germany and Wagner, a principal focus of the drive for a prestigious Czech culture was a national theater. Both the rationale and the exhortations that nationalists employed in the national theater project rely heavily on the ideas of competition and status, as a pronouncement of 1850 from the Committee to Build a National Theater illustrates:

> Since we have been delayed and retarded by fate in our national development, we must now exert our full efforts in order to catch up with others, and to present a good example to all who will, perhaps, follow us and attempt to reach the same goal...The Czech patriot can now view with inspiration and hope the progress which our fresh national spirit has already made in education and culture...Yet we are still lacking something without which Europe will hardly regard us as an educated and cultured nation. We mean an independent *national theater*—that school of both life and morals in which many strands of culture and education are intertwined to form a living wreath which will testify to our national culture before the world, and which will strike new sparks and plant new seeds of noble aspirations and undertakings.[19]

Only a prestigious theater would ensure the Czechs "national equality with the other nations within the Empire," the Committee added.[20] In addition to the themes of competition and status, this citation also clearly enunciates the idea that a national culture must stand before the world, looking inward but also directed outward. Part of the program for a national theater naturally was to present Czech works of art—and to this end a competition was held in the early 1860s. This competition, which has become known after the name of its main sponsor, Count Harrach, called for the creation of a Czech opera that would show the world that the Czechs, known far and wide as virtuosic musicians, were also capable of great musical compositions.

Smetana entered the Harrach competition with his first opera, *The Brandenburgers in Bohemia,* and won. The goal that the Harrach prize committee promoted in the competition announcement was one that Smetana explicitly shared as well. In a letter he wrote to an old friend in

1880, Smetana said that his goal in his career had been "to prove that we Czechs are not mere practising musicians as other nations nickname us, saying that our talent lies only in our fingers but not in our brains, but that we are also endowed with creative force, yes, that we have our own and characteristic music. How far I have succeeded in this hitherto, not I but the world will judge."[21] Or, as Smetana wrote in his article outlining the artistic development that the Czech opera should take, only through developing a Czech opera of high musical standard would "complete the honor that belongs to our nation, as a naturally musical nation, before all of Europe."[22] Smetana's reference to honor in particular implies that the Czechs' great artistic talent needed to be more widely acknowledged abroad.

If the national theater was the concrete goal, another focus of this effort to produce a prestigious national culture was the city of Prague itself. Czech nationalists sought to turn Prague from a provincial, predominantly German city into a world-class capital that was thoroughly Czech. In an article of 1862, Smetana demanded that musical life in Prague be boosted so that it would compare favorably to that in other cultural capitals such as London or Paris. He says again that the Czechs' honor depends upon them supporting a great musical life in Prague: "I believe that our good name as a musical nation is quite old and renowned; it is the role of the artist enthused with the true love of his homeland to edify our name even more. I will make such a step."[23] When he became the director of Prague's Provisional Theater, one of Smetana's primary objectives was to bring its standard of performance up as much as possible to international levels. He was determined that even though the Czechs were a small nation of relatively limited resources, their theater would stand on an equal footing, in terms of its artistic quality and prestige, with the national theaters of the large European nations.

Finally, Czech nationalists' preoccupation with prestige is also strongly linked to the "originality" value of nationality in art: one reason why their nation should take its place at the table of great European cultures is because it has something unique and particular to offer. This idea played a role in Smetana's career, as an entertaining anecdote demonstrates.

It concerns a debate that took place in Weimar, among Franz Liszt's circle of "musical brains" (as the relater of the anecdote, Václav Juda Novotný, terms them) regarding national music.

> In the Weimar music circle of that time there was, apart from Smetana, the well-known Viennese composer [Johann, Ritter von] Herbeck, who was a confirmed enemy of everything Czech. They fell to discussing what various nations had done in the great sphere of music, and Herbeck began, pointedly and maliciously, to attack the honour of the Czech nation. "What have you achieved up to now," he scoffed, turning to Smetana. —"All that Bohemia can bring forth is fiddlers, mere performing musicians who can brag only of their perfection in craftsmanship, in the purely mechanical side of music, whereas on the real artist's path of truth and beauty your creative strength dwindles; indeed hitherto you have not done anything for the dent and progress of musical art, for you have not a single composition to show which is so purely Czech as to adorn and enrich European music literature by virtue of its characteristic originality."[24]

This barb succeeded in riling Smetana, who protested that the Czechs indeed had made important contributions to European music. Herbeck continued to deny it, however, only angering Smetana further. The story concludes:

> Liszt, who had followed the quarrel with a silent smile, bent slightly forward, took a bundle of notes from the table, and with the words: "Allow me, gentlemen, to play you the latest, purely Czech music," sat down at the piano. In his enchanting, brilliant style he played through the first book of Smetana's character pieces.
>
> After he had played the compositions, Liszt took Smetana, who was moved to tears, by the hand and with the words "here is a composer with a genuine Czech heart, an artist by the grace of God," he took leave of the company.[25]

There is more than a trace of mythologizing here, of course. However, even if the story were not true, it would still be valuable for its portrayal of the period's conceptions of nationality, originality, artistic quality, and how these elements were supposed to grant a nation cultural prestige.

For Edvard Grieg, the analog to Smetana's aims for a national theater was the music festival he organized in Bergen in 1898. The desire to put on a festival that met international standards was a guiding impulse behind Grieg's plans. Grieg described as his vision a "Norwegian music festival" consisting of Norwegian musical works given "the most ideal performance possible, and doubly here, where it concerns an international gathering that Europe will be attending."[26] Grieg's intent was not only to showcase Norwegian art, but also to show Europe that Norwegian art was as good as that of any other nation. The same arguments for the prestige of Norwegian culture show up in Grieg's 1874 application (coauthored with Johan Svendsen) for a stipend from the Storting (the Norwegian parliament). In this document, Grieg and Svendsen take the tone of, "other countries support their composers with stipends, so how can Norway not do it too?" There is even a hint of shaming the Storting into supporting them, by exposing the lamentable state of Norwegian music. "Here in our beginning artistic conditions," they write, "nothing of that can be found, which abroad works so fruitfully upon the creative artist's fantasy, because we are lacking the fundamental support that lies in a national opera with an orchestra and chorus that corresponds to art's and our time's requirements."[27]

Their implication is obviously that Christiania needed an opera and an orchestra that would be at a level equal to that found in other European capital cities. As Wagner and Smetana did, Grieg argues here for the establishment of a prestigious cultural institution so that Norway could have a thoroughly "national" culture. Interestingly, regardless of whether we can attribute it to Grieg and Svendsen's insistence, the parliament members did seem to be convinced by the challenge to keep up with other countries. Johan Sverdrup, the Storting president, described how in the debate over whether to award the stipends, the perception that other nations had developed a "well-rounded and complete" cultural life through an "artistic treatment" of "national melodies" indeed played its part in the decision in favor of the stipend.[28]

Apart from these two examples, the theme of prestige actually makes relatively few appearances in Grieg's discourse. Nonetheless, it was a recurring theme for Norwegian nationalists, including Grieg's friends. Ole Bull, for one, was intent that Norway should aspire to the standards of other countries in forming a national theater. Surveying what he perceived as the sorry status of theater in Norway, he wrote, "Among other nations that can serve as a model for us, one sees...that the national art is also advantageously fostered on the stage, while foreign art finds encouragement only rarely, or in a lesser extent and as a break in routine from the dominant national."[29] Bull's idea is that once Norwegian theater became truly Norwegian, it would merit recognition and prestige. Bjørnson was also a major campaigner for developing a high culture that would allow Norway to participate as an independent culture-nation on the world stage.[30] In his own artistic efforts, Bjørnson explicitly acknowledged that other countries provided a model that Norwegian culture had to live up to.[31] If overall, Grieg was not as preoccupied as Smetana with the prestige of the national art, he nonetheless did agree with a biographer who wrote that in his career, he "secured for Nordic music rank alongside the other culture lands."[32]

## DISSEMINATION

In order to attain prestige and recognition it was, of course, necessary that the products of the new national culture go out into the world as evidence of the nation's creative power. However, beyond just the goal of these cultural products achieving a place on the world stage, they were also supposed to communicate to the rest of the world what the values of the nation were. Disseminating the nation's art internationally was a further means of both cementing a national style and positioning the artist's people as a *Kulturnation*. Nationalist composers' art was disseminated in three main ways. First, concert tours by the composers allowed them to personally present their works and their nation's culture to audiences abroad. Second, their works were obviously performed abroad even without the composer present; Wagner and Grieg especially came to enjoy great fame this way. Lastly, dissemination was also effected through print: sales of musical scores, and in Wagner's case the publishing of his prose works, played a major role in the spread of these composers' national art.

Much as with prestige, dissemination is accomplished in large part through the application of international forms to the national culture. Where in the drive for prestige these forms are things like a national theater, in the case of dissemination they are primarily musical forms such as opera, concerti, and piano music. These forms are easily "consumable," in that a market existed for them. Opera houses were always looking for new works to produce, performers were seeking new music, and even the general public would pay to see performances or to purchase the score for their own enjoyment. This consumability is what really facilitated dissemination. Such works are conceived to be universally communicable: a string quartet, as an established art form, thus becomes an excellent vehicle for disseminating the supposedly unique national style contained within the form. And for all the particularity or distinctly "national" musical content of these forms as Wagner, Smetana, and Grieg use them, they are still in an important sense cosmopolitan because they come from a wider European culture. Also, as Grieg will suggest, dissemination is predicated on the idea that music itself, as an art, can communicate across borders. It communicates to people regardless of their national background because of its universality.

These three composers actually experienced highly varying degrees of success in their dissemination efforts. Smetana attained relatively little success, particularly in comparison with Wagner and Grieg. Nonetheless, Smetana was unquestionably aware of the utility of dissemination, and early in his career he worked hard to achieve international recognition for his art. He felt that it would have been a benefit to the whole Czech nation if his works became known abroad.[33] As with the other two composers, performance tours played a role here. In a letter to his wife of 1861, Smetana declares that with his tours, "the intention to become known quickly, and to be sent out in all the papers to all the corners of the world, is being achieved, and can be of great use later on."[34] These tours also served a patriotic goal. For instance, before Smetana embarked on one of his trips, his cousin and former teacher František Smetana reminded him, for the good of his country, to "travel as a Czech artist" and not as a German (Smetana did often go by the name of Friedrich Smetana when he traveled abroad, though).[35] Smetana was sensitive to admonitions such as his uncle's, and at his concerts abroad he usually performed his own "Czech compositions" side by side with pieces by the likes of Liszt, Chopin, and Schumann. In this way the ambition of gaining fame for himself and his own works went hand in hand with the dissemination of a Czech art.

Once his career was more firmly established, Smetana continued to be concerned with means of assuring the spread of his own Czech music. For instance, he insisted on having a decent German text of *The Bartered Bride* so that it could be performed in German theaters, "which we are striving for in every way possible," as he says in a letter.[36] Similarly, in 1869 he had the opera translated into French so that it could "go out into the world and gain recognition beyond our frontiers and perhaps earn some money for me too."[37] He in fact sent a copy of the score to the Paris Opera, but was unsuccessful at getting *The Bartered Bride* performed there during his lifetime. It did, however, reach St. Petersburg as early as 1871, though it was not well received by Russian critics. Smetana said that the libretto of his final, uncompleted opera had attracted him because he thought that with its subject matter it would more easily "reach beyond the frontiers of Bohemia."[38]

Though the Paris Opera was not interested in producing Smetana's operas, later in his life another possibility arose of having his works performed in Paris, at the so-called *concerts populaires*. That prospect spurred him to write to a friend, "But if this venture were successful and he [the producer of the *concerts populaires*] accepted and performed my compositions then not only I but also our Czech art would profit, and that is the main thing."[39] He was similarly excited by the possibility of his tone poems *Vyšehrad* and *Vltava* being performed in London— though not only the prestige of having his works heard in one of the major world cities, but also a hope of significant profits seem to have stoked his excitement.[40] Smetana also tried to get *Vyšehrad* and *Vltava* published by the Schott firm in Leipzig in 1875, but could not come to an agreement with them.

Sadly, after various such failures, Smetana in his last years became embittered and resigned about the chances of his music being heard abroad. His friends continued to pressure him to send his works to foreign publishers and not to rely just on Czech ones, since the Czech firms were much too small ever to distribute Smetana's music properly or even to pay him adequately for it.[41] As we have seen, his motives were not always exclusively national-political, since he would have seen some financial gain if theaters outside the Czech lands had started performing his operas. In fact, it is in a discussion of the financial situation for Czech composers that Smetana laments that whereas German, French, and Italian composers have many theaters where their works can be performed, "we Czech composers have only one stage that can and should encourage the supply of good works and the elevation of national art."[42] Czech composers, Smetana wrote on another occasion, suffer because of how small their country is, which significantly hinders the possibility of their works becoming well-known abroad. As he complained in a letter of 1877, "it's terrible that our domestic compositions go across the borders with such difficulty, while in Germany every bit of trash is not only published, but also spread by performances. And of those foreign composers apart from Wagner, Liszt, and Brahms we Czechs have absolutely nothing to fear."[43]

The reasons for Smetana's failed dissemination are partly personal. His deafness and the accompanying financial insecurity in which he lived his last years eliminated the possibility of trips abroad to promote his music. His increasing mental instability in this time also inhibited touring. He was thereby robbed of the same kind of peak in fame that both Wagner and Grieg enjoyed in their last decades. Even prior to his deafness and mental decline, his directorship of the Provisional Theater left Smetana little time for guest appearances abroad. He was simply unable to promote his music personally in the way that both Wagner and Grieg did. His failure to secure a contract with a major foreign publisher also hampered the spread of his works; Grieg's contract with the Peters publishing firm in Leipzig proved of immense importance in furthering his own career.

Another difficulty in the dissemination of Smetana's music was posed by the limitations of the "national language." This is a problem he was aware of, as his concern for good translations of his operas shows. Ironically, though one goal of establishing a national art was to demonstrate that the national language was capable of a full range of emotional and artistic expression, "minor" languages such as Czech and Norwegian have been an obstacle to international audiences coming to know vocal music and operas in these languages. Very few performers who are not Czech or Scandinavian can cope with the texts. This is a shame, since it prevents some of Smetana's and Grieg's best works (such as Smetana's operas *Dalibor* and *The Two Widows* or many of Grieg's Lieder, like his song cycle *Haugtussa*) from being heard outside of their native lands.

So, while some of Smetana's music is internationally known today, much of the best of it is very seldom heard outside the Czech lands. Dvořák has instead become the most famous international representative of the Czech "national school," despite the fact that Smetana was actually more of a nationalist and not notably an inferior composer in comparison with Dvořák. However, Dvořák succeeded where Smetana failed, namely in securing a foreign publisher and touring widely. Also, Dvořák's much greater output in the consumable classical forms of symphonies and chamber music facilitated his extensive dissemination.

Wagner today certainly suffers none of the recognition problems that obscure many of Smetana's gems. Perhaps surprisingly, however, Wagner first became known abroad for his prose writings, as Hannu Salmi demonstrates.[44] It was only later in the 1850s that Wagner's operas gained worldwide fame. For Wagner, though, his prose and his music were *supposed* to spread together, as they were closely and essentially linked. A letter of 1849 indicates that he wanted people to read his "philosophical" writings early on so that they would understand his music:

> It is absolutely necessary for me to complete these [philosophical] works and to send them out into the world before I continue in

> my immediate artistic production: I must, and those who are
> interested in my artistic nature must come with me to a precise
> understanding. Otherwise we will all grope about in a repellant
> half-light that is even worse than the absolute, narrow-minded
> night in which one sees nothing at all and only clings religiously
> to the same old handrail.[45]

His aesthetic philosophy was supposed to blaze the trail for his art.
Nonetheless, he did also rely on performances of his works to herald
his achievements in the "reform" of dramatic music. He gave concerts
throughout the German lands, especially later in his career when he
was attempting to drum up support for his Bayreuth plans. To some
extent, he also took his works abroad, as with the Paris production
of *Tannhäuser* in 1860. However, his presence was not necessary to
secure performances of his operas, since beginning in the later 1850s,
they were frequently given in houses throughout Germany.

Wagner's concern with dissemination applies first and foremost to
dissemination in his own country in order to establish a national style.
In a letter of 1845 he proclaims an urgent need for such dissemination,
announcing that "I now consider it very important for the entire future
of our dramatic music that a figure appear from Germany's heart and
disseminate itself throughout Germany."[46] In this regard, Wagner saw
himself as carrying on Beethoven's achievements: whereas Beethoven
had shown to the world the glories of the "German artistic spirit" in the
realm of purely orchestral music, Wagner would do the same for dramatic music. The function that the spread of works such as *Tannhäuser*
and *Lohengrin* would fulfill would be "to form the starting-point to a
truly German style for musical-dramatic performances—of which no
trace currently exists."[47] To *Tannhäuser* specifically, he assigned the task
"to win for me the hearts of my German compatriots to a greater extent
than my earlier works have yet been able to!"[48] Wagner thought that
thanks to his operas, a truly German style would become known, and
hopefully take hold, throughout Germany. Once it was firmly established
in Germany, then, this national style would take its place in the international operatic world as a beacon for the reform of dramatic music.

Ironically, however, at least earlier on in his career, Wagner's popularity *outside* of Germany was higher than within, as Martin Gregor-Dellin shows.[49] One example is with the 1860 Parisian performances of *Tannhäuser*, which apparently actually helped increase Wagner's profile within Germany. The slowness, as he perceived it, of his works becoming popular in his native land is doubtless responsible for some of Wagner's insistence on the need for dissemination of a German style within Germany. The borders of the many German states first had to be surmounted before the national art could truly travel abroad. Nonetheless, as his fame increased, some evidence does suggest that the reception (in both Germany and abroad) of his works as specifically German also increased. Such, at least, was the case with the premiere of *Die Meistersinger* in 1868, which attracted attention throughout Europe as a new German "national opera."

The way in which his aspirations for art within Germany to transcend borders and go out into the world becomes clear from a passage in his proposal to Ludwig II for building a national theater. "The completion of this important institution of magnificent model performances of noble German original works," Wagner writes, "would thereby, if all the arrangements to this end proved worthwhile, lead to the official opening of a noble festival theater, which would stand as an exemplary realization of its goal to the entire cultured world, a monument of the German artistic spirit."[50] This, then, is a paradigmatic expression of the power and purpose of the dissemination of the national art: not only do the artworks make a national art in the first place, but they serve as ambassadors to "the entire cultured world" for what the nation is capable of creatively.

Grieg, despite the international success his music achieved, was actually acutely aware of the difficulties of his works finding their way to audiences outside of Norway. As for Smetana, language was an issue; Grieg recognized early on that his Norwegian songs' texts had to be translated (into German, English, and French) in order to make them performable abroad.[51] Often he found that the translations were quite bad, which in turn hampered the public's appreciation of his music. Not surprisingly, then, he was deeply concerned with getting better translations.[52] Still, though, Grieg saw a special role for music in the dissemination of Norwegian culture, particularly music that was not based on a text. Music's power was to communicate beyond any linguistic level, to speak to every person in the universally comprehensible language of tones. Grieg agreed with the following description of his efforts to disseminate Norwegian culture:

> On his many concert tours Grieg has had the opportunity to acquaint the best orchestras and the most gifted musicians with his muse's particular national spirit. As he gets across his intentions in a musical sense, at the same moment the national spirit is present and permeates the entire ensemble. In this way the traveling Grieg has accomplished a quiet mission, since with his tones and his conductor's baton he "spiritualizes" Bjørnson's and Ibsen's thoughts and thereby sinks into the depths of foreigners' hearts the finest and tenderest soul-feelings in Norwegian folk life, that do not allow themselves to be expressed in words.[53]

As that quote suggests, Grieg's concert tours were of central importance in the spread of Norwegian music—much more important, relatively speaking, than either Wagner's or Smetana's were for their countries. Grieg was a huge concert draw, and in the last twenty years of his life, invitations to come perform constantly poured in. On these tours, Grieg very often brought other Norwegian musicians along with him. He thereby not only spread his own work and the fame of Norwegian music abroad, but also furthered the careers of his fellow countrymen and -women. There is no doubt that Grieg saw this dissemination as a patriotic project. As he himself said, at the end of a concert abroad when he had lowered the conductor's baton, and the audience was responding with a storm of a applause, "yes, then they come over me, the tears from the love of my fatherland."[54]

Grieg's piano concerto played a major role in establishing his reputation and subsequently in winning him admirers. With this concerto, Grieg realized a masterpiece in one of the major genres of Western art music, and it was the piece that first brought him into concert halls worldwide. Later, most of his major works became famous in all the musical capitals of Europe; the incidental music to *Peer Gynt* in particular enjoyed enormous popularity. Grieg's fame was such that he and Tchaikovsky were reportedly the two most-performed composers in the world around 1900.[55] Beyond the concert hall, however, Grieg's chamber music also helped disseminate his idea of a Norwegian art. His solo piano music became very popular even early in his career. On a visit to Berlin in 1866, for example, he went into a music store and found that all the copies of his *Humoresker* had sold out.[56] Similarly, he once remarked happily that his edition of *Norges Melodier* ("Norway's Melodies") had sold "many thousand copies" by 1905.[57] His *Lyric Pieces* were and remain one of Grieg's most popular compositions, and it was these that really brought Grieg into thousands of homes in Norway and abroad, above all by amateur pianists wanting to play them.[58]

Thus within his own lifetime, Grieg's importance in making Norwegian culture known throughout the Western world was already acknowledged. The flood of tributes to him surrounding his sixtieth birthday in 1903 often make reference to Grieg's role as a sort of cultural ambassador for Norway.[59] Grieg was certainly aware of the idea that he both presented and represented Norwegian music, and even espoused this idea himself.[60] He was conscious of following in the footsteps of his predecessor Ole Bull, the violinist who had first brought an idea of Norwegian music to European capitals with his many tours earlier in the century.[61] Unlike Wagner, however, Grieg was not a committed self-promoter, and so he also worked on behalf of other Norwegian composers, most decisively perhaps with the 1898 Bergen festival. One of the greatest accomplishments of this festival, he wrote, was that the lesser-known Norwegian composers whose works had been performed there would receive more artistic recognition abroad, going from Bergen out "to Europe's concert halls."[62]

## UNIVERSALITY

The theme of universality is closely linked in this discourse with cosmopolitaneity because universality is what makes cosmopolitaneity possible. The idea that music is a "universal language" means that it can communicate to everyone. So, music can in theory travel anywhere and be understood; it becomes the possession of all peoples regardless of nationality. More specifically, nationalist art becomes cosmopolitan when it goes out into the world to proclaim, through the universal intelligibility of music, the values of the national culture. It is this universal power to communicate to the world at large that makes art both national and cosmopolitan. However, nationalist art could only become cosmopolitan in this way when it attained the universal standards of all great art.

In Wagner, the theme of universality takes a somewhat different tone than it does in either Smetana or Grieg. The demand for universality—and, in its way, cosmopolitaneity—is there, above all as an emphasis on producing dramatic truth. As do Smetana and Grieg, Wagner wants to produce art that will speak to everyone—that reveals basic truths about human existence. Similar, also, is the fact that these three composers all couple universality with nationality, in that nationality is the vehicle to achieving the goal of an audience beyond the composer's own nation. Wagner, however, takes a more radical (one might also say a more chauvinistic) step than Smetana and Grieg by insisting that *only* German nationality is the proper vehicle for achieving universality in dramatic music. Chauvinistic, then, because despite his embrace of the "purely human," he absolutely attributes to the German spirit, and to it alone, the power to overcome the sorry state of the modern world and its art.

To begin with, Wagner undeniably praises the national in music. He believes that all culture proceeds from nationality.[63] Hence he rails against the idea of the "absolute artwork," that is, "the artwork that is neither bound to place or time, nor presented by particular people under particular circumstances to equally particular people in order to be understood by them—is a complete absurdity, a shadow-image of aesthetic philosophical fantasy."[64] The truth is, according to Wagner, that a work of art must spring from its own place and time in order to be great. This claim is linked with his idea that all art should stem from Volk inspiration. Also, given that Wagner's preferred Volk inspiration—myth—is inherently "true," and universal, with a "purely human" content, these Volk inspirations can be simultaneously national and universal.

However, Wagner (and for that matter, the other two composers as well) also stresses the need for art to rise above the bounds of nationality. In what might seem a preposterous bit of hypocrisy, Wagner does even criticize patriotism—he says it makes the citizen blind to the interests of "humanity above all," blind to the relations "human to human."[65] As we have seen in previous chapters, on a number of occasions in his writings, Wagner actually criticizes national styles in music, which he says amount only to "the particular," lacking any true connection to the Volk or any authentic aspirations to universally communicable art. Given, then, that patriotism prohibits people from communicating with one another on a purely human level, it follows that Wagner rejects patriotism in art. The ideal art form, he wrote, transcends "the restrictive moment of narrower nationality" in order to produce an art that is "commonly understandable, accessible to every nation."[66]

Drama can realize this goal, according to Wagner: its purpose is to show society its "purely human nature" or "purely human individuality."[67] As he says, in the theater, "the whole human, with his lowest and highest passions, is presented to himself in alarming nakedness."[68] However, the dramatic art in its present form is so degraded (principally through the deleterious French influence) that it must itself be perfected in order to realize its universality. Thus Wagner's project of perfecting drama aims at benefiting all humanity, based on drama's power to reveal the "purely human," the universal aspects of human existence.[69] His own means of depicting this "naked human" is primarily through myth, because, as mentioned previously, myth is universal, "true at all times."[70] In this regard, he praises the Greeks' method of using myth in their art, and particularly the "self-eradication of their national particularity" that they achieved.[71] Wagner writes that once he began investigating German myths, he finally found in the German spirit "the potential that leads over the narrower barriers of nationality to a comprehension of the purely human, to me seeming so closely related to the Greek spirit."[72] He sees the German *Geist* as a kind of rebirth of the Greek, in that both "national spirits" were endowed with delivering universality to the world.

It is through art, then, that the national and the universal are interwoven so that they become something transcendent. To the extent that the knot of Wagner's thinking on this matter can be untangled, the formula seems to be this: art must be national, but it must also rise above national particularism. It accomplishes this by being based in the Volk, since art stemming from the Volk is *in its nature* also universal. Though it retains its unmistakable national coloring, that origin in the Volk—its naturalness—is precisely what makes the art universal. He illustrates this idea perhaps most clearly in his description of the universality of the "folk melody." The folk melody, he wrote in *Oper und Drama*, is

> free of all local-national particularity, it contains a broad, general expression of feeling, it has no other embellishment than the smile of the sweetest and most natural sincerity, and it speaks thus, through the power of undistorted grace, to the heart of a person, regardless of what national particularity he might belong to, precisely because in that melody the purely human comes so directly to light.[73]

The folk melody is "the authentic language of the heart, true and unfaked."[74] It is able to communicate to everyone regardless of nationality, precisely because it is "purely human," the natural expression of human creativity. Indeed, this is the great property of music, that it is the most universal of the arts, a "language equally understandable to all people."[75]

However, this universality is not quite so easy to achieve as it might seem. Not all art, for Wagner, really manages to be universal. Similarly, not all Volk inspirations really attain the "purely human." And here is where Wagner's nationalism collides with his aspirations to universality, in that he privileges the German Volk or spirit as alone capable of delivering artistic universality to the world. A passage from *Deutsche Kunst und deutsche Politik* announces this unique property of the German spirit: "Universal, as the destiny of the German Volk announces itself since its entry into history, is the talent of the German spirit also for art.

The example of the activation of this universality on the most important fields of art has been shown in the experience of the rebirth of the German spirit since the second half of the previous century."[76] Hence the folk melody he describes in the previous paragraph is actually only the *German* folk melody, as in Weber's operas. Only in the German folk melody is found "the happy property of naive sincerity without the stifling national particularity."[77] So in terms of artistic inspiration, German sources are superior because it is specifically in German myths that one finds "the real, naked human...the true human above all."[78]

Wagner's insistence on the German spirit's messianic power to achieve universality is one of the stranger themes in his entire discourse about art and nationality. Strange, but not without precedent: in fact, messianic, universalistic claims for German culture are relatively common themes within German nationalist discourse. Friedrich Meinecke has shown in great detail how a fixation on universality pervaded the German movement, beginning with Novalis and Friedrich Schlegel, and espoused influentially by Fichte as well.[79] So, this is the intellectual tradition that Wagner inherited and applied to his own artistic and social thinking. He was in fact conscious of the historical pedigree here, attributing to Goethe, Schiller, and the whole German literary rebirth the following mission: the German movement "pressed resolutely for the discovery of an ideal, purely human form that did not belong exclusively to nationality."[80] And of course, what Goethe and Schiller achieved in the literary realm, Wagner aspired to in the musical. In this way he would also follow Mozart's model, since through his music Mozart was able to elevate the Italian form of opera to universality.[81]

Within this messianic, universalistic theme, we see wrapped up together Wagner's nationalism, his concerns about the decline of civilization, and his obsession with salvation, all of which appear throughout both his prose and his dramatic works. The German spirit's "calling in the council of peoples" is to create "something common" for the entire world.[82] The "something common" that the Germans would accomplish is no small task: Wagner describes it as nothing less than as "a thoroughgoing regeneration of the European peoples' blood [*des europäischen*

*Völkerblutes*]," a "rebirth of the spirit of peoples," and "reconciliation" of nations.[83] The place to start with this rebirth is the arts. The German spirit will "save" not only the "spirit of European peoples" from its "artistically-led depravity," but moreover the "human spirit" from its "deep shame."[84]

Here, though, is where the role of artists such as himself (and, he claims, Beethoven, Goethe, and Schiller) enters the picture. As I show in the second chapter, the artist will present the nation with its true nature. So, once the German Volk has realized itself through the "development of its national character," it will also realize the salvationary potential inherent in its spirit.[85] Therefore, in helping the German Volk to realize itself, the artist works toward the "salvation of his human brothers across the world."[86] Needless to say, Wagner claimed this as his own goal.

In this sense, Wagner's own mission is the same as that of the German Volk as a whole. He insists in *Mein Leben* that his ideas are for the good of all of human society.[87] He wants to save the world from itself, and he can do it because he is a German. And in his seemingly contradictory, chauvinistic way, he claims that the ultimate goal toward which humanity should develop is to the "unnational universal."[88] This is another argument for the dissemination of German art, then: the greatest, "purely human," world-saving achievements of German culture would educate all of humanity toward meeting the Germans' high standards in art, and all of human culture would be miraculously redeemed. He sees this goal realized in Beethoven, whose music is the "world-redeeming proclamation of the most exalted innocence."[89] Music is indeed a universal language, one capable of communicating to all peoples. However, *German* music, in particular, has "something special, yes divine," it "teaches all the heathens," alone attaining true, transcendent universality.[90]

Where Wagner locates universality ultimately only in the German spirit, Smetana finds it in all great art. Smetana actually had relatively little to say about universality per se, but it is nonetheless clear that a universal standard for high art undergirds his own cultural and social goals. Hence for all the value of nationality in art, if that art falls short of the universal measures of greatness, then it is ultimately worth little. One important manifestation of Smetana's aspirations to universality was his insistence on being open to wider European influences. Together with his circle of friends, Smetana believed that in order to create a truly valuable Czech art, Czech culture had to learn from the best foreign artistic trends. As one example, the writer Jan Neruda—one of Smetana's closest friends—was particularly concerned with orienting Czech poetry after European models.[91] This outlook is what makes Smetana and his circle cosmopolitan.

For his part, Smetana rejected a music that was "only" national, based exclusively on allegedly national/folk forms, since such forms (and hence the music that would result) did not live up to his conception of the universal standards of a high art. In this way, for all his undeniable patriotism, Smetana rejected particularism and did aspire to values that he conceived as transcending those of the nation. While he said he preferred to set to music stories taken from Czech history, he also envisioned eventually making use of international subjects for his operas.[92] His last opera *Viola* was based on Shakespeare, for example. By choosing this subject, Smetana, as Guy Erismann suggests, wanted to work with material from an author who was "universal."[93] For Smetana, there was simply no contradiction between nationalism and the cosmopolitan receptivity to foreign trends: "The opinion that art in its cosmopolitaneity excludes every *national* direction is already long since defeated and finished," he wrote.[94]

A major element in Smetana's campaign to keep Czech culture open to cosmopolitan trends was his programming as director of the Provisional Theater. The operas he programmed and his writings on the topic show that he was adamant about bringing the best of international opera to Prague. From the classics such as Mozart's *Figaro* and Beethoven's *Fidelio* to the best recent operas, Smetana wanted to present the greatest works of art, regardless of their national origin.[95] Interestingly, Wagner expressed much the same idea about presenting the greatest international works in his own plans for a national theater.[96] In view of the art Smetana wanted to present to Czech audiences, he firmly rejected the notion that Czech culture must be exclusively Czech, free of foreign influences. We have seen in the third chapter how in his own art he resisted the *prostonárodní* ("simple folk") strategy of basing Czech music solely on folk forms. Instead, Smetana's own receptivity to "neo-German" models, and particularly to Wagner's style, is the best example of his openness to outside influences in Czech music—particularly given that Germans were otherwise the main foes for Czech nationalists.

However, the ferocious storm of criticism Smetana suffered for acknowledging Wagner's influence must be read as evidence of the extent to which certain key figures in Czech musical life desired to "shut off Czech art into its own domestic track," to retain the *prostonárodní* character of Czech music, as Petr Vít has written.[97] The cosmopolitan attitude of Smetana, Neruda, and their ilk was one side of a deep rift within Czech nationalism. On the other side, patriots often from an older generation continued to adhere to this *prostonárodní* idea that any art that was Czech had a value just for being Czech. They emphasized the "self-sufficiency" of Czech music, whereas the advocates of Europeanness such as Smetana believed that it was the task of Czech art "to open a window to the world."[98] Christopher Storck has provided an excellent summary of the dispute:

> The "isolationists" wanted to strengthen the particular character of Czech music in order to protect it from "foreign infiltration"; they considered outside influences permissible only when they came from another Slavic culture. Their opponents, for whom there was only a single "world-art," pursued instead the goal of bringing Czech music to equal a western European level. That, however, was only possible if the composers showed themselves to be open to all the important innovations in musical life. Such an attitude brought upon them the accusation of the "national purists" that they were striving for a "cosmopolitan" art, hindering the nation in its development toward independence. Conversely, the representatives of the model of an open culture wanted to show precisely through the production of artworks of an international caliber that the Czechs in this regard were an equal member in the society of European culture-nations.[99]

Storck explains that the "isolationists" feared that a cosmopolitan art could not be national—though Smetana, as we have already seen, denied this incommensurability.

The nationalists who feared cosmopolitaneity are in a sense under-standable, in that they represent the traditional view that the national culture must be built up entirely from within, that foreign influences are only corrupting. This is the view that has come to be taken for granted in many accounts of nationalism. However, those nationalists concerned with building a national high culture of *international* quality believed, like Smetana, that any sort of artistic integrity for that culture would be impossible without responding to broader trends—the same trends that inspired artists in the great *Kulturnationen* of Europe. So, Smetana and his cohort are cosmopolitan both through their receptivity to foreign influences and through their idea that Czech culture properly belongs *in* the world, where it can be appreciated by all people *as Czech*. Indeed, these international trends run deep in the program of constructing a national high culture perhaps above all because many artists maintained a notion that their works, for all their national character, should also be universal. They should say something about the human condition and thereby have a worth not just to Czechs but to everyone.

In much the same way as Smetana, throughout Grieg's career we see him trying to find a way to be both thoroughly national and cosmopolitan at the same time. Indeed, the artistic conflict between nationalism and cos-mopolitanism "in many ways came to stamp his life's work," as Benestad and Schjelderup-Ebbe remark.[100] So as much as he loved Norway and desired to contribute to a uniquely Norwegian culture, Grieg also wanted to see Norway open to the world. Small nations, he once wrote, have to have a "wider horizon"—they must know "everything."[101] The idea of being open to cultural influences from "outside" was one Grieg shared with other Norwegian nationalist intellectuals. For instance, he and his composer colleague Johan Svendsen both espoused the goal of commu-nicating not just with their nation but with "universal humanity," which for them was the mark of any true artist.[102]

However, as in the Czech lands, there were some for whom being international meant not being national, as if cosmopolitan tendencies were a threat to Norwegian patriotism. This is exactly the sort of atti-tude Grieg combated in, among other spheres, his attempt to bring a high-quality concert life to Norway. These battles are direct parallels to Smetana's problems in programming for the Provisional Theater. For example, Grieg rejected the accusation that a Bergen musical group with which he was involved was too "cosmopolitan" to be of use for "a national-political objective."[103] In the same way, Grieg's insistence on hiring Amsterdam's Concertgebouw Orchestra for the 1898 Bergen music festival—over a storm of protest that it was unpatriotic to do so— was prompted by his belief that Norwegians would benefit more from a highest-quality performance of their art than they would if an inferior orchestra from Christiania were engaged. Grieg saw here that "artistic and national considerations" collided—and he opted to let the artistic goals take precedence.[104]

In this instance, we see Grieg letting letting chauvinistic anxieties be superseded by a greater goal of securing the best possible display of Norwegian art. The Bergen festival is thus an excellent representation of how Grieg's artistic goals transcended restrictive national consider- ations. In an article for the Bergen newspaper summarizing what the festival had accomplished, Grieg stresses that the Norwegian national music the festival showcased was capable of communicating to every- one, that is, not just to Norwegians.[105] In this sense, the festival realized what Grieg on another occasion called his "youthful dream:" that art "just as in ancient Greece will now go out to everyone, precisely because its calling is to bring a message from heart to heart."[106] Throughout his life, as with the Bergen festival, Grieg drew a line between nationalism and chauvinism. He admitted that he did not know "a greater joy than to vex chauvinists, those trolls, whom I hate like the plague."[107] For both Grieg and Smetana, one could perfectly well be a patriot without being close minded about international influences on the national culture.

As his career progressed, Grieg became convinced of the imperative never to let the national trump the cosmopolitan. In a famous letter that has become known as Grieg's "cosmopolitan profession of faith," he declared, "in my later works I have more and more sought out a broader, more general outlook on my own individuality, an outlook that has been influenced by the age's great concerns—in other words by cosmopolitaneity."[108] He wrote this statement in response to a German critic's accusation that Grieg viewed himself as Norwegian music's "messiah." Grieg's aspiration corresponded to the way he described Verdi's career in his obituary for the Italian composer in 1901. He says that Verdi's great triumphs from his earlier period "all denote a national perspective." However, he writes, "then the remarkable happens, and Verdi as a fully mature man expands his horizon, and still retaining the national in his art he becomes a cosmopolitan."[109] Grieg admires how, beginning with *Aida*, Verdi becomes both an Italian and a European, progressing toward the profound universality of *Otello*.

While never denying the nationality of his music—even in the "cosmopolitan profession of faith" he admits that the "roots that tie me to the fatherland" cannot be ripped up—he stresses that the real goal of art should be the universal. This, he insisted, was his goal, too: "as a modern artist the universal is my goal."[110] Side by side with his goal of creating a national music, Grieg of course maintained the ideal of creating great art. And great art, according to him, "is in any case never so national, but rather raised high above the mere national level. It's cosmopolitan."[111] He proclaimed that he never sought only "the Norwegian" with his music but rather that he always aimed at "the great."[112]

Likewise, Grieg said that in his art, "[I] did not want to be just Norwegian, and even less so Norwegian-Norwegian—but rather—myself. I wanted to find expression for something of the best in me."[113] And this "best of himself" was both a product of his own individuality and of the social influences upon him. So, according to Grieg, since he as an individual was both nationalist and cosmopolitan, so, too, was his art. "My opinion is that just as a person is *individual* and *social*, so the artist is both national and cosmopolitan," Grieg wrote in 1889.[114] Grieg recognized that his background as an artist was in no way "purely" Norwegian. He claimed that his familial and social connections to Denmark had impacted his life and art, and also that "a good portion of my individuality is due to my Germanization" since he was trained in Leipzig.[115] All these influences made up his own personality, and together with the fact that he always kept his eyes open for what was going on beyond the borders of Norway, Grieg saw himself as thoroughly cosmopolitan. He was too aware that "national pride can be the most beautiful and the most disgusting, that's for sure, it can make you *dumb*" ever to be a chauvinist.[116]

In Grieg's mind, then, the national was a means to an end, but should never be an end in itself; "that which was great in the national idea just could be united with what was universal, and it could not have a future by getting lost in the particular."[117] The nationality in his music was, in a way, only a part of its artistic worth. Grieg wrote that without doubt, "cultural history shows us that every art that remains vital has been national."[118] However, it was thanks to the "blending of cosmopolitan and national factors" that his work truly won a place for itself in the world.[119] Grieg indicates that the particularly national features of his work made it original and attention getting, but at the same time his striving for the cosmopolitan standards of great art enabled his work to communicate with everyone, regardless of nationality.

And despite the avowedly local purposes behind his music—that is, the endeavor of creating a national music—Grieg's conception of the power of music, even the power of national music, surpassed any mere localism. Music should belong to everyone, in Grieg's view; it should be universal by being *human*, much as Wagner maintained.[120] In a letter to his close friend Frants Beyer, Grieg dreamily wishes about great music that "*[e]veryone* could feel these beauties! That would indeed be 'the new heaven and the new earth, in which bliss dwells!' No! It would not be just an *earth*, since we would all come to embrace each other out of pure jubilation!"[121] He in fact experienced the power of his music to bring people together, and rejoiced in that. This was especially so in the late 1890s, as tensions in the Swedish-Norwegian Union rose. After a concert in Stockholm in 1896, he wrote, "I have—as unbelievable as it sounds—fulfilled a national mission in Stockholm, in that I really contributed to bringing the Swedish and Norwegian people nearer to each other."[122] In much the same way, he described the enjoyment he took at a Prague concert at smoothing over the bitterness—however temporarily—between Czechs and Germans: "How glorious there as a musician to be able to gather the quarreling parties in the same hall and to compel them with the tones' power."[123]

## CONCLUSION

As the discourse on creating a national music shows, nationalism and ideas that transcend nationalism—universality, cosmopolitaneity—need not be contradictory. Indeed, there is no unavoidable conflict between particularism and universality at all. Nationalism in itself is in fact cosmopolitan, a kind of universal. The universalistic aspects of nationalism include, first, the assumptions justifying national particularity, and second, the presumed universal applicability of the nation form.

The ideology of nationalism rests on certain basic assumptions and demands, namely for sovereignty and recognition of each individual nation that claims to itself such rights. These demands or rights are assumed to be universal. As Ernesto Laclau explains, "To assert...the right of all ethnic groups to cultural autonomy is to make an argumentative claim which can only be justified on universal grounds. The assertion of one's own particularity requires the appeal of something transcending it."[124] So, the demand for political or cultural autonomy is predicated on a universal value that *every* group deserves autonomy. Additionally, this demand rests on a belief that particularity is a good, a fundamental of human existence that is also universal. It is universal because every human social community is conceived to be entitled to some claim to particularity, and to the right to realize that claim. We in fact see such thinking in the drive to create a national culture: the assumptions behind national prestige in art presuppose a benefit to all humanity in disseminating the unique characteristics of each nation's cultural expression.

Complicating the equation, however, Laclau points out further that even universalisms are particularistic. This is so because, in his view, there is no such thing as a true universal. Rather, there are various, differing conceptions of universals. Laclau uses this particularity at the heart of universalist claims to argue that the universal and the particular are not only *not* opposites, but that they actually go together:

> The particular and the universal are not mutually exclusive, but rather mutually inclusive and in fact, constitutive. The universal requires the demarcation of its outer limit, or more specifically, that which it does not name [i.e., the non-universal]...The particular, if it wishes to argue for the freedom to be, must appeal to 'universal' values of independence as a strategic necessity, even as it forces the recognition of its particularity. Yet this is not a contradiction within the particular, but precisely the laying open of the contradictions of the universal.[125]

Applied to our examples of nation-building movements, we can see that, indeed, the claims of universality for these national cultures or arts are *based on* particularity. In Grieg's career, for instance, it is the unique nationality of his music that on the one hand grants it some entrée into a broader, international music. On the other hand, Grieg himself always emphasized that his music was not merely particular but that it was also simultaneously universal because it adhered to the transcendent values of great art.

The second universal aspect of nationalism is the privileging of the value of the nation form. Equating nationalism with religion, as many writers have done, either implicitly or explicitly acknowledges this universalistic bias. Many religions are notoriously universalist, making absolute claims to truth. However, the nation has replaced religion as "the most universally legitimate value in the political life of our time," in Anderson's words.[126] Nationalism is the new, ostensibly universally applicable truth system for which people are willing to die. It has become the main principle by which human political communities on a large scale are organized, in the system of nation-states. So, nationalism, while once presumed to be opposed to universalisms such as Enlightenment culture, is itself seen to make a universalistic claim as a principle of human social organization. Nonetheless, it is just one of multiple competing universalisms—possible nominees for other "truth-systemic" modes of human social organization could be fundamentalist Islam, market capitalism, or, formerly, Marxism. Yet as Laclau reminds us, multiple universalisms inherently presume particularity. Thus even nationalism is ultimately predicated on both particularity *and* universality.

Moreover, nationalism is itself a cosmopolitan form, as a widespread, internationally dominant ideology with some local variation. The strategies of nation building are themselves very often "foreign," in that they come from "outside" of the nation but are applied to constitute the nation "from within." In this way, inescapably, the entire nationalist movement is impregnated with a certain cosmopolitaneity. Similarly, nationalist art is in a sense inherently cosmopolitan because it is responding to wide international aesthetic trends. Far from ever being exclusively or "purely" national, the national culture enshrines particularity in cosmopolitan forms to which are attributed universal validity.

It is interesting that Wagner, Smetana, and Grieg seemed to realize the internationality of nationalism already in the nineteenth century. And though each adopted a slightly different strategy for being both uniquely national and transcendently universal, we can judge all of them to have succeeded. The fact that they did succeed reinforces the ineluctable association of particularity and universality: they succeeded because they are all three unique products of their time and place, but they (or their art) simultaneously belong to the whole world for all times.

## ENDNOTES

1. Amanda Anderson, "Cosmopolitanism, Universalism, and the Divided Legacies of Modernity," in *Cosmopolitics: Thinking and Feeling Beyond the Nation*, ed. Pheng Cheah and Bruce Robbins (Minneapolis: University of Minnesota Press, 1998), 265–289. *See esp.* p. 267.
2. Kwame Anthony Appiah, "Against National Culture," in *Text and Nation*, ed. Laura García-Moreno and Peter C. Pfeiffer (Columbia, SC: Camden House, 1996), 175–190. *See esp.* p. 175.
3. Isaiah Berlin, *The Crooked Timber of Humanity* (Princeton: Princeton University Press, 1990), 243.
4. Ibid., *Against the Current: Essays in the History of Ideas* (New York: Viking Press, 1980), 343–344.
5. See Elie Kedourie, *Nationalism* (London: Hutchinson, 1985).
6. Hughes, *Nationalism and Society: Germany 1800–1945*.
7. Křen, *Konfliktní společnosti: Češi a Němci 1780*–1918, 49, makes this argument.
8. Bruce Robbins, "Comparative Cosmopolitanisms," in *Cosmopolitics: Thinking and Feeling Beyond the Nation*, ed. Pheng Cheah and Bruce Robbins (Minneapolis: University of Minnesota Press, 1998), 246–264. *See esp.* p. 260.
9. Cited in Echternkamp, *Der Aufstieg des deutschen Nationalismus*, 435.
10. Cited in Pheng Cheah, "The Cosmopolitical—Today" in *Cosmopolitics: Thinking and Feeling Beyond the Nation*, ed. Pheng Cheah and Bruce Robbins (Minneapolis: University of Minnesota Press, 1998), 20–41. *See esp.* p. 25.
11. Ottlová and Pospíšil, *Bedřich Smetana a jeho doba*, 83.
12. Hugh LeCaine Agnew, *Origins of the Czech National Renascence* (Pittsburgh: University of Pittsburgh Press, 1993).
13. See Wagner, "Vorwort zur Herausgabe," 279, for one example.
14. Cited in Gregor-Dellin, *Richard Wagner*, 202.
15. Wagner, *Bericht an Ludwig II*, 5.
16. Wagner, "Vorwort zur Herausgabe," 279.
17. Wagner, *Deutsche Kunst und deutsche Politik*, 34.
18. Jiří Kořalka, *Tschechen im Habsburgerreich und in Europa 1815–1914* (Wien: Verlag für Geschichte und Politik, 1991).
19. Kimball, *Czech Nationalism*, 38–39.

20. Ibid.
21. Bartoš, *Bedřich Smetana*, 210.
22. Smetana, *Kritické dílo*, 89.
23. Ibid., 37.
24. Bartoš, *Bedřich Smetana*, 45.
25. Ibid., 47.
26. Grieg, *Brev* Bind I, 313.
27. Ibid., 480.
28. Cited in Benestad and Schjelderup-Ebbe, *Edvard Grieg*, 144.
29. Herresthal, *Med spark i gulvet og quinter i bassen*, 94.
30. Per Amdam, *Bjørnstjerne Bjørnson 1832–1880* (Oslo: Gyldendal, 1993).
31. Ibid., 264.
32. Rojahn, "Edvard Grieg som national tonedigter," 94.
33. So reports V. V. Zelený in Bartoš, *Bedřich Smetana*, 221.
34. BS: Bettina Smetanová, October 30 and 31, 1861. MČH #146.
35. Bartoš, *Smetana ve vzpomínkách a dopisech*, 20.
36. Séquardtová, *Bedřich Smetana*, 144.
37. Letter cited in Large, *Smetana*, 168.
38. Letter to Krásnohorská of January 31, 1878, cited in Bartoš, *Bedřich Smetana: Letters and Reminiscences*, 188.
39. Bartoš, *Bedřich Smetana*, 194.
40. Letter in ibid., 221.
41. Smetana, *Smetana-Procházka korespondence*, 30.
42. BS: Rudolf Wirsing, September 22, 1876. MČH #2140.
43. BS: Karel Bendl, December 20, 1877. MČH #184.
44. See Salmi, *Imagined Germany*, 5.
45. Cited in Gregor-Dellin, *Richard Wagner*, 325.
46. Wagner, *Briefe* Band II, 433.
47. Wagner, "Vorwort zur Herausgabe," 278.
48. Ibid., 434.
49. Gregor-Dellin, *Richard Wagner*, 463.
50. Wagner, *Bericht an Ludwig II*, 47.
51. Finck letter in Gaukstad, *Edvard Grieg*, 56.
52. See ibid., 43; and Grieg, *Briefwechsel mit Peters*, 620.
53. Rojahn, "Edvard Grieg som national tonedigter," 93–94.
54. Ibid., 92.
55. Cited in Nils Grinde, "Grieg as a Norwegian and a European Composer," 127.
56. Grieg, *Dagbøker*, 91.
57. Benestad and Schjelderup-Ebbe, *Edvard Grieg*, 155.

58. Ibid., 101.
59. See the Grieg tribute issue of *Bergens Tidende* from June 13, 1903, for example.
60. See the letter to Hans Lien Brækstad in Grieg, *Brev* Bind I, 110, for example.
61. See Gaukstad, *Edvard Grieg*, 100.
62. Grieg, *Brev* Bind I, 315.
63. Cosima Wagner, *Tagebücher* Band II, 827.
64. Wagner, *Eine Mitteilung an meine Freunde*, 234.
65. Wagner, *Über Staat und Religion*, 13.
66. Wagner, *Zukunftsmusik*, 95.
67. Wagner, *Oper und Drama* Parts II and III, 70–72.
68. Wagner, *Deutsche Kunst und deutsche Politik*, 60–61.
69. Ibid., 212.
70. Wagner, *Oper und Drama*, Parts II and III, 64.
71. Wagner, *Kunstwerk der Zukunft*, 142.
72. Wagner, *Mein Leben*, 221.
73. Wagner, *Oper und Drama* Parts II and III, 261–262.
74. Ibid., 262.
75. Wagner, *Zukunftsmusik*, 95.
76. Wagner, *Deutsche Kunst und deutsche Politik*, 53.
77. Ibid., 263.
78. Wagner, *Eine Mitteilung an meine Freunde*, 312.
79. Friedrich Meinecke, *Cosmopolitanism and the National State*, Robert B. Kimber, tr. (Princeton: Princeton University Press, 1970); Hughes, *Nationalism and Society: Germany 1800–1945*; and Düding, *Organisierter gesellschaftlicher Nationalismus in Deutschland (1808–1847)*.
80. Wagner, *Zukunftsmusik*, 93.
81. Wagner, *Über deutsches Musikwesen*, 97.
82. Wagner, "Einleitung zum dritten und vierten Bande," 6, and *Über deutsches Musikwesen*, 94.
83. Wagner, *Deutsche Kunst und deutsche Politik*, 31–32.
84. Wagner, *Beethoven*, 84. The reasons for this shame are sundry, and they vary somewhat throughout the course of Wagner's prose. In his earlier writings, he lays the blame on the corrupting influence of property and greed, in the later writings, on the degeneracy of the French, the Jews, and race mixing.
85. Ibid., 123.
86. Wagner, *Oper und Drama* Parts II and III, 228.
87. Wagner, *Mein Leben*, 402.

88. Wagner, *Kunstwerk der Zukunft*, 60.
89. Wagner, *Beethoven*, 126.
90. Wagner, "Zur Einführung in das Jahr 1880," 30.
91. Jörg K. Hoensch, *Geschichte Böhmens* (München: C.H. Beck Verlag, 1992).
92. Bartoš, *Bedřich Smetana*, 202.
93. Erismann, *Smetana l'éveilleur*, 403. This conclusion can be drawn from Smetana's comment about wanting to "reach beyond the borders" of the Czech lands with *Viola*, a comment cited previously in the section on dissemination.
94. Smetana, *Kritické dílo*, 165. Italics in the original.
95. Ibid., 88.
96. Wagner, *Bericht an Ludwig II*, 32.
97. Vít, "Hudba v programu českého národního hnutí doby předbřeznové a po Říjnovém diplomu," 61.
98. Petr Pithart, Petr Příhoda, and Milan Otáhal, *Podiven: Češi v dějinách nové doby* (Praha: Rozmluvy, 1991).
99. Christopher P. Storck, *Bedřich Smetana in der tschechischen Nationalbewegung 1860–1884*. Magisterarbeit. Universität zu Köln, 1991.
100. Benestad and Schjelderup-Ebbe, *Edvard Grieg*, 16.
101. Grieg, *Dagbøker*, 115.
102. Benestad and Schjelderup-Ebbe, *Johan Svendsen: mennesket og kunstneren*, (1990b), p.108.
103. Gaukstad, *Edvard Grieg: artikler og taler*, 101.
104. Grieg, *Brev* Bind I, 451.
105. Gaukstad, *Edvard Grieg*, 171.
106. Ibid., 180.
107. Ibid., 198.
108. Benestad and Schjelderup-Ebbe, *Edvard Grieg*, 336–337.
109. Gaukstad, *Edvard Grieg*, 187.
110. Grieg, *Brev*, Bind I, 248.
111. Grieg, *Dagbøker*, 144.
112. Grieg, *Breve til Frants Beyer*, 52.
113. Cited in Benestad and Schjelderup-Ebbe, *Edvard Grieg*, 51.
114. Cited in Benestad and Schjelderup-Ebbe, *Edvard Grieg: mennesket og kunstneren* (1990), 338.
115. Cited in ibid., 339.
116. Grieg, *Brev* Bind II, 246. Italics in the original.
117. Gaukstad, *Edvard Grieg*, 74.

118. Ibid., 51.

119. Ibid.

120. See his "Tale til arbeiderne" in Gaukstad, *Edvard Grieg*, 180.

121. Grieg, *Breve til Frants Beyer*, 98.

122. Grieg, *Röntgen Briefwechsel*, 174.

123. Grieg *Brev* Bind I, 679.

124. Ernesto Laclau, "Subject of Politics, Politics of the Subject," *differences* 7.1 (spring 1995): 147.

125. Cited in David Palumbo-Liu, "Universalisms and Minority Culture," *differences* 7.1 (spring 1995): 199.

126. Cited in Bruce Robbins, "Actually Existing Cosmopolitanism" in *Cosmopolitics: Thinking and Feeling Beyond the Nation*, ed. Pheng Cheah and Bruce Robbins (Minneapolis: University of Minnesota Press, 1998), 1–19. *See esp.* p. 4.

# CONCLUSION

On a summery day in early May some years ago, I was in Riga, Latvia, strolling through the lovely main park that sits between the medieval old town and the nineteenth-century neighborhoods. Suddenly, through the trees, I glimpsed the city's gleaming ivory opera house, and I couldn't resist investigating. They were doing an opera called *No Rozes un Asinīm* ("Rose and Blood"), a work I had never heard of—but I bought a ticket anyway. What I experienced that night, much to my comingled surprise, satisfaction, and befuddlement, turned out to be an eye-popping combination of nationalism and art. The opera, as it happened, was nothing less than a contemporary national opera, a *Freischütz* two hundred years tardy, based on an old Latvian folk tale about the tragic love story of a beautiful maiden known as "the rose" of the Turaida region. But as I sat there during the scene changes, in a time-warped reverie plotting how I could work this into my book, I was at once rudely interrupted by confusing announcements made in Latvian over the PA system. At each of these announcements, people in the audience began cheering. What on earth is that all about, I wondered?

At the interval I found an usher who spoke good English, and she told me the announcements were keeping people apprised of the latest score in that night's world hockey championship match, which pitted the beloved Latvian national team against the United States. She also told me a bit about the opera, that it was written by Zigmars Liepiņš, who was known mostly for his pop songs. The opera had premiered the previous year to great fanfare. She agreed with me *sotto voce* that the music was pretty weak, a sort of lowest-common-denominator Disney accessibility, rock banality hungering to be taken seriously. To its credit, though, the opera seemed quite popular, and indeed it incorporated so many of the obligatory features of any worthy national folk opera that I was fascinated in spite of myself: it was sung in the national language, based on an old legend, set among identifiable places in the Latvian landscape, and featured boisterous crowd scenes in a pub as well as a climactic wedding. *Rose and Blood* was even apparently created with the intent of establishing a Latvian operatic repertoire. So, though it did not measure up to *Der Freischütz*, it was nonetheless a gallant, if anachronistic, effort. When the performance finally ended, I heard that the outcome of the hockey game had been a tie—and that was apparently reason enough for celebration. Walking back to my hotel as the night erupted in cheers, chants, and car horns honking, I reflected on the absurd collision between two expressions of nationalism: the rejoicing in the national team's nonvictory, nonloss, right in the middle of an opera that disinterred the hoary conventions of nineteenth-century national opera, all on the threshold of the twenty-first century in a young country still struggling to assert its independence.

What conclusions did I come to in my reflective walk that night? First, the Latvians can get excited about hockey *and* opera, and you have to admire them for that. More importantly, though, the example of *Rose and Blood* demonstrates that the ideas, conventions, and goals of nationalist music are still very much alive today. Cultural nation building by no means stopped in 1900. This endeavor occupied composers both before and since Wagner, Smetana, and Grieg. It is time, then, to bring these other composers into the story, albeit briefly, to demonstrate that the constitutive elements of nationalist music that appear in Wagner's, Smetana's, and Grieg's discourse appear in others' as well. The concerns for constructing a national culture, and the view of music's role in that project, attained not only a major historical significance but continue to ripple into the present.

Though my inquiry has centered on the German, Czech, and Norwegian nationalist movements, a glance at other nationalist composers confirms the generalizability of the key tropes of creating national music. Naturally, different themes become variously salient in the different cases, though some themes do indeed reach an almost universal importance. Also, not every composer espoused a concerted commitment of the type we see in Wagner, Smetana, and Grieg to building a national culture per se, but a patriotic desire to depict some element of the nation in music is always present. Glinka and Chopin, for instance, were never as deeply involved as was Smetana in a nation-building project. However, all three—together with colleagues from England, Italy, Hungary, Poland, and Finland—do nonetheless express many of the same ideas about how "the national" enters into music.

The trope of decline is one of the most widespread: many nationalist composers complain about the degradation of public taste in their homelands. Isaac Albéniz, for one, repeatedly lambasted urban Spaniards' preference for light and worthless music over ambitious art music. Alexander Borodin also lamented the low standards of taste that predominated in the Russia of his day, and declared his determination to try to raise those standards. The theme of education, then, is also a common cause for other nationalist composers. Musical training as a means of improving the general public's appreciation for art was a central, life-long concern of Zoltán Kodály's career. As did many composers, he contributed to the founding of institutions to realize these educational goals. Mili Balakirev started the Free Music School in St. Petersburg, for example, and Albéniz tried to create a Catalan national theater in Barcelona. Even when they did not directly contribute to institution building, composers such as Ralph Vaughan Williams often argued for the utility of such institutions for the national artistic life; to such an end, Giuseppe Verdi called for governmental support for the theaters in Milan, Rome, and Naples.

Some of the most consistent actuations of the typical tropes are the works that nationalist composers produced. Some, such as Carl Maria von Weber and Cesar Cui, authored prose tracts about the need, respectively, for German and Russian national styles in music. Enshrining the national language through musical setting was a principal tenet here, as we have seen: Mihály Mosonyi set works by Hungarian nationalist poets, Balakirev set Russian, and Frédéric Chopin set Polish poets. Ostensibly national myth and history preoccupied virtually every nationalist composer. Balakirev's symphonic work *Rus*, and Borodin's and Musorgsky's operas *Prince Igor* and *Boris Godunov* all evoke Russian history. Several of Verdi's works, such as *La battaglia di Legnano*, put Italian history on stage. Jean Sibelius' choral symphony *Kullervo* relies on material from the *Kalevala*. Béla Bartók's early symphony *Kossuth* attempts to depict musically both a great Hungarian patriot and the life of the entire Hungarian people. National opera was of course a major concern to generations of composers, from Weber to Stanisław Moniuszko to Mikhail Glinka to Ralph Vaughan Williams, and including even Sibelius. The national landscape was often depicted in operas as well as other works. Borodin's *The Steppes of Central Asia*, Balakirev's *On the Volga*, Manuel de Falla's *Nights in the Gardens of Spain*, Albéniz's *Iberia*, Vaughan Williams' *London Symphony*, Mosonyi's *Puszta-Life*, and Kodály's *Matra Pictures* are just a few of very many examples.

The adoration of the folk and the translation of folk culture into the realm of high art is such a common and obvious trend that it is not hard to corroborate other composers' ideas and works in this area. More interesting is how many nationalist composers actually undertook their own collections of folk materials. Weber, Balakirev, de Falla, Vaughan Williams, Kodály, and Bartók all gathered folk songs firsthand. And seemingly all composers subscribed to the idea that folk songs must be "lifted up" into the artwork. Hence rather than directly quoting folk songs, they typically preferred to evoke folk style through imitation. Cui wrote of the necessity to elevate folk songs, and Borodin agreed that direct quotations were the wrong approach. Albéniz and Vaughan Williams also treated folk songs as in themselves insufficient for constituting a national art. Bartók, too, though a devoted student of folk music, insisted that direct quotation was not the ideal way to bring a folk character into a work of art.

Almost equally common in the discourse on creating national music is the recurrence to boundary construction and "Othering." Most often this takes the form of protests against foreign domination of the national cultural scene, in exact parallel to Wagner's complaints against the French and Italians. Indeed, Italian music was the focus of resistance and scorn for composers throughout the nineteenth century and on into the twentieth. Successively, Weber, Glinka, the Russian Five, Albéniz, and de Falla all railed against the influence of Italian music. In that ironic reversal of Wagner's complaints, however, like Grieg many later composers also protested the way that Germans and their art claimed for themselves the peak of musical achievement. Balakirev and other leading figures in Russian musical circles such as Vladimir Stasov repeatedly attacked the prominence of German music, fearing attempts to "Germanize" Russian culture. English composers also resisted the "cultural hegemony" of German style and urged their countrymen to avoid being "colonized" in this way.[1] Even Verdi lived long enough to see German music rise from what Wagner portrayed as its subjugated position earlier in the nineteenth century—thus by the 1880s, Verdi was himself warning against "Germanism" infecting students and teachers at Italy's conservatories.

The themes of prestige, dissemination, and universality are relatively more difficult to substantiate in other composers. I suspect that with more detailed research into other composers' discourse, these preoccupations would turn out to be relatively common. In any event, the prestige component at least is apparent in several cases. De Falla was concerned with securing a place for Spanish music internationally, just as Russians sought prestige and recognition for their own culture. Likewise, men such as George Grove argued for the need of English music to attain a standard of achievement comparable to that of the great musical nations such as Germany. Kodály had much the same thoughts for Hungarian music, and he was also actively concerned with promoting Hungarians' culture abroad. Albéniz, too, did his part for the international dissemination of Spanish music, much like Grieg always including "national" pieces on his wide-ranging tours. Already early in his career, Sibelius' music was traveling beyond Finland as a representative of Finnish culture, as with the Helsinki Philharmonic's tour around Europe in 1900. The belief in the universality of art was customary enough that most nationalist composers probably adhered to it. Liszt certainly espoused it, and Balakirev also believed that national expression could simultaneously be universal, citing Chopin's music as an example.

Probably the best confirmation of both the importance and relevancy of these tropes is again the power they continue to exert today. For instance, many of the same old arguments about the theater's role as the high temple of the nation's artistic culture were trotted out at the opening in 2002 of the new Hungarian National Theater in Budapest. Or consider the Latvian opera *Rose and Blood*, so resolutely incorporating many of the key features of a national folk opera. Built patently on models like *Der Freischütz* and *The Bartered Bride, Rose and Blood* demonstrates how composers still rely on familiar patterns to make their works "national." In 2000 for Zigmars Liepiņš as in 1866 for Bedřich Smetana, the recipe remains the same.

In the Introduction chapter, I referred to the three creative processes that form the central subjects of this book. These were, first, the creation of nationalist music, second, the creation of the national culture, and third, the creation of the sociopolitical role of nationalist artists. Having examined these phenomena in my case studies, it is finally time to discuss all three together as intersecting elements of the culture, politics, and history of nineteenth-century Europe. My aim is to demonstrate how these three elements were to a certain extent mutually constitutive, and thereby to argue for the ultimate significance of nationalist music and nationalist composers.

The effort to create a national culture coincides with the rise of the artist as a major social actor. With the Romantic era comes a new, Olympian conception of the artist and his creative power. That power was viewed as little short of divine: creativity and the inspiration behind it were heaven-sent. The artist thus assumed the power to invent a world (whether in music, literature, or the visual arts) and then to give that world form through the artwork. And through his vision as realized in the artwork, the artist could effect social change. This new conception of the artist was in fact advanced by influential artists themselves, men like Byron and Wagner, who insisted upon the artist's almost mystical ability (even duty) to change society. Geniuses fed the cult of genius, with their works elaborating for themselves this new social role of the artist and inculcating such an understanding of art and the artist among the wider public.

In the Romantic understanding, art was to be not a mere pastime or amusement, but rather a social force: this is the new place and function of art that I discussed in the second chapter. Art would be democratic, belonging not just to the aristocracy but equally to all classes. So, despite the artist's heaven-sent powers, he still belongs in an important way to his community. In the ideology of nationalism above all, the community that inspires and honors the artist was the national community. The nation, then, would be the artist's patron, as both the subject and support for his work. Nationalist artists were of course the ones who most passionately argued for the community (whether the nation-state or just the nation) to support their creative endeavors—it was these endeavors, after all, that were creating the nation's culture. Beyond even that, nationalist artists argued for their ability to create national citizens.

We have seen a striking juxtaposition in this discourse on how the nation would be created, however. Wagner, Smetana, and Grieg do believe in an eternal, primordial origin of nationality—this origin is essentially the Herderian idea of the *Volksgeist*. At the same time, though, they also believe that the nation must be constructed. The Volksgeist, with its mystical content, is not enough to actually constitute the national culture. Rather, that culture must be *made*, and it must be made specifically into a high culture. The high culture, unlike the national spirit, is not a given. Similarly, then, national citizens are not givens: they too must be made. The discourse on the role of folk sources in the national music is one of the best examples of this simultaneous primordialist-constructivist juxtaposition. Nationalist intellectuals, particularly in the early stages of the movement, are obsessed with preservation of the untainted nationality as found in the peasantry: all the eternal values of the nation reside there. Subsequently, other nationalists such as artists call not just for preservation but also for elevation of these cultural values. Nationalist artists demanded that the products of the folk culture be re-created, and thereby raised up into the realm of a high art. These high artworks they produced would then establish an elevated national culture.

It was this process of elevation that would in turn create the national citizens. Effectively all nationalist intellectuals, artists included, stress the need for education. The people would be educated into the rights, duties, and culture of national citizenship. The national culture was essential here for its unifying power. Through the fusion of the lower but inherently national folk forms with the higher, sophisticated art forms, the national culture would enshrine in the artwork the principal of unity that is the core of the nation idea. The national culture was to bridge the community's social divides by belonging equally to all the people. This mammoth task of creating the unified and unifying national culture was the paramount goal of nationalist artists, and thus the defining element of their social role.

In addition to securing the internal unity of the nation, though, the national culture also faced an external challenge in relation to the cultures of other nations. The perceived need to situate the national culture *internationally* gave rise to the discursive strategies on both boundary drawing and the transcendence of those boundaries through the principles of cosmopolitaneity and universality. The discourses on boundary drawing and "Othering" were products of what I have called the fetishization of difference, which in turn stems from the Volksgeist belief that each people should and does have a distinct communal cultural expression. Creating boundaries between national high cultures, then, was a means of securing the distinction of the culture. These boundaries would serve as the markers for the vertically integrated culture, that is, the unified culture shared among the national populace that would replace the older, horizontally integrated culture shared transnationally by elites, regardless of country.

The desire for boundaries between cultures is an assertion of particularity. However, nationalist artists also expressed a desire for universality; indeed, in their thought, universality would proceed from particularity. With Grieg's as well as many other nationalist composers' music, it was the particular nationality of that music that gained it recognition and encouraged its spread internationally. Yet that international dissemination was ultimately only possible, in these composers' view, when the music adhered to the universal standards of great art. National particularity was thus the vehicle for a universal artistic expression. In this way art could be both national and cosmopolitan: national, because it originated in a distinct Volksgeist, but cosmopolitan, because it would go out and take its place in the world as the representative of the nation's culture.

The deep and simultaneous universality and particularity of nationalism is quite starkly revealed by the discourse on nationalist music. The claims of nationalism are predicated on an assumption of universal validity, that every people deserves independence. There is also the insistence that every culture, universally, has a unique, inherent worth. So, particularity appeals to universality as its justification and legitimation. Most obviously, the tropes and strategies of nation building are universal because they appear universally, in one form or another, in virtually every nationalist movement. Thus these strategies themselves become cosmopolitan, the property not of any one nation but of all, applied in this case and borrowed from that one.

These strategies are part of what we should conceive as the intellectual structure of nation building. The intellectual structure is made up first of the beliefs about the nation: the folk is the repository of the nation's culture, the national spirit is in decline and must be reawakened, a national culture is necessary to create citizens and a prestigious art that gives the people their identity, and so on. This is the universe of meaning in which nationalist intellectuals operate—the understandings of life, society, and art that serve as the fundament for their own ideas.

The intellectual structure is also made up of the strategies for realizing the particular social-political goals of the nationalist. In the case of nationalist composers, these strategies include a national opera, works that figuratively unify the populace by incorporating and elevating folk materials, and the discursive and artistic production of difference. So, by definition, such strategies constitute the practice of the nationalist artist. The attempt to build nations, which is the goal of the nationalist's activism, proceeds according to these strategies.

As with all social structures, this ideational universe of the strategies of nation building is both constraining and enabling. It constrains because the ideas on the efficacy and validity of these strategies determine the nationalist intellectual's practice. This practice takes place within the realm of possibility framed by beliefs about the nation and how nations are built. Simultaneously, of course, these beliefs actualize the nationalist intellectual's practice, making possible the attempts to realize the promise of the nation-building strategies. Also, typically for social structure, the ideational universe results partly from nationalist intellectuals' own agency. Nationalists produce and reproduce the beliefs about the nation that become the structure for their activism. This intellectual structure is partially inherited, of course, as the product of earlier thinkers (whether nationalists or not) or the result of ideas that are held throughout society. However, men such as Wagner, Smetana, and Grieg also contribute to this structure both through their reproduction of it and through their own works. The works of earlier nationalist artists serve as models for later artists, amounting to a pantheon of possibility and inspiration for creating a national musical culture.

As these ideas and strategies constitute the *practice* of the nationalist artist, so they inevitably constitute the *category* of the nationalist artist as well. Nationalist intellectuals are defined by what they think and do, and what they think and do is determined largely by the intellectual structure. This, then, is the widest historical and analytical scope of my examination of nationalist music. The intellectual history of the meeting between nationalism and music reveals the drive to create a uniquely national culture. The meeting of nationalism and music also resulted in the typical ideas and strategies that nationalist composers used to make music national. In tracing the origins and applications of these ideas, we perceive the elaboration of the practice of the nationalist composer, and from that practice the emergence of the category itself. Hence through the creation of nationalist music, we also finally witness the creations of the national culture and the role of nationalist artists.

One of the goals in my examination of nationalism and music has been to fire another salvo in the seemingly yet-unwon battle to convince people that culture is not somehow "separate" from politics, as if art were some sort of autonomous, hermetically sealed realm, isolated from struggles for power. Such misconceptions of the nature of politics, culture, and the relationship between the two need to be corrected by the understanding that art can just as much be the subject of political struggles as can money, voters, state boundaries, or nuclear weapons.

For those involved in them, debates about the content of the national culture are every bit as heated and vital as a fight over, say, congressional redistricting. Indeed, if we accept as the most basic, pithy definition of politics that it is about power (how to get it and how to keep it), then the drive to create a national culture is in its very essence also about power. This is the power to establish for a community of people a particular, unique, ostensibly "national" set of symbols, beliefs, works, and practices. The national culture is essential in actually drawing the boundaries of this community, and in determining who does and does not belong, and who has the right to rule. Moreover, as a monopoly, the national culture excludes alternatives, perpetuating itself as it delegitimizes contesting claims for what binds the community, and what binds that community to a territory. Art plays a role in all of these things, and all of them, in short, involve politics as a means of producing human social groupings.

Nationalist artists are both soldiers and generals in this battle: but not only do they erect the fortifications around the community, they also fight among themselves over what the content of the culture must be. Politics takes place even *within* the national culture. Nationalist artists are integrally linked with other nationalists—even those most "political" who stand and speechify in parliament or who land a blow on the oppressor with their fists, bullets, or words. Those nationalists who endeavor in the cultural realm are thus also concerned with politics, just as nationalist politicians are frequently obsessed with culture. And finally, the work of nationalist artists demonstrates that cultural nationalism is not somehow passive, not a sleepy backwater in contrast to the dynamics of other forms of nationalist agitation. To the contrary, cultural politics can be every bit as vital, energetic, and essential as political activism in other spheres.

Beyond merely preaching to the converted, I hope the interaction of nationalism and music has revealed to the doubters how political art and culture can be. Not isolated, not tangential, but as the examples of Wagner, Smetana, and Grieg show, the artist's national activism is an absolutely fundamental element of the nationalist movement, since without it, the culture that actually communicates nationality would be almost empty, like a stave with no notes.

## ENDNOTE

1. Stradling and Hughes, *The English Musical Renaissance*, 99.

# BIBLIOGRAPHY

## PRIMARY SOURCES

### Wagner

Wagner, Cosima. *Die Tagebücher*. Volume I: 1869–1872. Volume II: 1873–1877. Volume III: 1878–1880. Volume IV: 1881–1883. München: Piper, 1976.

Wagner, Richard. *Bericht an seine Majestät König Ludwig II*. Tutzing: Hans Schneider, 1865 (1998).

———. *Das Braune Buch*. München: Piper, 1988.

———. "Die deutsche Oper." In *Dichtungen und Schriften*. Volume 5. Frankfurt: Insel Verlag, 1983.

———. *Ein deutscher Musiker in Paris*. München: Deutcher Taschenbuch Verlag, 1987.

———. "Das Judentum in der Musik." In *Gesammelte Schriften und Dichtungen*. Leipzig: Breitkopf und Härtel, 1888.

———. *Mein Leben 1813–1868*. München: List Verlag, 1994.

———. *Sämtliche Briefe*. Volumes 1–8. Edited by Gertrud Strobel, Werner Wolf, Hans-Joachim Bauer, Johannes Forner. Leipzig: Deutscher Verlag für Musik, 1967–1993.

———. *Sämtliche Schriften und Dichtungen*. Volumes 1–12. Leipzig: Breitkopf und Härtel, 1907. All references to Wagner's prose works come from this edition, apart from the exceptions that follow.

———. *Was ist deutsch?* München: Rogner und Bernhard, 1975 (1865–1878).

### Smetana

Bedřich Smetana Letters. Muzeum České Hudby. Listed as "BS" to recipient. Cited according to the MČH letter number in the museum's archive.

Deník Bedřicha Smetany. Muzeum České Hudby. Cited according to the MČH document number in the museum's archive.

Smetanovy zápisky v Kalendáři Koruny České.

Jiránek, Josef. *Vzpomínky a korespondence s Bedřichem Smetanou.* Praha: Státní nakladatelství krásné literatury, hudby a umění, 1957.

*Eliška Krásnohorská—Bedřich Smetana: vzájemná korespondence.* Ed. Mirko Očadlík. Praha: Topičova edice, 1940.

*Listy B. Smetany E. Zünglovi.* Nymburk: Nákladel L. Zelenky-Lerando, 1903.

*Bedřich Smetana a Dr. Ludevít Procházka: vzájemná korespondence.* Ed. Jan Löwenbach. Praha: Umělecká beseda, 1914.

*Z dopisů Bedřicha Smetany.* Praha: Pourova edice, 1947.

*Smetana ve vzpomínkách a dopisech.* Ed. František Bartoš. Praha: Topičova edice, 1948.

*Kritické dílo Bedřicha Smetany 1858–1865.* Ed. V. H. Jarka. Praha: Nakladatelství Pražské akciové tiskárny, 1948.

*Bedřich Smetana: Letters and Reminiscences.* Ed. František Bartoš. Prague: Artia, 1955.

### Grieg

Benestad, Finn, and Hanna de Vries Stavland, eds. *Edvard Grieg und Julius Röntgen: Briefwechsel 1883–1907.* Amsterdam: Koninklijke Vereniging voor Nederlandse Muziekgeschiednis, 1997.

Carley, Lionel. *Grieg and Delius: A Chronicle of their Friendship in Letters.* London: Marion Boyars, 1993.

Gaukstad, Øystein, ed. *Edvard Grieg: artikler og taler*. Oslo: Gyldendal Norsk Forlag, 1957.

Grieg, Edvard. *Brev i utvalg 1862–1907. Bind I*. Ed. Finn Benestad. Oslo: Aschehoug, 1998.

———. *Brev i utvalg 1862–1907. Bind II*. Ed. Finn Benestad. Oslo: Aschehoug, 1998.

———. *Breve til Frants Beyer 1872–1907*. Ed. Finn Benestad and Bjarne Kortsen. Oslo: Universitetsforlaget, 1993.

———. *Briefwechsel mit dem Musikverlag C.F. Peters 1863–1907*. Frankfurt am Main: C. F. Peters, 1997.

———. *Dagbøker*. Bergen: Bergen Offentlige Bibliotek, 1993.

## SECONDARY SOURCES

Agnew, Hugh LeCaine. *Origins of the Czech National Renascence*. Pittsburgh: University of Pittsburgh Press, 1993.

Amdam, Per. *Bjørnstjerne Bjørnson 1832–1880*. Oslo: Gyldendal, 1993.

Anderson, Amanda. "Cosmopolitanism, Universalism, and the Divided Legacies of Modernity." In *Cosmopolitics: Thinking and Feeling Beyond the Nation*, edited by Pheng Cheah and Bruce Robbins. Minneapolis: University of Minnesota Press, 1998. 265–289.

Anderson, Benedict. *Imagined Communities*. London: Verso, 1983.

Appiah, Kwame Anthony. "Against National Culture." In *Text and Nation*, edited by Laura García-Moreno and Peter C. Pfeiffer. Columbia, SC: Camden House, 1996. 175–190.

Applegate, Celia. "How German Is It? Nationalism and the Idea of Serious Music in the Early Nineteenth Century." *19th-Century Music* XXI/3 (1998). 274–296.

———. "What Is German Music? Reflections on the Role of Art in the Creation of the Nation." *German Studies Review* (winter 1993): 21–32.

Arbusow, Leonid. "Herder und die Begründung der Volksliedforschung im deutschbaltischen Osten." In *Im Geiste Herders*, edited by Erich Keyser. Kitzingen am Main: Holzner-Verlag, 1953. 129–256.

Ashley, Mark. "Nations as Victims: Nationalist Politics and the Framing of Identity." Paper presented at the annual meeting of the American Political Science Association, 2001.

Barth, Frederik, ed. *Ethnic Groups and Boundaries*. Boston: Little, Brown and Company, 1969.

Beckerman, Michael. "In Search of Czechness in Music." *19th-Century Music* X/1 (1986): 61–73.

Benestad, Finn, and Dag Schjelderup-Ebbe. *Edvard Grieg: mennesket og kunstneren*. Oslo: Aschehoug, 1980.

———. *Edvard Grieg: mennesket og kunstneren*. 2nd edition. Oslo: Aschehoug, 1990.

———. *Edvard Grieg: The Man and the Artist*. Translated by William H. Halverson and Leland B. Sateren. Lincoln: University of Nebraska Press, 1988.

———. *Johan Svendsen: mennesket og kunstneren*. Oslo: Aschehoug, 1990.

———. "Norsk musikk—en kamp for frigjøring." In *Norge ad notam: en kulturhistorisk innføring*, edited by Nanna Segelcke. Oslo: Aventura Forlag, 1992.

Berlin, Isaiah. *Against the Current: Essays in the History of Ideas*. New York: Viking Press, 1980.

———. *The Crooked Timber of Humanity*. Princeton: Princeton University Press, 1990.

Beyer, Harald. *Henrik Wergeland*. Oslo: Aschehoug, 1946.

Bless, Marion. *Richard Wagners Oper 'Tannhäuser' im Spiegel seiner geistigen Entwicklung*. Eisenach: Verlag der Musikalienhandlung Karl Dieter Wagner, 1997.

Bohlman, Philip V. *The Music of European Nationalism*. Santa Barbara, CA: ABC-Clio, 2004.

―――. *The Study of Folk Music in the Modern World*. Bloomington: Indiana University Press, 1988.

Bradley, John F. N. *Czech Nationalism in the Nineteenth Century*. Boulder: East European Monographs, 1984.

Bredal, Dag, and Terje Strøm-Olsen. *Edvard Grieg: 'Musikken er en kampplass'*. Oslo: Aventura Forlag, 1992.

Bresgen, Cesar. *Der Komponist und die Volksmusik*. Vienna: Universal Edition, 1970.

Brock, Hella. *Edvard Grieg*. Leipzig: Reclam-Verlag, 1990.

―――. *Edvard Grieg als Musikschriftsteller*. Altenmedingen: Hildegard-Junker-Verlag, 1999.

Brown, David. *Mikhail Glinka*. London: Oxford University Press, 1974.

Brusatti, Otto. *Nationalismus und Ideologie in der Musik*. Tutzing: Hans Schneider, 1978.

Bujic, Bojan, ed. *Music in European Thought 1851–1912*. Cambridge: Cambridge University Press, 1988.

Cambell, Stuart, ed. *Russians on Russian Music, 1830–1880*. Cambridge: Cambridge University Press, 1994.

Černý, František. "Diváci českého divadla v 19. století." In *Umění a veřejnost v 19. století*. Plzeň: Albis International, 1998.

―――. "Idea národního divadla." In *Divadlo v české kultuře 19. století*. Praha: Národní galerie, 1985.

Cheah, Pheng. "The Cosmopolitical—Today." In *Cosmopolitics: Thinking and Feeling Beyond the Nation*, edited by Pheng Cheah and Bruce Robbins. Minneapolis: University of Minnesota Press, 1998. 20–41.

Clark, Walter Aaron. *Isaac Albéniz: Portrait of a Romantic*. Oxford: Oxford University Press, 1999.

Dahlhaus, Carl. *Between Romanticism and Modernism*. Berkeley: University of California Press, 1980.

————. *Die Idee der absoluten Musik*. Kassel: Bärenreiter Verlag, 1978.

————. *Nineteenth-Century Music*. Berkeley: University of California Press, 1989.

————. *Richard Wagners Musikdramen*. Hildesheim: Friedrich, 1971.

Danckert, Werner. *Das Volkslied im Abendland*. Bern: Francke Verlag, 1966.

Danielsen, Rolf, Ståle Dyrvik, Helle Grønlie and Edgar Hovland. *Norway: A History from the Vikings to Our Own Times*. Oslo: Scandinavian University Press, 1995.

Day, James. *Vaughan Williams*. Oxford: Oxford University Press, 1997.

DeNora, Tia. *Beethoven and the Construction of Genius*. Berkeley: University of California Press, 1995.

Derry, T. K. *A History of Modern Norway 1814–1972*. Oxford: Clarendon Press, 1973.

Deutsch, Karl W. *Nationalism and Social Communication*. Cambridge: MIT Press, 1953.

Dolanský, Julius. *Karel Jaromír Erben*. Praha: Melantrich, 1970.

Donakowski, Conrad L. *A Muse for the Masses*. Chicago: University of Chicago Press, 1977.

Duara, Prasenjit. "Historicizing National Identity, or Who Imagines What and When." In *Becoming National*, edited by Geoff Eley and Ronald Suny. New York: Oxford University Press, 1996. 151–178.

————. *Rescuing History from the Nation*. Chicago: University of Chicago Press, 1995.

Düding, Dieter. "The Nineteenth-Century German Nationalist Movement as a Movement of Societies." In *Nation-Building in Central Europe*, edited by Hagen Schulze. Leamington Spa: Berg Publishers, 1987. 19–49.

———. *Organisierter gesellschaftlicher Nationalismus in Deutschland (1808–1847)*. München: R. Oldenbourg Verlag, 1984.

Echternkamp, Jörg. *Der Aufstieg des deutschen Nationalismus (1770–1840)*. Frankfurt: Campus Verlag, 1998.

Einstein, Alfred. *Music in the Romantic Era*. New York: W. W. Norton & Co, 1947.

Eley, Geoff, and Ronald Grigor Suny, eds. *Becoming National*. New York: Oxford University Press, 1996.

Engel, Carl. *An Introduction to the Study of National Music*. London: Longmans, Green, Reader, and Dyer, 1866.

Erben, Karel Jaromír. *Próza a divadlo*. Praha: Melantrich, 1939.

Erismann, Guy. *Smetana l'éveilleur*. Arles: Actes Sud, 1993.

Falnes, Oscar J. *National Romanticism in Norway*. New York: AMS Press, 1933.

Finck, Henry T. "Grieg's Influence on the Musical World." *The Musician* III, no. 7 (July 1898). Philadelphia: The Hatch Music Company.

Fink, Gonthier-Louis. "Das Wechselspiel zwischen patriotischen und kosmopolitisch-universalen Bestrebungen in Frankreich und Deutschland (1750–1789)." In *Volk—Nation—Vaterland*, edited by Ulrich Herrmann. Hamburg: Felix Meiner Verlag, 1996. 151–184.

Finkelstein, Sidney. *Composer and Nation: The Folk Heritage in Music*. New York: International Publishers, 1989.

Finscher, Ludwig. "Die Entstehung nationaler Stile in der europäischen Musikgeschichte." In *Europäische Musik zwischen Nationalismus und Exotik*. Winterthur, Switzerland: Amadeus Verlag, 1984. 33–56.

Garden, Edward. *Balakirev*. New York: St. Martin's Press, 1967.

Gazi, Stephen. *A History of Croatia*. New York: Barnes and Noble Books, 1993.

Gellner, Ernest. *Nations and Nationalism*. Oxford: Blackwell, 1983.

———. *Thought and Change*. London: Weidenfeld and Nicholson, 1964.

Giesen, Bernhard. *Die Intellektuellen und die Nation: eine deutsche Achsenzeit*. Frankfurt am Main: Suhrkamp, 1993.

Goswami, Manu. "Rethinking Modularity: Beyond Objectivist and Subjectivist Approaches to Nationalism." Paper presented at the Nations and Nationalism Workshop, University of Chicago, 1998.

Gregor-Dellin, Martin. *Richard Wagner*. München: Piper, 1991.

Greini, Liv. *Rikard Nordraak*. Oslo: Johan Grundt Tanum Forlag, 1942.

Grinde, Nils. "Grieg as a Norwegian and a European Composer." *Studia Musicologica Norvegica* 20 (1994): 125–135.

Grunfeld, J. *Manuel de Falla: Spanien und die neue Musik*. Zürich: Verlag der Arche, 1968.

Gutman, Robert W. *Richard Wagner: The Man, His Mind, and His Music*. New York: Harcourt, Brace, Jovanovich, 1990.

Hale, Philip. "Edvard Grieg." In *Famous Composers and Their Works*, edited by John Knowles Paine, Theodore Thomas, Karl Klavser. Boston: J. B. Millet Company, 1892.

Haugen, Einar, and Camilla Cai. *Ole Bull. Romantisk kunstner og kosmopolitisk nordmann*. Oslo: Universitetsforlaget, 1992.

Havlíček Borovský, Karel. *Lid a národ*. Praha: Melantrich, 1981.

Herder, Johann Gottfried von. *Ausgewählte Werke*. Stuttgart: J. G. Cotta-'scher Verlag, 1844 (1807).

Herresthal, Harald. *Med spark i gulvet og quinter i bassen*. Oslo: Universitetsforlaget, 1993.

Hobsbawm, Eric. *Nations and Nationalism since 1780*. Cambridge: Cambridge University Press, 1990.

Hobsbawm, Eric, and Terence Ranger, eds. *The Invention of Tradition*. Cambridge: Cambridge University Press, 1983.

Hodne, Bjarne. *Norsk nasjonalkultur: en kulturpolitisk oversikt*. Oslo: Universitetsforlaget, 1994.

Hoensch, Jörg K. *Geschichte Böhmens*. München: C. H. Beck Verlag, 1992.

Holden, Anthony. *Tchaikovsky*. New York: Random House, 1995.

Hostinský, Otakar. *Bedřich Smetana a jeho boj o moderní českou hudbu*. Praha: Jan Laichter, 1941.

Hroch, Miroslav. "Das Erwachen kleiner Nationen als Problem der komparativen sozialgeschichtlichen Forschung." In *Sozialstruktur und Organisation europäischer Nationalbewegungen*, edited by Theodor Schieder. München: R. Oldenbourg, 1971. 121–139.

————. "From National Movement to the Fully-Formed Nation: The Nation-Building Process in Europe." In *Becoming National*, edited by Geoff Eley and Ronald Suny. New York: Oxford University Press, 1996. 60–78.

————. "Social and Territorial Characteristics in the Composition of the Leading Groups of National Movements." In *The Formation of National Elites*, edited by Andreas Kappeler. New York: New York University Press, 1992. 257–276.

Hughes, Michael. *Nationalism and Society: Germany 1800–1945*. London: Edward Arnold, 1988.

le Huray, Peter, and James Day, eds. *Music and Aesthetics in the Eighteenth and Early-Nineteenth Centuries*. Cambridge: Cambridge University Press, 1981.

Jeismann, Michael. "'Feind' und 'Vaterland' in der frühen deutschen Nationalbewegung 1806–1815." In *Volk—Nation—Vaterland*, edited by Ulrich Herrmann. Hamburg: Felix Meiner Verlag, 1996.

————. "Stereotypen für nationale Identität und politisches Handeln." In *Nationale Mythen und Symbole in der zweiten Hälfte des 19.*

*Jahrhunderts*, edited by Jürgen Link and Wulf Wülfing Stuttgart: Klett-Cotta, 1991. 84–93.

Jiránek, Jaroslav. *Dílo a život Bedřicha Smetany: Smetanova operní tvorba I*. Praha: Editio Supraphon, 1984.

————. "Regarding the Question of Smetana's Originality." In *Report of the International Musicological Conference on Bedřich Smetana, 24 to 26 May 1994*. Praha: Muzeum Bedřicha Smetany, 1995.

Johannesson, Lena. "1800-talskonsten. Nationell mobilisering på internationella villkor—några strukturer." In *"Hjemländsk Hundraårig Sång": 1800-talets musik och det nationella*, edited by Henrik Karlsson. Göteborg: Kungliga Musikalska akademien, n.d.

Kappeler, Andreas, ed. *The Formation of National Elites*. New York: New York University Press, 1992.

Kedourie, Elie. *Nationalism*. London: Hutchinson, 1985.

Kimball, Stanley Buchholz. *Czech Nationalism: A Study of the National Theater Movement, 1845–1883*. Urbana: University of Illinois Press, 1964.

Klima, Arnošt. *Na prahu nové společnosti*. Praha: Státní pedagogické nakladatelství, 1979.

Kořalka, Jiří. *Tschechen im Habsburgerreich und in Europa 1815–1914*. Wien: Verlag für Geschichte und Politik, 1991.

Křen, Jan. *Konfliktní společnosti: Češi a Němci 1780–1918*. Praha: Academia, 1990.

Kuhn, Ernst, ed. *Alexander Borodin: Sein Leben, seine Musik, seine Schriften*. Berlin: Ernst Kuhn Verlag, 1992.

Laclau, Ernesto. "Subject of Politics, Politics of the Subject." *differences* 7, no. 1 (spring 1995): 146–164.

Large, Brian. *Smetana*. New York: Praeger Publishers, 1970.

Laube, Heinrich. *Kritiken*. Edited by S. D. Stirk. Breslau: Verlag Priebatsch's Buchhandlung, 1934.

Lebl, Vladimír, and Jitka Ludvová. "Nová doba (1860–1938)." In *Hudba v českých dějinách: od středověku do nové doby*. Praha: Editio Supraphon, 1989.

Ling, Jan. *A History of European Folk Music*. Rochester: University of Rochester Press, 1997.

Maciejewski, B. M. *Moniuszko: Father of Polish Opera*. London: Allegro Press, 1979.

Macura, Vladimír. "Paradox obrozenského divadla." In *Divadlo v české kultuře 19. století*. Praha: Národní galerie, 1985. 36–43.

———. *Znamení zrodu: České obrození jako kulturní typ*. Praha: Československý spisovatel, 1983.

Martin, George. *Verdi: His Music, Life and Times*. New York: Dodd, Mean and Company, 1963.

Maurer, Michael. "Nationalcharakter und Nationalbewußtsein. England und Deutschland im Vergleich." In *Volk—Nation—Vaterland*, edited by Ulrich Herrmann. Hamburg: Felix Meiner Verlag, 1996. 89–100.

Meinecke, Friedrich. *Cosmopolitanism and the National State*. Translated by Robert B. Kimber. Princeton: Princeton University Press, 1970.

McColl, Sandra. *Music Criticism in Vienna 1896–1897*. Oxford: Clarendon Press, 1996.

Motyl, Alexander J. "Inventing Tradition: The Limits of National Identity Formation." In *Intellectuals and the Articulation of the Nation*, edited by Ronald Grigor Suny and Michael D. Kennedy. Ann Arbor: The University of Michigan Press, 1999. 57–75.

Nejedlý, Zdeněk. *O Bedřichu Smetanovi*. Praha: Academia, 1980.

Neruda, Jan. *Česká společnost III*. Praha: Státní nakladatelství krásné literatury, hudby, a umění, 1960.

Newman, Ernest. *The Wagner Operas*. Princeton: Princeton University Press, 1949.

Nipperdey, Thomas. *Deutsche Geschichte 1800–1866*. München: Verlag C. H. Beck, 1983.

Novotný, Jan, ed. *Obrození národa*. Praha: Melantrich, 1979.

Orozco, Manuel. *Manuel de Falla*. Barcelona: Destinolibro, 1985.

Ottlová, Marta, and Milan Pospíšil. *Bedřich Smetana a jeho doba*. Praha: Nakladatelství Lidové noviny, 1997.

———. "Konce ideje české národní hudby." In *Čechy a Evropa v kultuře 19. století*. Praha: Ústav pro českou a světovou literaturu ČSAV, 1993. 81–86.

Palumbo-Liu, David. "Universalisms and Minority Culture." *differences* 7, no. 1 (spring 1995): 186–200.

Pešková, Jaroslava. "Divadlo jako způsob vědomí sebe." In *Divadlo v české kultuře 19. století*. Praha: Národní galerie, 1985.

Pilková, Zdeňka. "Doba osvícenského absolutismu (1740–1810)." In *Hudba v českých dějinách: od středověku do nové doby*. Praha: Editio Supraphon, 1989. 211–284.

Pithart, Petr, Petr Příhoda, and Milan Otáhal. *Podiven: Češi v dějinách nové doby*. Praha: Rozmluvy, 1991.

Plantinga, Leon. "Dvořák and the Meaning of Nationalism and Music." In *Rethinking Dvořák: Views from Five Countries*, edited by David Beveridge. Oxford: Clarendon Press, 1996. 117–124.

Pletsch, Carl. *Young Nietzsche*. New York: The Free Press, 1991.

Pynsent, Robert B. *Questions of Identity: Czech and Slovak Ideas of Nationality and Personality*. Budapest: Central European University Press, 1994.

Racek, Jan. *Idea vlasti, národa a slavy v díle Bedřicha Smetany*. Praha: Nákladem Hudební matice Umělecké besedy, 1947.

Rak, Jiří. "Divadlo jako postředek politické propagandy v první polovině 19. století." In *Divadlo v české kultuře 19. století*. Praha: Národní galerie, 1985.

————. "Udatný národ holubičích povah." In *Čechy a Evropa v kultuře 19. století*. Praha: Ústav pro českou a světovou literaturu ČSAV, 1993. 87–91.

Ramsten, Märta. "'Ur forntida djup stige svenskmanna sang.'" In *"Hjemländsk Hundraårig Sång": 1800-talets musik och det nationella*, edited by Henrik Karlsson. Göteborg: Kungliga Musikalska akademien, n.d.

Raynor, Henry. *Music and Society since 1815*. New York: Schocken Books, 1976.

Robbins, Bruce. "Actually Existing Cosmpolitanism." In *Cosmopolitics: Thinking and Feeling Beyond the Nation*, edited by Pheng Cheah and Bruce Robbins. Minneapolis: University of Minnesota Press, 1998.

Röder, Martin. "Edvard Grieg. Biographische Skizze." *Neue Musik-Zeitung*, Volume 5, no. 11 (1 June 1884) .

Rojahn, Ferdinand. "Edvard Grieg som national tonedigter." *Nordisk Musik-Revue*, Volume 3, no. 12 (15 June 1903): 90–95.

Roverud, Lars. *Et Blik paa Musikens Tilstand i Norge*. Christiania: Forfatterens Forlag hos Thr. Grøndahl, 1815.

Salmi, Hannu. *Imagined Germany: Richard Wagner's National Utopia*. New York: Peter Lang, 1999.

Schieder, Theodor. *Nationalismus und Nationalstaat*. Göttingen: Vandenhoeck und Ruprecht, 1991.

Schjelderup, Gerhard. "Edvard Grieg." *Allgemeine Musik-Zeitung*, volume 30, no. 26 (26 June 1903).

Schneider, Louis. "Edvard Grieg." *Musica*, Volume 6, no. 62 (November 1907).

Scholes, Percy A. *The Oxford Companion to Music*. Oxford: Oxford University Press, 1970.

Schulze, Hagen. *Der Weg zum Nationalstaat*. München: Deutscher Taschenbuch Verlag, 1985.

Séquardtová, Hana. *Bedřich Smetana*. Praha: Editio Supraphon, 1988.

Seroff, Victor I. *The Mighty Five: The Cradle of Russian National Music*. New York: Allen, Towne and Heath, Inc, 1948.

Smith, Anthony. *National Identity*. London: Penguin, 1991.

————. 1996. "The Origins of Nations." In *Becoming National*, edited by Geoff Eley and Ronald Suny. New York: Oxford University Press. 106–131.

Snyder, Louis L. *The New Nationalism*. Ithaca: Cornell University Press, 1968.

Sørensen, Øystein. *Bjørnstjerne Bjørnson og nasjonalismen*. Oslo: J. W. Cappelens Forlag, 1997.

Steinmetz, Horst. "Idee und Wirklichkeit des Nationaltheaters. Enttäuschte Hoffnungnen und falsche Erwartungen." In *Volk—Nation—Vaterland*, edited by Ulrich Herrmann. Hamburg: Felix Meiner Verlag, 1996. 141–150.

Stenseth, Bodil. *En norsk elite: Nasjonsbyggerne på Lysaker 1890–1940*. Oslo: Aschehoug, 1993.

Štěpánek, Vladimír. "Historická tragédie a historismus v období národního obrození." In *Uměnovědné studie. III: Historické vědomí v českém umění 19. století*. Praha: Ústav teorie a dějin umění ČSAV v Praze, 1981. 124–132.

Storck, Christopher P. *Bedřich Smetana in der tschechischen Nationalbewegung 1860–1884*. Magisterarbeit. Universität zu Köln, 1993.

————. "Bedřich Smetanas Weg zum 'Nationalkomponisten' und 'Begründer der tschechischen Musik." In *Report of the International Musicological Conference on Bedřich Smetana, 24 to 26 May 1994*. Praha: Muzeum Bedřicha Smetany, 1995.

Stradling, Robert, and Meirion Hughes. *The English Musical Renaissance 1860–1940*. London: Routledge, 1993.

Střítecký, Jaroslav. "Tradice a obrození. Bedřich Smetana." In *Povědomí tradice v novodobé české kultuře (doba Bedřicha Smetany)*. Praha: Národní galerie, 1988. 65–76.

Suny, Ronald Grigor, and Michael D. Kennedy, eds. *Intellectuals and the Articulation of the Nation*. Ann Arbor: University of Michigan Press, 1999.

Szabolcsi, Bence, ed. *Béla Bartók: Weg und Werk*. Kassel: Bärenreiter Verlag, 1972.

Szulc, Tad. *Chopin in Paris*. New York: Scribner, 1998.

Taruskin, Richard. *Defining Russia Musically*. Princeton: Princeton University Press, 1996.

———. "Introduction." *repercussions*, 5, nos. 1–2 (spring-fall 1996): 5–20.

———. "Nationalism." In *The New Grove Dictionary of Music and Musicians*, edited by Stanley Sadie, 689–706. New York: Grove's Dictionaries, 2001.

Tawaststjerna, Erik. *Sibelius: Volume I 1865–1905*. Berkeley: University of California Press, 1976.

Tichý, Vladimír. "The Structural Role of Kinetics in Bedřich Smetana's České Tance." In *Report of the International Musicological Conference on Bedřich Smetana, 24 to 26 May 1994*. Praha: Muzeum Bedřicha Smetany, 1995.

Titzmann, Michael. "Die Konzeption der 'Germanen' in der deutschen Literatur." In *Nationale Mythen und Symbole in der zweiten Hälfte des 19. Jahrhunderts*, edited by Jürgen Link and Wulf Wülfing. Stuttgart: Klett-Cotta, 1991. 118–143.

Tomberg, Friedrich. "Das Theater als politische Anstalt betrachtet." In *Philosophie und Kunst: Kultur und Ästhetik im Denken der deutschen Klassik*. Weimar: Hermann Böhlaus Nachfolger, 1987.

Treitler, Leo. *Music and the Historical Imagination*. Cambridge, MA: Harvard University Press, 1989.

Ujfalussy, József. *Béla Bartók*. Boston: Crescendo Publishing Company, 1971.

Ullrich, Johann. *Heinrich Laubes politischer Entwicklungsgang bis zum Jahre 1834*. Berlin: Friedrich-Wilhelms Universität, 1934.

Vaughan Williams, Ralph. *National Music and Other Essays*. Oxford: Clarendon Press, 1934.

Vít, Petr. "Doba národního probuzení (1810–1860)." In *Hudba v českých dějinách: od středověku do nové doby*. Praha: Editio Supraphon, 1989.

———. "Hudba v programu českého národního hnutí doby předbřeznové a po Řijnovém diplomu." In *Povědomí tradice v novodobé české kultuře (doba Bedřicha Smetany)*. Praha: Národní galerie, 1988. 54–64.

Vollsnes, Arvid O. "'Tysk' mot 'norsk' og 'nasjonalt' i norsk musikk: Eksemplet Halfdan Kjerulf belyst ved romansene 'Murmelndes Lüftchen,' 'Mit hjerte og min lyre,' 'Lokkende toner' og 'Venevil'." In *"Hjemländsk Hundraårig Sång": 1800-talets musik och det nationella*, edited by Henrik Karlsson. Göteborg: Kungliga Musikalska akademien, n.d.

Wagner, Wolfgang Michael. *Carl Maria von Weber und die deutsche Nationaloper*. Weber-Studien. Vol. 2. Mainz: Schott, 1994.

Walker, Alan. *Franz Liszt: The Virtuoso Years 1811–1847*. New York: Alfred A. Knopf, 1983.

———. *Franz Liszt: The Weimar Years 1847–1861*. New York: Alfred A. Knopf, 1988.

Warrack, John. *Carl Maria von Weber*. New York: Macmillan, 1968.

———. *Richard Wagner: Die Meistersinger von Nürnberg*. Cambridge: Cambridge University Press, 1994.

Wehler, Hans-Ulrich. "Nation und Nationalstaat in Deutschland seit dem ausgehenden 18. Jahrhundert." In *Volk—Nation—Vaterland*, edited by Ulrich Herrmann. Hamburg: Felix Meiner Verlag, 1996. 269–277.

Weiner, Marc A. *Richard Wagner and the Anti-Semitic Imagination.* Lincoln: University of Nebraska Press, 1995.

White, Harry, and Michael Murphy, eds. *Musical Constructions of Nationalism: Essays on the History and Ideology of European Musical Culture 1800–1945.* Cork: Cork University Press, 2001.

Willms, Johannes. *Nationalismus ohne Nation.* Düsseldorf: Claassen, 1983.

Wiora, Walter. *Das echte Volkslied.* Heidelberg: Müller-Thiergarten-Verlag, 1962.

———. *Europäische Volksmusik und abendländische Tonkunst.* Kassel: Johann Philipp Hinnenthal-Verlag, 1957.

———. "Herders Ideen zur Geschichte der Musik." In *Im Geiste Herders,* edited by Erich Keyser. Kitzingen am Main: Holzner-Verlag, 1953. 75–125.

Young, Percy M. *Zoltán Kodály.* London: Ernest Benn, 1964.

Závodský, Artur. *František Ladislav Čelakovský.* Praha: Melantrich, 1982.

# INDEX